JEWS IN BRISTOL

In memory of my father, Frank Alfred Benedictus (1903–1978) whose encyclopædic knowledge encouraged me to seek and enquire. I believe he would have been overjoyed to have seen these results of my research.

JEWS IN BRISTOL

The History of the Jewish Community in Bristol
from the Middle Ages to the Present Day

JUDITH SAMUEL

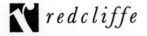 *redcliffe*

First published in 1997 in the Redcliffe imprint by
SANSOM & COMPANY
81g, Pembroke Road, Bristol BS8 3EA

© Judith Samuel

ISBN 1 900178 16 8

British Cataloguing-in-Publication Data.
A catalogue record for this book is available
from the British Library.

Typeset by Mayhew Typesetting, Rhayader, Powys
Printed in Great Britain by Bookcraft, Midsomer Norton

CONTENTS

Plate illustrations appear between pp 80–81, 128–129 and 176–177

LIST OF ILLUSTRATIONS

IN PLATE SECTIONS

PREFACE

W hen one considers the importance of the city of Bristol and its position in history, it is surprising that its Jewish population has not appreciated its heritage. Better late than never, however, Judith Samuel has devoted a decade to this labour of love and historians will greet her efforts with delight. She has taken us from the very beginnings of the medieval community to that of the Resettlement and through to modern times. It will be revealing to many that the city had so many prominent medieval figures and the fact that we now know so much about them is due in great measure to the present writer's efforts. Jews were said to have come very early to the area, perhaps because of the slave trade; but if the story of Joseph of Aramathea is to be believed, then Jewish presence dates from the start of the Christian Era. Centuries of demolition and rebuilding have obliterated the Bristol Jewry, with the exception of the oldest Mikveh (ritual bath) in Europe, but Judith Samuel has made it come alive again in her early chapters.

Equally, the number of household names, in the Jewish world and outside it, should make us realize the possibilities we all have. Famous families like the Jessels, the Jacobs, the Alexanders, in our own time the Sacoffs, have all been part of the congregation. Some of the most notable ministers of the Victorian age – the great preacher and scholar, David Meyer Isaacs, Abraham Barnett and, of course, the almost legendary Aaron Levy Green – have occupied the pulpit. Nor should we forget the connection with the city of the writers, the Zangwills and Isaac Rosenberg . . . and this list is far from exhausted. It has never been a large community: at its height it did not exceed 2,000 souls, but its contribution to society at large and the attractions of the region, have guaranteed an unending supply of businessmen and professional people as charted by Judith Samuel in a careful and interesting fashion.

CYRIL P. HERSHON, M.A., Ph.D., M.I.L.,
University of the West of England
April 1997, Nisan 5757

INTRODUCTION

I came to the task of historical research as a complete amateur, having no formal training. It all started when Raphael Emanuel remarked that he thought the money obtained from selling the Synagogue in Bath should have gone to the upkeep of its Cemetery. I looked into this in some detail and found that the Synagogue was leased from St. John's Hospital in Bath so there was no money for the Cemetery. This encouraged me to write about the small community in Bath which otherwise had been completely forgotten. This was done with Malcolm Brown's help and the story of the Jews in Bath appeared in Jewish Historical Studies (previously known as the Transactions) of the Jewish Historical Society of England and Bath History I, 1986.

Writing *Jews in Bristol* grew out of the exhibition '200 Years of Bristol Jewry' held at St. Nicholas Church, Bristol in 1986. Those of us who were involved in the project, and I had only a very small part in it, realised that there must be more to the story than we were able to find at the time.

Previously Alix Schlesinger had written a summary of Bristol's Jewish history in the 'Save our Shul' brochures of 1971 and Raphael Emanuel had produced 'The History of Bristol Jewry' for Temple Local History Group, published in volume 4/88. Remembering that the cemetery of the pre-1290 congregation on Brandon Hill is now covered by the buildings of Queen Elizabeth Hospital School which gave rise to the quotation that 'whatever the state of the boys' Greek or Latin, they have a good Hebrew foundation', I have a similar feeling that this work is firmly founded on that of my predecessors.

In addition, the creation of the Bristol Jewish History Group helped to lay the foundations for this book but for much of the time I have been working on my own. Nonetheless, without the History Group's valuable support, I would never have started in the first place.

At the time, I thought that unlike Bath, Bristol must still have all their records since they had been going strong since the eighteenth century. This time I would not have to put the story together from census records, rate books, the local and Jewish press and occasional personal memories. But I was wrong. The absence of minute books and similar material belonging to Bristol Hebrew Congregation was identical to Bath except that most, if not all, of their losses were recorded. Part of the deficiency is explained in a report in the *Jewish Chronicle* of 22nd July, 1910, which states that:

The old minute book of the Congregation, extending back eighty years, has unfortunately been mislaid and all attempts to recover it have hitherto failed.

The rest of the deficiency was due to the Jewish Historical Society of England's request for congregations who had old record books to send them to their newly refurbished Mocatta Library at University College, London. In the preface to *Transactions* XI, 1924/1927, the Society recorded that:

> The Bristol Congregation has taken advantage of the facilities and a large quantity of records relating to the Congregation in the nineteenth century is now in the Library.

The College received a direct hit during the Second World War and an enormous amount of very valuable records (including those from Bristol but excluding those already lost in 1910) went up in smoke. The only useful book of the nineteenth century still extant in Bristol is a register of births from 1829/30 and 1849 to 1893 and deaths from 1828/9 and 1848 to 1862.

The first extant ledger of general meetings starts in December 1901 and for committee meetings in February 1938. Both are then continuous to the present day. I read them as far as 1971, thus covering the Mayoralty of Helen Bloom and the creation of the Bristol and West Progressive Jewish Congregation.

The 1986 exhibition, '200 Years of Bristol Jewry', listed the three members of the Bristol Hebrew Congregation (then in Temple Street) who had been members of the Town Council. So I read the Council's minute books for the period and, relating to the move from Temple Street to Park Row, those for the Improvement Committee and the New Streets Committee (part of the Local Board of Health).

I also consulted the local press from 1836 to 1874 and spasmodically thereafter. I started in 1836 because that was when Bristol Town Council first petitioned their Members of Parliament to vote for the bill for the removal of the Disabilities of the Jews. This was repeated on three subsequent occasions. I ceased reading the local papers from 1874, the year when William Wolfe Alexander died and his place as alderman was taken by another. Also at this time, the reports in the Jewish press on affairs in Bristol vastly improved. It provided all the information in the chapter on the social and artistic life of the community and much else besides.

In those days the press reported sittings of Parliament and local Council meetings verbatim, relating matters not recorded in the briefer Council minutes. Would it were so nowadays! When I performed a similar exercise to find out about Lord Mayor Alderman

Mrs. Helen Bloom, the only reports were 'photo opportunities' for the press when she met the public for some City occasion. Unfortunately I failed to contact members of Helen Bloom's family at that stage. What the local press in the nineteenth century also carried were advertisements which provided a great deal of valuable information about members of the Congregation and how they earned their living as well as the occasional comment in the news paragraphs relating to events and people of public interest.

Joseph Alexander, who came to Bristol in the 1740s, created a family of shipowners and shipbrokers. As far as I can tell, they appear to have taken no part in the slave trade. In addition, it is worth noting that, unlike other towns such as Portsmouth and Plymouth, there have been no Jewish ships' chandlers in Bristol.

My thanks are due to Bob Emmanuel (President of Bristol Hebrew Congregation at the time) for allowing me to read the Synagogue's minute books from 1901 to 1971, those of the Bristol Hebrew Ladies' Benevolent Society from 1909 to 1952 and the Literary Society from 1938 to 1947.

More formally, to Raphael Emanuel and the Temple Local History Group for information about Temple Parish and the Mikveh; John Adler, Simon Ferguson and Michael Wagen for coming out, sometimes at short notice, to take photographs for me; Bristol City Museum and Art Gallery, who provided the copy of Ashmead's map of Bristol and the drawing of the Stone Kitchen; Bristol Central Library and Bristol City Archives, both of whom put up with my many questions and, for several years, constant visits; the Newspaper Library at Colindale, without which the story would have been impossible to write and who provided many of the illustrations; the library at University College, London, which has taken over the Mocatta Library of the Jewish Historical Society.

My thanks to Rabbi Dr. Bernard Susser who pulled the book into shape and had been asked to write the Preface but very sadly died on 11th April, 1997, 4th Nisan, 5757, before he could complete the task. Also to Dr. Cyril Hershon for his proofreading, without which the work would be much less complete than it is and for stepping into the breach and providing the Preface. In addition, to Ms. Madge Dresser, who also read the book with a critical eye. She recently co-edited *The Making of Modern Bristol*.

On a fleeting visit to Bath from his home in New York, my son, Maurice J. Samuel gave an expert look at the glossary and improved it in many ways. And last but not least, my thanks to my husband, Woolf Samuel, without whose patience over the last ten years this book would never have happened.

JUDITH SAMUEL April 1997, Nisan 5757

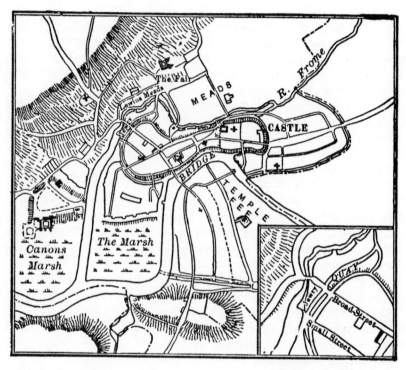

Plan of City of Bristol showing situation of Jewry in the mid-thirteenth century.

A Brief Summary of
Anglo-Jewish History

J ews first appear in English history shortly after the Norman conquest. William of Malmesbury states they were brought over from
Rouen. The Duke of Normandy, like most European rulers of his
day, used his Jewish subjects as a source of finance. This was necessary
as the Church of those days officially would not permit lending money
at interest. Certainly it is clearly forbidden in Jewish law:

> You shall not deduct interest from loans to your countryman,
> whether in money or food or anything else that can be deducted
> as interest. You may deduct interest from loans to foreigners; but
> do not deduct any from loans to your countryman, – so that the
> Lord your God may bless you in all your undertakings in the
> land which you are about to invade and occupy.[1]

The very early records that remain from those days are documents
which were found in a room in the old Domus Conversorum (now the
Public Record Office in Chancery Lane). There is one Pipe Roll for
the years 1130–1131 during the reign of Henry I and a complete set
from the second year of the reign of Henry III to that of Edward I,
covering the period 1218 to 1290. These records are of financial
transactions between all kinds and conditions of men of affairs but
they give the impression that Jews in Norman England were all money
lenders. But the number of people mentioned would not make a
community in any town where they lived. There would still need to
have been the hewers of wood and drawers of water, the butcher, the
baker, the candlestick maker and so on. But such people were not
permitted to do business outside the Jewish community. Thus we have
a very one-sided picture of life among Jews and Christians of those
days.

At the coronation of Richard I on Sunday, 3rd September, 1189,
some leading Jews came with gifts from their communities and were
rudely ejected by a door keeper. The rumour spread that the King
had ordered a general massacre of Jews and an eager mob, egged on

---

[1] Deuteronomy 23: 20–21. Similar verses exist in Exodus 22: 24, Leviticus 25: 35–
37.

by some of his courtiers, set to work. The unfortunate Jewish deputation was beaten and left for dead outside the hall. There was a rush to the Jewry, where finding that all doors were barred and bolted, the rioters set fire to the houses. Some of the inhabitants perished in the flames and others by the sword as they attempted to escape. The authorities tried to reason with the mob, but they shrank from using force on Coronation Day and the massacre continued until the supply of victims gave out. Richard could not punish so many wrong-doers. He contented himself with a proclamation announcing that the Jews were in his 'special peace' and there the matter rested.

But this misplaced indulgence had a worse outcome. The provinces began to emulate the crimes committed in London. The Jewish community in York had been active from the middle 1170s when Jews began to acquire property in the city. Early York Jewry supported a number of scholars, the most notable of whom was Rabbi Yomtob of Joigny, a famous doctor of law who came from beyond the sea to teach English Jews. But its most successful financiers were Josce and Benedict of York. They had travelled to King Richard's coronation. Josce survived the violence but Benedict was severely wounded by the mob and died the following day. At first, Josce joined Aaron of Lincoln (the richest Jew of his time) in lending money and then continued on his own. He also worked with Benedict of York, a money lender who seems to have been even more active and wealthy than Josce until his untimely death.[2]

The bloodiest event took place at York on Friday, 16th March, 1190, the eve of the Sabbath before Passover. The plot was laid by some crusaders and knights, including the Sheriff of Nottingham, whose debts to the Jews were more than they could cope with. They started a fire in York which distracted the citizens and ended by plundering the house and killing the family of Benedict who had already perished in London. The remainder of the Jews benefited by the warning and took refuge in the castle. But their panic made them suspicious of the castle keeper who had befriended them. They locked him out of Clifford's Tower where they stayed; he appealed to the sheriff for assistance, the troops were called to arms and the conspirators found themselves, to their gratification, acting under the mantle of the law. The Jews were besieged in the castle. They realised their hopeless position. Led by Rabbi Yomtob of Joigny, their spiritual leader, they met in council and agreed that the only course was to destroy their wealth in a great pyre, kill their wives and children and

---

[2] R.B. Dobson, *The Jews of Medieval York and the Massacre of March 1190*, Borthwick Papers, No. 45, 1974, pp.11–13,15,24.

14

finally themselves. The fire they lit took hold of the tower and destroyed them all.[3]

A few months after the massacre, Benedict's sons paid 700 marks for the inheritance of their father's landed property and his debts. From this time, the Jews of York waxed wealthy and often paid the largest amount in the many tallages recorded in this period. But in the lean years after 1250, many York Jews left for other towns in England or abroad.[4]

The result of these frightful events was the 'Ordinances of the Jews' which ordered that all financial contracts with Jews had to be registered under the supervision of Christian and Jewish Chirographers. Charters were made; one part of each contract was sealed by the person to whom the money was lent, which would be held by the Jew and the other to be kept in the Common Chest or Archa. Later, in 1240, these rules were changed so that the document with the seal was kept in the Archa and both borrower and lender had a copy.[5]

The Hebrew for a deed is 'Starr' and the room in the Exchequer of the Jews, which regulated this system, was known as the Starr Chamber. By the time the Exchequer of Elizabeth I met in that room for their own nefarious purposes the reason for its name was long forgotten.

The myth that Jews were in the habit of sacrificing little boys to gratify their hatred of Christianity goes back to the time of Josephus and Philo. In modern times, it recurred in the story of William of Norwich. Thomas of Monmouth, a monk of the Benedictine Priory in Norwich, wrote the story within a decade of the boy's death, not only as history but also to attack those who did not believe the story and to recount the miracles wrought at the shrine of St. William as his proof.

William was born in 1132 or 1133, son of a well-to-do farmer. At the age of eight, he was apprenticed to a skinner in Norwich. He had frequent dealings with the Jews of the town who were said to regard him with special favour.

According to Thomas, on 20th March, 1144 (the Monday before Easter) the 12 year-old William called on his mother with a stranger who said he was the cook of William, Archdeacon of Norwich and

---

[3] R.B. Dobson, *The Jews of Medieval York and the Massacre of March 1190*, Borthwick Papers, No. 45, 1974, pp.18,24–28.

[4] R.B. Dobson, *The Jews of Medieval York and the Massacre of March 1190*, Borthwick Papers, No. 45, 1974, pp.38,41,44.

[5] From the Introduction to Israel Abrahams, M.A., and the Rev. Canon H.P. Stokes, Ll.D., Litt.D., F.S.A., *Starrs and Jewish Charters*, for the Jewish Historical Society of England at the University Press (Cambridge) 1930.

offered William a place in the Archdeacon's kitchen. The next time William was seen was when his body was found in Thorpe Wood to the east of Norwich, dressed only in his jacket and shoes with his head shaved and punctured with countless stabs. The suggestion was that William had been received kindly by the Jews on the Tuesday and early Wednesday, the first and second days of Passover. But after the service on Wednesday morning the boy was seized, gagged, bound and pierced to the heart. On Good Friday (a day when Jews did not normally stir abroad) the body was taken to Thorpe Wood. When he was found on the Saturday by a forester, he wanted it to be buried but this was not done until Easter Monday.

Although William's mother and uncle went round the town saying his death was the fault of the Jews, nothing much was done against them at this time. Much later, the Jews were brought before the synod, to be tried by ordeal. Since the inevitable result would be a guilty verdict, the Sheriff escorted them to the castle where they remained till the danger was passed.

Subsequently, William became a saint who performed miracles, caused visions and wonderful occurrences although the local clergy at the time were opposed to the cult of William as a holy martyr. Jews continued to live in Norwich untroubled by their neighbours until 1190 when Jews in England all suffered after the coronation of King Richard I.

Many explanations have been proposed for William's death and subsequent canonization. Lipman observes:

> My own inclination is to regard the case as a sexual crime against a child, of the kind unfortunately so prevalent today. . . . But the most likely culprit would surely be the mysterious stranger who took the boy away with the promise of a post in the archdeacon's kitchen. Had this mysterious person been a local Jew, or even had he looked like a Jew, this would surely have been recorded. Silence on this point would indicate that the mysterious stranger was a Christian.[6]

There were similar cases in Gloucester in 1168, Bury St. Edmunds in 1181 and Bristol in 1183. In each case the consequences for the local Jews were not serious. It was much later that the idea of the blood libel, that the blood was used for ritual purposes such as making matzah, made this accusation so much worse for the Jews who were

---

[6] V.D. Lipman, *Medieval Norwich* (Cambridge, 1967), W.E. Heffer & Sons for the Jewish Historical Society of England, pp.50–57.

accused of the crime. Indeed, the accusation was repeated with monotonous regularity and has recurred even in the present century.[7]

From the reign of Henry III (1216–1272) conditions for English Jews worsened. The Fourth Lateran Council of 1215, attended by Stephen Langton, Archbishop of Canterbury, affected Jews seriously. They were thought to have been responsible for an alarming spread of heresy. Therefore all the degrading restrictions proposed by the earlier Lateran Council were re-enacted and others were added. Jews now had to pay tithes to the Church and the practice of usury was prohibited. But usury by Jews was very useful to the Treasury and this instruction was resisted by Henry III. In addition they had to wear a badge, which in England was in the form of tablets of stone. Resulting from regulations of 1253, Jews could only remain in England if they performed the King's service, new Synagogues could not be built, prayers had to be silent, Jews could not employ Christian servants. Life became increasingly difficult.

The reign of Edward I (1272–1307) saw conditions getting even worse. He was a correct and religious man, greatly influenced by Church policy. The attitude of Pope Honorius IV hardened against Jews wherever they were living. In 1286, he sent a Papal Bull to the Archbishops of York and Canterbury forbidding free intercourse with the perfidious Jews, to avoid it having a similar effect on English Christians.[8] Finally, at the Council of London in 1290, there was much discussion about the expulsion of the Jews. It was agreed that a public edict be issued so that the Jews, 'that miserable people' be ordered to leave, taking their goods with them, which they did.

When the Jews left England the task of providing funds to the King was taken over by the Lombards. Very few Jews remained in this country. These were the converts to Christianity who were living in the Domus Conversorum (House of Converts) in London. Their families considered them as if they were dead and the English as subjects for charity.

The English Jews went to France or Germany and joined other communities. However, Edward I put pressure on Philippe the Fair to expel all English Jews from his realm, and they moved to Aragon (i.e. Narbonne) or Catalonia. Conditions in Europe were always hard and discrimination followed them wherever they went. The only country where Jews were well off was Spain. Jews lived in Iberia, then part of the Roman Empire, from the destruction of the Second Temple in 70

---

[7] The blood libel makes no sense, since Matzah are made only from flour and water.
[8] To the Archbishops of Canterbury and his Suffragans (Reg. Vatican, 43, fol. 208v, no. 42) dated 30th November, 1286.

C.E. When Rome fell the area was overrun by the Visigoths and the problems of the Jewish residents continued. In 711 the Muslims conquered the land and the Golden Age for Spanish Jewry began. Although in political terms the Jewish subjects were second class citizens they could use their talents to the best advantage. They flourished as politicians, lawyers, doctors, poets and at least one military leader.

THE MIKVEH IN BRISTOL

A medieval Mikveh was found in Bristol in autumn 1986 when the Avon Wildlife Trust took over the nearby Old Brandon Hill Police Station in Jacob's Wells Road, near Brandon Hill. Bob Vaughan of Temple Local History Group visited and saw a well in the entrance courtyard. (See ill. 1.) It might have been a fresh-water cistern with an open well top, but the original plan showed a well in that position.

The building had been purchased by a developer. While he was rebuilding the antique workshop at the back of the site, some unexpected features were found by the workmen. A cast iron pump close to the rear wall indicated the well site. A few feet to the left of the pump was an opening about two feet in height in the wall, filled with rubbish. Members of Temple Local History Group decided to observe progress and take photographs in the hope that this would indeed be the site of the old Jacob's Well. As the debris was cleared a strong flow of water quickly removed the disturbed slurry. The water went down a drain running beneath building directly towards Constitution Hill. The water was tepid and during a spell of freezing weather in January 1987, steam could be seen rising from the opening (later tested and found to be about 53 degrees F).

One of the workmen employed on the building noticed some 'hieroglyphics' on the front of the massive stone lintel supporting the superstructure. It was decided to cut an opening in the newly-built concrete retaining wall to investigate. In case these letters were significant, Robert Vaughan informed Temple Local History Group. Raphael Emanuel, a long-standing member of the Group and a lecturer on Architecture at Bath University, recognized the letters as Hebrew and that it might be a 'Mikveh'. Realizing the importance of this find, he informed the British Museum. The one word inscription, much hacked about to provide a key for later plaster which still survives on the upper half of the lintel, reads 'Zochalim' or flowing. The plaster may well cover the word 'Mayim' or water, the two words together are used in the Mishnah to designate a bath of flowing water which can be smaller than the more common static water which has a statutory minimum size. The inscription was no doubt placed there to inform the user of the difference.

The problem of dating the structure remained. Michael Ponsford of the City Museum noted similarities in the lintel and other stonework to Romanesque masonry found in the excavation of St. Augustine's Church, College Green. As the land surrounding Jacob's Well was acquired by St. Augustine's Abbey (now the Cathedral) in 1142, the Mikveh must be earlier. Therefore it is earlier than that discovered in Cologne in 1956 which dates from 1170 and at that time was thought to be the oldest in Europe. The inscription is also the only medieval Hebrew one yet discovered in Britain. This could put the Jewish settlement in Bristol from about 1100. At the expulsion of the Jews from England in 1290, all Jewish property passed to the Crown, enabling Edward III to present it to the City in 1373.[9]

---

[9] The Mikveh is reprinted from R.R. Emanuel, 'The History of Bristol Jewry', in the Newsletter, No. 4/88, of the Temple Local History Group, Bristol.

The Jews in Bristol Before 1290 [1]

T he Jews who came to England after the Norman Conquest
settled in the principal towns and villages in various parts of
the country. In those days Bristol (or Bristowe or Bricgstow,
'the fenced place of the bridge')[2] was the chief centre of trade in the
West country and second only to London.[3] From the river Avon, and
its tributary the Frome, English and foreign ships sailed to Ireland and
all parts of Europe. Norman Jews found a congenial market in this
busy seaport town for the practice of money-lending. Rigid control
over their financial dealings was exercised by the King of England
who was an apparently sleeping though in fact an active partner in
their business affairs.[4]

At the time of the Expulsion in 1290, Bristol was one of the
authorised Jewries in which there existed not only a synagogue and a
Jewish quarter, but also the royal chirograph chest or *archa*[5] in which
were preserved the bonds and tallies registering financial transactions.
The Bristol community was one of the smallest in England, but is
none the less of interest. It was also one of the earliest.[6]

The Jewry was situated on the Quay between Broad Street and
Small Street (see map on page 12), outside the inner city walls but
within the outer wall. The Synagogue was situated in Small Street,
under the emplacement of the later St. Giles' Church and can possibly
still be excavated. The cemetery was, of course, outside the walls and
was traditionally on a hill under today's Queen Elizabeth Hospital
School on Brandon Hall. The Normans referred to Jewish cemeteries
as 'Mont Juif' ('Jews' Hill'), even when they were not on a hill. As the

---

[1] Much of this chapter is based on the paper by Michael Adler, 'The Jews of Bristol
in Pre-Expulsion Days', Jewish Historical Society of England's *Transactions* (hereafter
JHSE *Trans.*), 1928–1931, with additions by C.P. Hershon.

[2] J.F. Nichols & John Taylor, *Bristol Past and Present*, vol. i, p.14; William Hunt,
Historic Towns, Bristol, Longman Green, 1902 & 1909, p.4; John Evans, *A
Chronological Outline of the History of Bristol*, 1824, p.7.

[3] William Hunt, *Historic Towns, Bristol*, Longman Green, 1902 & 1909, p.2.

[4] Joseph Jacobs, *The Jews of Angevin England* introduction p.15, David Nutt, London,
1893, (hereinafter Jacobs, *Jews of Angevin England*); C. Gross, *Exchequer of the Jews of
England in the Middle Ages* (hereinafter *Exchequer of the Jews*) p.202, etc.

[5] *Exchequer of the Jews of England*, p.182 etc.; J.M. Rigg, *Calendar of the Plea Rolls of the
Exchequer of the Jews*, vol.ii, introduction p.xiv, (hereinafter *Plea Rolls*).

[6] Cecil Roth *Short History of the Jewish People*, 1953, p.169.

Jews probably came from Rouen, they would have had all the usual offices – a school, though the Synagogue was also called 'Scola', a ritual bath, a butcher, a communal baker (for matzah) and possibly some philanthropic buildings too.

The connection between the ancient Jewry and St. Giles' Church is important. The local tradition, repeated in all histories of Bristol, relates that the Jews' synagogue was in a room beneath Great Giles' Church. The main entance to the church was inside the wall while the entrance to the vaults and the synagogue was outside the wall. Thus the two faiths could share the same building without coming in contact with each other. The church was demolished during the reign of Queen Elizabeth, but it is recorded that it had previously been disused as a place of worship since 1301.[7] When Michael Adler wrote his history, the site was covered by the printing works of Messrs. J.W. Arrowsmith, Ltd. and the room could still be identified. This building was destroyed with so much else in the area in the bombing in 1940.

In the thirteenth century there was also a group of houses in Wine Street owned by Jews. This site had the advantage of being near the Castle and therefore Royal protection – although the history of York Jewry shows that that was not always satisfactory.

The Reeve or Mayor, the most famous Bristolian of his day, was Robert FitzHarding (1085–1170)[8] who married a niece of William the Conqueror. He found the presence of Jews in his city troublesome so, with Robert, Earl of Gloucester, he founded a Domus Conversorum[9] in 1154, probably the first in England. Others were founded in Southwark in 1213 (not called a Domus), in Oxford in 1221 and London in 1232. The House was run by the Guild of Kalendars,[10] a religious fraternity of clergy and laity, whose work included the healing arts and popular education. No evidence has come to light concerning the results of the labours of the Kalendars in the local Domus Conversorum. The only Bristol Jews who are known to have become converts are John and his sister Joan who, in 1235, were ordered to be

---

[7] J.F. Nichols & John Taylor, *Bristol Past and Present*, vol.ii, p.246; S. Seyer, *Memoirs, Historical and Topographical, of Bristol*, vol.i. p.264 and John Evans, *A Chronological Outline of the History of Bristol*, 1824, p.77.

[8] J.F. Nichols & John Taylor, *Bristol Past and Present*, vol.i, p.71.

[9] Leland's *Itinerary*, p.76 states that '. . . in the time of King Henry . . . schools were ordained in Brightstow by the two Roberts for the conversion of the Jews and put in the order of the Calendaries and the Mayor'.

[10] J.F. Nichols & John Taylor, *Bristol Past and Present*, vol.ii, p.91; W. Barrett, *History of the Antiquities of Bristol*, pp.449,452. He compares the work of the Kalendars with that of the Master of the Rolls in London.

admitted into the London Domus[11] and Christiana of Bristol[12] who resided in the same Home in 1280 and continued to enjoy the royal patronage many years after the expulsion. It may be that Fitz-Harding's Domus was not a residential home, but a school of instruction, or it may not have continued its operations owing to lack of scholars.

The earliest recorded Jew of Bristol was Moses, son of Rabbi Isaac. He was born in Germany, moved to Normandy and later came to England. He traced his ancestry back to Rabbi Simeon ben Isaac ben Abun the Great, who flourished in Mainz in 1000.[13] He was an exegete and a most important liturgical writer of the tenth and eleventh centuries. Also he was known as a miracle-worker. His descendant, Moses ben Isaac, was an important textual critic and grammarian.[14] About 1279 Moses (his great-great grandson) compiled a Calendar, at the end of which he gave a genealogical table, which traced the origin of this eminent Anglo-Jewish family. The first to settle in England was Moses of Bristol, father of the more famous Yom-Tob, author of the 'Sefer Ha-Tannaim' [Book of the Tanna teachers] who came to Bristol prior to 1170. He was grandson of Rabbi Simon of Trier (Trèves), a martyr of the Second Crusade. He subsequently moved to Oxford where he owned land in the Jewry and died about 1184.

A friend of Moses must have been Benedict (in Hebrew Berachyah), who died about 1184, leaving a widow, Leah and two sons, Moses and Joseph.[15] Benedict of Bristol was a wealthy man and before they could have their inheritance, King Henry claimed 40 marks from his widow in death duties and Moses had to pay one ounce of gold, of which he paid all except 15s. The balance was not forthcoming because he disappeared. Leah had also to pay the Royal Treasury 20 bezants (today equivalent to £65[16]) to enable her to draw up agreement between them and the local Beth Din (Coram Judaeis).

---

[11] *Close Rolls*, 1235, p.124.

[12] Michael Adler, 'History of the "Domus Conversorum"', JHSE *Trans.* vol.iv, 1899–1901, p.54.

[13] Jacobs, *The Jews of Angevin England*, p.253; H.P. Stokes, *Studies in Anglo-Jewish History*, p.57.

[14] A.M. Hyamson, *A History of the Jews of Oxford*, 2nd ed., London, 1928, p.95.

[15] *Pipe Roll 31*, Henry II, 1185; Jacobs, *The Jews of Angevin England*, pp.97,(86); and pp.95,(76) and *Pipe Roll 34*, Henry II; Jacobs, *The Jews of Angevin England*, pp.142,(105), *Pipe Roll 3*, Richard I.

[16] I am grateful for the approximate figures here and later in this chapter supplied by the Economics Section, Market Intelligence Department, NatWest Group, London.

The only other reference to the Bristol Ecclesiastical Court appears seven years later, when Judah of Bristol paid two ounces of gold for an inquiry to be made in the 'chapter of the Jews' whether a Jew ought to take usury from another Jew.[17] The importance of this Court proves that the Bristol community was an important one at this time. The existence of these Courts in Jewish communities is well established in the early pages of Anglo-Jewish history, and later King John confirmed their privileges in a charter fully legalising these tribunals of Jewish law.

Leah's second son, Joseph, succeeded his father as tax-collector on behalf of the King. In 1191 he was responsible for the payment of 100 shillings of the second 1,000 marks which the Jews of England promised the King in connection with the tallage levied at Guildford in 1188 to the total of 60,000 marks.[18] He is probably the Jose of Bristol in the Fine Rolls of 1205 who lent money to two Somerset gentlemen, and appears to have been the communal Rav.[19]

There was a man named Sturmis, considered by Bristol historians to have been a Jew. In 1177:

> the burgesses of Bristol were at the mercy of the King and were fined 80 marks for Sturmis, the usurer.[20]

It is not clear whether he was really a Jew or what was the outcome of his story. For a man with such an improbable Jewish name to be described an a usurer when only Jews could practise usury seems curious.[21] The royal intervention suggests that Sturmis was killed or ill-treated in some way by the local people and they had to pay his debts. In 1286 Robert Sturmy obtained royal protection against the alleged demands of a Norwich Jew and in 1314 Sir John Sturmy was

---

[17] Jacobs, *The Jews of Angevin England*, p. 155 (128); *Pipe Roll 4*, Richard I; H.P Stokes, *Studies in Anglo-Jewish History*, p.49.

[17] Jacobs, *The Jews of Angevin England*, p. 155 (128); *Pipe Roll 4*, Richard I; H.P Stokes, *Studies in Anglo-Jewish History*, p.49.

[18] The tallage was a special tax levied on Jews (and sometimes Christians) by the Kings. T. Madox, *Exchequer of the Jews*, ch.vii,(i), p.223; Jacobs, *The Jews of Angevin England*, p.142.

[19] Michael Adler, *Jews of Medieval England*, JHSE *Trans.*, London, 1939, p.191.

[20] T. Madox, *Exchequer of the Jews*, vol.vi., p.2, note 1 where the original Latin quotation is recited. S. Seyer, *Memoirs, Historical and Topographical, of Bristol*, vol.i. p.499.; J.F. Nichols and John Taylor, *Bristol, Past and Present*, vol.i. p.98; John Evans, *A Chronological Outline of the History of Bristol*, 1824, p.48.

[21] Tovey, *Anglia Judaica*, p.121; Joseph Jacobs, *The Jews of Angevin England*, Intro. p.xiii. T. Madox, *Exchequer of the Jews*, Ch.x, p.346, names three Christian men and two women described as usurers in the reign of Henry II. In all probability Sturmis was not a Jew.

an admiral of the fleet. It has been suggested that these men were descended from Sturmis, who entered the Domus Conversorum and were there converted. If that is so, they were the only known successes of that establishment.

The first list of Bristol Jews is in the Northampton Donum of 1194,[22] which names the Jews of England who contributed to the 'Gift' of 5,000 marks promised to King Richard I on his return from the Crusades and his subsequent captivity at the hands of Leopold, Duke of Austria, and Henry VI, Emperor of Germany. The total amount of the tallage of £1,803 came from twenty-two Jewish communities. Bristol was fourteenth in order and contributed £22.16s.2d. In comparing this with London's £486, Lincoln's £287 and Canterbury's £241, one can surmise that the community was now smaller, or certainly less affluent. Why? Because the Guilds were preventing them carrying on crafts and services. The donors are Isaac son of Jesse, Isaac le Eveske, Isaac son of Judah, Abraham Gabbai, Benlivinger, Preciosa, Isaac Furmager, Abraham son of Vives, Isaac Episcopi, Manasser, Salaman son of Isaac, Jacob son of Josce, Dieulecresse Furmager, Judas Gabbay and Samuel le Pointur. The last named may have been a scribe. The question is discussed in detail in Michael Adler's paper.[23] In old French, its meaning can be 'a number of points', hence it can refer to vocalization, therefore a scribe seems a reasonable description of Samuel.

The lady Preciosa is a typical example of the picturesque Norman-French names which Anglo-Jews of that time gave their daughters, whilst retaining the more Biblical names for men.

There are two men, Isaac and Dieulecresse (Gedalya) with the surname Furmager, which Adler suggests comes from the Norman-French fourmagier (in French fromage); hence they were cheese-mongers or at least dealt in farm produce. (They may have been the community's grocers.) Two contributors are called Isaac le Eveske and Isaac Episcopus; both no doubt, were Cohanim.[24] Although the name Benlivinger is said to be a variation on Levy it could equally well be ben Le Viguier, son of a tax collector. He was in Lincoln in 1221 owing money in the 1210 'Tallia Judaeorum' with his son Sammekin.

It is curious that there are two Gabbai's in the list, but it is suggested that Abraham was Gabbai of Gloucester, at that time a

---

[22] JHSE's *Miscellanies*, part I, 1925, p.lix; Jacobs, *Jews of Angevin England*, p.162.

[23] Michael Adler, *Jews of Medieval England*, JHSE *Trans.*, London, 1939, pp.197–199.

[24] Levites and Cohanim were the priests in the Temple. It is worth noting that the names given to certain Jews, such as l'Eveske or Episcopus (priest) and Arch-Presbyter (archbishop) are equivalent to Levi or Cohen in meaning. They were likely to be acting as the King's tax collectors.

larger community than Bristol. Gabbai indicated a tax-collector on behalf of the community, but it is more likely that by this period it was a surname only. His name appears in two cases of murder, in both of which he was acquitted. The first took pace in 1220 and involved several Jews of Gloucester.

Abraham was accused of bribing others to murder a Gloucester Jew named Solomon Turbe.[25] Gabbay and Turbe had a violent quarrel, and Gabbay charged his brother Jew with 'maliciously wounding him in the King's peace'. The Sheriff of Gloucester brought Solomon before the Justices at Westminster, and after a partial hearing of the case, Solomon was sent back to Gloucester and lodged in the Castle. On a certain Friday[26] it chanced that the Sheriff was approaching the Castle gate with several royal officials when they saw something fall from the tower. They wondered whether it could be a man or a bundle of clothing? The Sheriff asked the porter to inquire, and he reported that it was the Jew who was in prison who had fallen to the ground. Turbe was seriously injured and died the next day, after telling the Sheriff that he had intended to kill himself like King Saul had done. On being asked whether he accused anybody of pushing him so that he fell, he answered, 'No'. Then, continues the Exchequer Plea Roll:

> there comes to him Comitissa, his wife, to whom he said, 'Flee hence, for it is by thy plot that I am slain.'

Next day, Saturday, Turbe, feeling himself to be on the point of death, sent for five prominent local Jews to make his will. In their presence, and that of the Constable and Coroner of Gloucester, Turbe was reported to have charged his enemy, Abraham Gabbay, of intending to kill him. His widow brought an action against Gabbay,[27] accusing him of hiring five men to throw her husband from the Castle wall. The officers of the law at once began to move. The Sheriff was ordered to take possession of the chattels, charters, tallies and chirographs belonging to Abraham. Comitissa stated that the Sheriff had confessed that he had accepted a bribe of £10 in one version, or 10 marks in another, from Gabbay to cause the death of her husband. An inquiry instituted into the event decided that Turbe had committed suicide.[28]

---

[25] The name Turbe was that of William, Bishop of Norwich in 1146. See Jessop and James, *The Life and Miracles of St. William of Norwich*, introduction p.xxi.

[26] *Plea Rolls*, vol.i, p.51.

[27] H.P. Stokes, *Studies in Anglo-Jewish History*, pp.45,50; *Plea Rolls*, vol.i, introduction, p.x.

[28] H.P. Stokes, *Studies in Anglo-Jewish History*, p.51.

A second charge of murder was brought against Gabbay in 1223. Abraham Folet, a Jew of Bristol, had a sister who appears to have met her death by foul play. Folet accused Gabbay, together with his nephew Leo, of having murdered his sister and a mandate was therefore issued to the Constable of Bristol Castle to arrest Gabbay and his nephew and bring them to trial before the Justices of the Jews. Twelve 'honest and lawful' men, six Christians and six Jews were to form a jury, according to the usual custom. No record is known of the result of the trial but as Gabbay appears in a tallage roll four years later the charge against him must have failed for a second time.

These were, of course, Crown Pleas, but in the case of differences between Jews, King John authorized them to be settled by Rabbinical Courts. No Jew could give evidence against another one. These and other privileges were bought by 4,000 marks annually, paid in four half-yearly instalments.[29]

> Gloucester remained the chief Jewish town in the region until 1275, when all were transferred to Bristol when every Jew in Queen Eleanor's dower was expelled. What sort of Jews were these in the first batch? Can we believe the French description of Bristol as a city of soap-boilers?[30]
>
> In fact, many benefitted from the slave-trade activities of the port – even in an indirect way – and after its decline most left the town, Moses going to Oxford, others to Nottingham and London. Bristol Jews also engaged in the cloth trade with Spain, for Hispanic-Jewish documents mention 'cloth of Vristol'.[31]

The future King John found it necessary to borrow money from Jews in Gloucester and Bristol.

> By the time of John's connection with Bristol there was that sure sign of an urban community, a small Jewish colony. Robert FitzHarding had founded an establishment in 1154 for the instruction of Jewish converts, but the Jews in Bristol were still few at the end of the century, fewer than Gloucester, Exeter or Hereford.[32]

After his coronation, he issued several orders protecting Jews against violence, confirming former privileges and granting new ones

---

[29] A.M. Hyamson, *A History of the Jews of Oxford*, 2nd ed., London, 1928, p.48.
[30] Jacobs, *Jews of Angevin England*, p.149.
[31] Jacobs, *Jews in Spain*, p.xxxix.
[32] Bryan Little, *The City and County of Bristol*, London, 1954, p.36.

for which he received grateful recognition from the community, expressed in tallages.[33] In 1210, on his return from Ireland, King John issued an order for the whole Jewish community to be arrested and brought to Bristol Castle, where he was then staying. A tallage of 66,000 marks (equivalent to £32,740,000 today) was levied. There were about 2,000 to 3,000 Jews in England at this time. The *archae* of each centre were closely inspected. The desired amount was not produced. One Bristol Jew refused to pay even though he was tortured. The King ordered his gaolers to pull out one of his molar teeth each day until he had paid 10,000 marks. This lasted for seven days, on the eighth he agreed to pay the amount demanded.[34] Three years later the total had not been paid and Bristol Jews were imprisoned once again and one of their number was sent to the Tower of London. King John's son, Henry (1216–1272) was still trying to collect this tallage after his father's death.

At the beginning of his long reign Henry III and his counsellors intended to treat his Jewish subjects kindly,[35] orders for their protection – even against the bishops – being issued by the regent, William Marshal, Earl of Pembroke. The latter had himself conducted financial dealings with Jews[36] and regarded the policy of the late King John as harmful to the welfare of the State. In response to a royal order, Hugh de Vivonia, the Constable of Bristol Castle, appointed twenty-four citizens as guardians of the local Jews. Even the institution of the Jew badge in 1218[37] was intended for their good, in order that no man could plead that he had assaulted a Jew in ignorance of his race. It also avoided anyone unknowingly having sexual intercourse with a Jew, the reason for the Pope's call for distinctive clothing.

But like all his predecessors, Henry was short of money. His first tallage was for his sister's dowry. Princess Joan was to marry Alexander, King of Scotland, and the Jews were called upon to contribute.[38] The total collected from seventeen communities was £654.3s.5d. (£21,416), of which Bristol, tenth on the list, gave £22.2s.9d. (£725). Many other tallages followed. By the year 1234

---

[33] Tovey, *Anglia Judaica*, p.65; Jacobs, *The Jews of Angevin England*, p.215.
[34] This story was recorded by Roger of Wendover and accepted by almost all historians of the day. However, Sir Lionel Abrahams noted in his *Economic and Financial Position of Jews in Medieval England*, JHSE, *Trans.* VIII, 1915–1917, p.179 that Robert of Wendover 'was a copious and inaccurate writer'.
[35] Tovey, *Anglia Judaica*, p.76.
[36] *Plea Rolls*, vol.i, pp.12,32.
[37] Tovey, *Anglia Judaica* , p.79.
[38] Hilary Jenkinson, JHSE *Trans.* VIII, 1915–1917, p.44.

amounts of 8,000, 6,000, 1,000, 10,000 and finally 18,000 marks (£8,930,000)[39] were levied and some Jews tried to escape by leaving the country. Among them were two leading men of Bristol, Lumbard and Isaac.[40] A royal mandate was issued in 1238 that these men were to be imprisoned in Bristol Castle until they had paid their full quota of the tallages and given security that they would not run away. They evidently satisfied the demands, for three years later, they were at Worcester among the six Bristol delegates to assist the officers of the King to raise new taxes.

This meeting in February 1241 included the 'richest and most powerful' Jews, as the King desired: 'to treat with them as well concerning his own as their benefit'.

The *Parliamentum Judaicum* (Jewish Parliament) found they had to raise a tallage of 20,000 marks (£9,920,000) by the end of September 'under pain of forfeiting their goods and estates and the greatest penalties to the terror of all others'.[41] The six representatives from Bristol were Lumbard, Bonefey, Solomon of Ivelcester (Ilchester in Somerset), Isaac son of Jacob, Milo le Eveske, and Isaac of Bath, the only time that town is mentioned in pre-Expulsion Jewish records.[42]

The Jewish chirographers (that is, the two men in charge of the *archa*) of Bristol in 1253 were Cresse (Gedalya), the son of Milo le Eveske (Cohen) and Isaac of Caerleon. These two men were the pledges for the whole of the Bristol community two years later[43] for the payment of the arrears due to the King: 45 marks from the tallage of 60,000 marks of 1244, 60 shillings on the debts of Aaron of York,[44] £10.10s. as their portion form the arrears of £1,000 owed by Lumbard of Cricklade and 15 marks from the arrears of 500 marks levied upon Bristol as a tallage for Richard, Earl of Cornwall, to whom his brother King Henry had mortgaged his Jews in that year.[45]

---

[39] The last three amounts appear as follows: JHSE *Trans.* III, 1896–1898, p.198; *Exchequer of the Jews*, p.195 and Tovey, *Anglia Judaica*, p.91.

[40] *Close Rolls*, 1238, p.31; W. Prynne, *A Short Demurrer*, 1655, vol.ii. p.25; S. Seyer, *Memoirs, Historical and Topographical, of Bristol*, vol.i, p.528.

[41] 'Parliament', as can be seen from this passage, was very different to what is understood by this term today. In the Middle Ages it was a method of extracting money from the Jews.

[42] It is unlikely that Isaac of Bath lived in that town, it is more probable that he had an occasional connection with it, maybe for money lending to its citizens. R.B. Dobson, *The Jews of Medieval York and the Massacre of March 1190*, Borthwick Papers, No. 45, p.16.

[43] *Patent Rolls*, 1255, pp.439,443.

[44] JHSE *Trans.* III, 1896–1898, p.157; *Jewish Encyclopædia*, vol.i, p.16.

[45] Tovey, *Anglia Judaica*, p.135.

Aaron of York was one of the richest Jews in England, being appointed Arch-Presbyter in 1236,[46] and at one time being named as one of four representative Jews for the whole country. In 1235 he was granted exemption for life from all royal taxes on payment of an annual sum of 100 marks, and a further 100 shillings per annum in order to be quit of all debts already owing to the King. His circumstances changed about 1255, when his Majesty, at the instance of his brother, the Earl of Cornwall, 'granted exemption to him this time from tallage because of his poverty'.[47] His co-religionists, including those of Bristol, were therefore called upon to pay his quota, as was also done in the case of the wealthy Lumbard of Cricklade. Bristol was the only Jewry taxed for Lumbard's debts, even those of Wiltshire, where Lumbard lived, being exempt. This habit ran through all Christendom, making Jews responsible for unpaid taxes by their fellows.

Of all the tallages that appear in the Rolls (and some Rolls are missing, so the list is far from complete), Bristol was always low down the list, but generally managed to contribute something towards the required sum.

To return to the chirographers of 1255: Cresse's father, Milo le Eveske, was one of the Bristol representatives at the Worcester Parliament, and he carried on extensive financial operations,[48] which engaged the attention of the Barons of the Exchequer even after his death. About 1266 he was accused of 'felony' and sentenced to death by hanging.[49] His ostensible offence was very possibly clipping coin of the realm, for which many Jews in the thirteenth century were executed.

The other chirographer, Isaac of Caerleon, belonged to a wealthy family who had moved from that town in South Wales to Bristol shortly before this date. His father Jose (Joseph) bought a tenement in a street near the Castle and two houses in Winch Street, one of which he gave to his son Cresse, who sold it. After Cresse was hanged, Samuel of Wilton was appointed in his place.[50] During the period

---

[46] H.P. Stokes, *Studies in Anglo-Jewish History*, p.29.

[47] *Patent Rolls*, 1237, pp.178,187; 1238, p.228; 1241, p.246; 1235, p.93; Tovey, *Anglia Judaica*, p.108; *Patent Rolls*, 1255, p.443.

[48] *Calendar of Fine Rolls*, vol.i, pp.192,202; *Select Pleas, Starrs, etc.*, from J.M. Rigg, *The Rolls of the Exchequer of the Jews* (hereinafter *Select Pleas*), p.129; *Plea Rolls* vol.i, p.309, vol.ii, pp.238,271; Hilary Jenkinson (ed.), *Plea Rolls*, 1276, p.127.

[49] *Calendar of Fine Rolls*, vol.i, p.197.

[50] *Patent Rolls*, 1266, p.13. There were three charters of the debts and chattels of Samuel of Wilton in the Bristol *archa* in 1275. Public Record Office, E.101, No. 249.19.

they held office, an attack was made upon the small Bristol Jewry, in which the *archa* of the chirographers was burnt. This assault upon the Jewish quarter occurred during the last year of the Barons' War (1266): a civil war that caused great misery to all, including English Jews. It especially affected Bristol Jews, who lived so close to the Castle (of which the Earl of Gloucester, Gilbert, was liege-lord), because much of the fighting took place in and around it. Gilbert was a turncoat, transferring his support from Simon de Montfort to Prince Edward, himself the Lord of Bristol. De Montfort's men fell on the Jewry, as they had done in Toulouse, and subsequently the *archae* were either taken away or destroyed.

At Bristol, the chirographers were required to testify before the royal officers about the bonds destroyed 'by the King's enemies at the time of the disturbance of the realm'.[51]

Two Jews were killed in the War and their affairs appear in the Rolls. One was recorded but his name is illegible. The other was the lady Belazez, for whom Hagin son of Isaac paid a fine of 26s. to one of the Justices of the Jews to obtain her property.[52] Hagin lived in Bridgwater under the name of Benedict Bateman. He carried on his business in Bristol as well as in other parts of the west of England,[53] two of his bonds appearing in the Westminster Abbey records.

> In 1269 the same Bristol Chirographers had to produce all debts to the Barons in London that were still owing so that they could be cancelled, to punish English Jews 'for the betterment of the realm'.[54]

Once Henry III grew up, he showed himself insensitive to the feelings of his people. At a Parliament at Oxford in 1258 he was compelled to accept a scheme of government which placed the conduct of affairs in the hands of the barons. But he did not, and never had, intended to observe the Provisions of Oxford. He knew the Pope would absolve him from an oath given under duress. But the outcome was the Barons' War of 1264–1266. He died in 1272 after a long and troublesome reign. However his son and successor, Edward I, was no more sensitive to 'his Jews' than his father had been although English historians regard him as a good ruler.

---

[51] *Patent Rolls*, Loc. Cit.
[52] *Plea Rolls*, vol.i, p.194.
[53] *Plea Rolls*, vol.i, pp.238 et seq.; Muniments of Westminster Abbey, Nos. 6937 and 6933.
[54] JHSE *Trans.* XII, 1928–1931, p.177.

Before 1273 Samuel of Wilton was replaced as chirographer by Cressaunt (Dieulecresse, Gedalya) son of Pictavin.[55] He did not hold office long[56] and was succeeded by Isaac (HaKohen?) le Prestre who now shared the office with Isaac of Caerleon. In 1274 the chirographers were accused of conspiracy to forge a bond and place it in the *archa*.[57] When this charge of 'trespass and deceit' was first brought before the Justices, neither of the dismissed chirographers appeared, Hak le Prestre being ill and Isaac of Caerleon absent without reason. The Constable of Bristol was instructed to bring them to court and seize their property. Two other Bristol Jews, Solomon, son of Isaac of Wilton, and Isaac Hariprud of Wilton, otherwise known as Isaac of Marlborough, were implicated.[58] Later that year they stood trial and denied that they were guilty of the 'said false and malicious practice, word by word'.

The court fined them collectively the sum of £10 and two bezants (£6.55) and the Constable of Bristol had to obtain this from their land and goods. Isaac of Caerleon probably lost his office as a result of this sentence, but continued to live in his house in Winch Street. In 1283 he appears as a representative Bristol Jew together with his father Jose in a dispute about a debt.[59]

Isaac le Prestre was arrested in 1278 on a charge of coin clipping and sentenced to death by hanging. Hanging for this crime was a common punishment. In that same year, 293 Jews were similarly put to death in London alone.[60] Twenty-seven were hanged in Bristol, Devizes and Winchester. Isaac le Prestre had been a rich man, as can be seen from an inventory of his property sold for the benefit of King Edward in a Pipe Roll of 1285. His property included 75 spoons, 14 gold rings, 8 brooches, 22 silver cups, 21 *mazer* wood bowls, 5 hoods, 30 silk belts, 1 crimson robe with a mantle, and 1 blue robe. Five books are listed – a poor volume worth 20s., which may have been the *Sefer Mitzvat Haktan* (the Book of Mitzvot) of R. Isaac of Corbeil or the *Cuavar Katan* of R. Nissim, a poor quality *Tanach*, the *Halachot Gedolot* and two Psalmers with commentaries. This shows that he was learned and that he was in contact with the works of the French Rabbis. It also implies that Isaac le Prestre was fully conversant with the French language, as Isaac de Corbeil's works are noted for the vast number of French words used in them. The alternate work, even if by

---

[55] *Plea Rolls*, vol.i, p.61.
[56] *Plea Rolls*, vol.ii, p.167, he was in Southampton in 1274.
[57] *Plea Rolls*, vol.ii, p.138.
[58] *Plea Rolls*, vol.ii, p.198.
[59] *Select Pleas*, p.129.
[60] Michael Adler, *Jews of Medieval England*, JHSE *Trans.*, London, 1939, p.222.

R. Nissim, is likely to be Isaac de Coucy's rewrite of it – well-known in England at the time.

Another victim of the gibbet – it was common in Europe to have a 'Jews's gibbet' – was Solomon (Salle) of Wilton who left two silver 'bechers' [kiddush cups?], three bronze lamps [shabbat candles?], one mantle (fur), two hoods, three pillows (goose-feathers?), two sheets, nine books of the Law of the Jews, valued at 30s. Again, where the rest of England might be illiterate, Jews by definition could not be.

In another trial in Bristol in 1274, a Jew was first the accuser and then the defendant. Manser (Manasseh), the son of Solomon of Calais, charged John of Berwick with breaking into his house and taking goods worth £40. John was a well-known citizen of Bristol, appearing in 1283 as a juror in a case against Jose and Isaac of Caerleon. John was arrested and imprisoned for breaking the peace. He pleaded 'not guilty' and was acquitted. Then he brought an action against Manser for false imprisonment and perjury. At the inquiry, six Christians swore that the Jew was to blame. But, there being no Jewish witnesses, the Constable of Bristol Castle had to look further into the matter. He summoned six Jews, since a Jew had the right to call people from his own community in trials between Jews and Christians. Manser did not attend this hearing and its outcome was not recorded.[61]

Returning to 1275, a momentous year in the story of Bristol Jewry, when theological hatred was rife. Such hatred had been concentrated by the Provincial Council of London, 1259, which sought power for Ecclesiastical Courts to try Jews for alleged offences against Church property or clerics, sacrilege, and especially violence against clerics. The same applies to the case of adultery with a Christian woman.[62] This was confirmed at the Council of Merton, 1258,[63] while the 1261 Council of Lambeth stated:

> Anyone who impedes Jews guilty of ecclesiastical crimes from appearing in Courts Christian is to be excommunicated.[64]

Eleanor, the Queen Mother, seems to have been caught by the religious wave of feeling against the Jews and to have applied to her royal son for power to expel them from her four dowertowns. Accordingly the Jews of Gloucester were deported to:

---

[61] Michael Adler, *Jews of Medieval England*, JHSE *Trans.*, London, 1939, p.223.
[62] F.M. Powicke and C.R. Cheney, *Councils and Synods*, OUP, London, 1964, p.545.
[63] Ibid, p.580.
[64] Ibid, p.679.

our town of Bristol with their chirograph chests and all their goods, and they henceforth to dwell and abide among our other Jews in that place.

No injury was to be done either to their persons or their goods during their removal. The arrival of their Gloucester neighbours must have taxed the accommodation in the small Bristol Jewry to the utmost, although the newcomers were not very many and their financial condition was poor. The 1274 tallage roll quotes their contribution as bottom of the list with £9.6s.8d. compared with £46.10s.11d. from Bristol out of a total of £1,425. However most Gloucester Jews did not remain in Bristol, for they reappear in 1290 in Hereford, Oxford and Norwich but none held property at the time of the expulsion.

Two events of this year may have contributed to the unwillingness of the Gloucester Jews to stay in the town to which they had been deported. The church was infuriated because of an unfortunate incident. It was said that Bishop Giffard issued a mandate to the Deans of Westbury and Bristol to excommunicate certain Jews of Bristol and to forbid all traffic with them. The reason given for this display of episcopal anger was:

> because the Jews were guilty of iniquitous insults, blasphemies and injuries and of an assault upon the Chaplain of St. Peter's when he administered the holy Eucharist to a sick person in the Jewry.

There are no more details about this case. Although the Jewry had moved to Winch Street by this time there may still have been Jews living in the old Jewry down by the churches of St. John, St. Laurence and St. Giles. It may be that the chaplain entered a Jewish house in the hope of obtaining a last minute conversion, or in error, but there is no way of finding out.[65]

Greater distress was caused to Bristol Jewry when twenty-two men and two women, whose names are recorded:[66]

> came by night with force and arms and attacked the Jews and broke their houses and entered the same and took and carried away the King's goods that were in the keeping of the Jews against the peace and to his damage £1,000[67]

---

[65] *Victoria County History of Gloucester*, p.17.
[66] *Close Rolls*, 1275, p.30; *Patent Rolls*, 1275, p.107. Those involved in the attack were William Giffard, William Maleden, Roger le Pessoner, Geoffrey Pistor and Simon le Waleys.
[67] *Plea Rolls*, vol.ii, p.297.

or in another version £100, which seems more likely. The Jewry was burned, but it seemed no-one died. The leader was William Giffard, whose earlier activities are worthy of note. Previously, he had been the Constable of Norwich Castle and Sheriff of Norfolk and Suffolk. For neglect of his official duties he was frequently fined, and in October 1274 he was dismissed.[68] He had many financial dealings with Jews, such as Moses of Clare, a well-known money-lender in Suffolk. In March 1270, proclamation had been made in various synagogues, including Bristol, about his liabilities.[69] Three Bristol Jews had claims against him. These were Preciosa, to whom he owed 44s. and 40 marks; Aaron son of Aaron, £16 and Isaac son of Jacob of Coutances, 50 marks, 100s., and £20. The amounts quoted are capital sums and do not include the interest that would have been due. On leaving Norwich, Giffard came to Bristol and planned to destroy the proofs of his debts by leading the raid on the Jewry. When arrested by order of the King, Giffard denied taking part in the riot. Again, the charges against him are not recorded. He seems to have escaped justice. In September 1276, he was still in Bristol paying off some of his debts.[70]

Another leader of the attack was William Maleden who, when charged with the offence, could not be found.[71] He had bought a house in Winch Street from Cresse, son of Isaac of Carleon, and was probably also in arrears with his payments. Jewish property had been stolen and was not returned. The Constable of Bristol Castle, Bartholomew le Jeune, and Henry de Montford, held an inquiry but he, too, seems not to have been punished.

Also in 1275, Parliament ratified the *Statute de Judaismo* (Statute of the Jews) which would, henceforth, make it impossible to obtain interest due on debts.[72] By doing this, Parliament was only coming into line with decrees passed by the Pope and the IVth Lateran Council. But at the same time the business of money-lending was severely damaged and Anglo-Jewry faced starvation. Most of the recent tallage was unpaid and a year later all Jews were imprisoned, those in Bristol were taken to the Castle.[73] All their goods not in the *archa* were sold and the money paid to the Treasury. They were to be dealt with as if they were outlaws who had taken the King's property.

[68] *Calendar of Fine Rolls*, 1274, p.33.
[69] *Plea Rolls*, vol.i, pp.220,266.
[70] *Calendar of Fine Rolls*, 1276, p.72.
[71] *Plea Rolls*, vol.ii, p.301.
[72] Tovey, *Anglia Judaica*, p.200; Lionel Abrahams, *Jewish Quarterly Review*, vol.vii, p.244.
[73] Hilary Jenkinson (ed.), *Plea Rolls*, 1276, p.104.

Their wives and children were to leave the country never to return. In Bristol, special demands were made on Isaac of Caerleon and Isaac of Sodbury in Gloucestershire, as well as on Saphira, daughter of Leke, for whom Isaac of Caerleon was responsible.[74] Two other Bristolians were named, Bonamy, son of Jose, and Isaac of Marlborough, known as Isaac Hariprud. Aaron son of Vives, a famous London Jew, had to ensure that their debts were paid. Haripud paid £20 the following year and was discharged.[75]

In 1276 and 1286 accused Jews were remanded in Bristol Castle. In the first, Hak (Isaac, son of Meyrot or Meir) and Swetman, his brother, were charged, together with a merchant of Gascony, with dealing in silver plates, valued at £17.[76] The Constable of Bristol Castle, Bartholomew le Jeune, claimed to have found these plates hidden under the merchant's bed. In the Gascon's possession there was another plate worth 50s. in an alloy which looked like silver. The merchant denied the accusation and asserted that he had bought the plate from Swetman, to whose brother Hak, he had paid 30s. on account. A goldsmith in Bristol had tested it and declared it to be false. The plates found under his bed he had brought with him from Normandy. Those accused denied all knowledge of the counterfeit plate, but were thrown into prison nevertheless. Swetman appears ultimately to have been freed, but Hak and his Gascon customer were sent for trial.[77]

The second case was also about counterfeit silver plate. Aaron, son of Benjamin, one of the heads of the Colchester community, had lived for a time in Ireland, and afterwards settled in Bristol.[78] One day he entered the shop of Robert of Arras, goldsmith, and offered a silver plate for sale in the presence of a number of Christians who were in the shop. The Bristol goldsmith weighed the plate and detected that it was fused from coin clippings. When Aaron heard him say this he ran off with the plate as far as the bridge over the River Avon. He was followed by some of the customers from the shop, who saw him throw the plate into the water. There was a hue and cry and Aaron was arrested and taken to Bristol Castle by the Constable. Three local Jews acted as his guarantors, Cresse, son of Isaac of Caerleon, Cresse le Prestre, and Abraham Hariprud (or Honiprud?).[79] After the usual

---

[74] Hilary Jenkinson (ed.), *Plea Rolls*, 1276, p.133.
[75] Hilary Jenkinson (ed.), *Plea Rolls*, 1276, p. 268.
[76] *Select Pleas*, p.91.
[77] Hilary Jenkinson (ed.), *Plea Rolls*, 1276, p.196.
[78] *Select Pleas*, p.120.
[79] Hilary Jenkinson (ed.), *Plea Rolls*, 1276, p.2.

fines had been paid, Aaron of Ireland was tried for this and 'divers other trespasses', and in his defence declared that 'the infamy is laid to his charge by persons who have a grudge against him, and he craves leave to acquit himself by Jews alone and not by Christians'. This refusal to be tried by a mixed Court was contrary to the law and custom of Jewry[80] and he was therefore committed to the custody of the Sheriff of Hereford to be detained in that prison. Some time later Aaron was set free and paid a fine of three bezants, as well as 8s. rent on property in his native Colchester for dropping his case. He was further ordered not to enter Bristol again without a special mandate from the King[81] and he probably returned to Colchester, where he possessed houses and other property which appeared four years later in the Expulsion inventory.[82]

Shortly before this event, Moses of Kent was executed outside Bristol Castle, though his crime was not stated. He owned a house in Bristol and a vacant piece of land adjoining it. For the house he paid 40d. a year to a certain John de Laygrave (worth 4s.8d. a year to the King). This property reappears in the Expulsion records below. The offence for which Moses of Kent was hanged is not mentioned. He first appeared in 1273 living in Canterbury, when he stood surety for a debt.[83] Several times, the law officers of the Crown were concerned with his affairs, suspecting him of performing evil practices. In 1276 he was fined for an offence against the Assize of the Jews.[84] Later that year, he was arrested for receiving goods which belonged to the King, including a golden cup which had been the property of the King of Scotland.[85] He had married Gyna (probably Regina, the Latin form of Malka) the widow of Abraham Russell of Huntingdon, who had been outlawed and most likely hanged. Some of the possessions of the deceased, now the property of the King, were kept by Gyna and her new husband. At the trial twelve of the most prominent Jews of the day were present including Benedict of Winchester. Moses succeeded in proving his innocence. A year later, the Prior of Barnwell in Cambridge brought an action against him about a plea of trespass and forgery. Moses did not appear and the Sheriff was ordered to arrest him and seize his goods.[86]

---

[80] Jacobs, *Jews of Angevin England*, p.331.
[81] *Select Pleas*, p.217; JHSE *Trans.* II, 1894–1895, p.90.
[82] JHSE *Trans.* II, 1894–1895, p.90.
[83] *Plea Rolls*, vol.ii, p.110.
[84] Hilary Jenkinson (ed.), *Plea Rolls*, 1276, p.92.
[85] Hilary Jenkinson (ed.), *Plea Rolls*, 1276, pp.92,211.
[86] Hilary Jenkinson (ed.), *Plea Rolls*, 1276, p.244.

The end of this story is the Expulsion from England. King Edward I ordered all the Jews of his kingdom to go to London, prior to their departure. All their property was left behind to be held by the King. The Sheriffs and officials of the Royal Exchequer compiled a register of their chattels which showed that the total value of the houses throughout England was about £130 and of the debts due to the expelled Jews about £9,100 made up as follows:

> in money about £4,000; in corn about £2,700 and wool about £2,400. This list should be increased to take into account those towns where the lists have not been preserved.[87]

With regard to Bristol, the inquiry about their property was made in the presence of Viscount (Earl) of Gloucester, in the nineteenth year of the reign of King Edward. It concerned the houses and holdings recently possessed by the Jews of the town. It was sent out by the King's edict via John of Wizth, Richard Hardcastle, William of Banwell, Jordanus the Long, Richard of Cumton, Walter at Street, Thomas the Welbetere, Laurence the Tanner, Robert of Tavistock, John the Marshal and Robert the Lorimer, as sworn assessors. They found as follows:

1. Benedictus of Wintonia, hanged, left property in Winchester worth 13 solidi, 4 denarii.[88] (The house itself was worth only 10 solidi.)
2. Hak the Priest, hanged, had two properties in fee and had built on it by Peter de la Mare, Constable, worth 25 solidi, for which Peter paid the King 4 denarii a year.
3. Moses (Mossi) of Kent, *hanged outside Bristol Castle*, a house and empty piece of land *once* held, which John of Leygrave owned and for which he paid 40d. and 4s.8d. annually to the King which would be worth more if the house were repaired.
4. Isaac of Caerleon held property in Winchester, held once from John of Woodstock, 6d. annually to the King, and on behalf of Langabulo owes the King a further 3d. obols, for a fourth part of the property. (Master Thomas of Bardeney Marescallus, Marshal, held it from the heirs of John of Woodstock, paying 20s. per annum because it was worth no more.)
5. Isaac the Jew held land in fee which he gave to Cresse, his son, who in turn sold it to William Mayleden and his heirs, giving the Jew annually 6s.

---

[87] Lionel Abrahams, *Jewish Quarterly Review*, vol. vii, p.447; JHSE *Trans.* II, pp.76 et seq.

[88] In this list solidi are shillings and denarii are pence.

37

6. Empty land previously belonging to Cressant, hanged, which brought the King in 6d.
7. Land next to the Castle held by Josse de Caerleon and held from John of Leygrave for 12d. annual rent and a further 40d. which the King was entitled to.

Finally the inquiry found that:

> They even say that a certain house in which the synagogue of the Jews was attached and rebuilt on the two empty spaces and that house was held by the heirs of Margery Toly recently deceased for 3s. annually returned, for which return the said Jews of Bristol gave that same Margery during her lifetime, for which sum of money into her hands we do not know and increasing yearly till it reached nil in twenty years, a term dating from the Easter following the late king's death – the 13th – for a future eighteen years, when it would also terminate at Easter, and for the ending of that (agreement) the king must receive 3s. annually. In the will of which king, the aforementioned assessors append their signature.

The Synagogue would not have been very large or elaborate as it was valued at 3s. per annum, compared with Oxford at 18s.9d., Canterbury at 11s.8d., Colchester at 7s., Norwich at 5s., Hereford at 4s. and Nottingham at 3s.11d.[89] This proves that during the attack (by Simon de Montfort?) on the Jewry, the Synagogue was destroyed and a second one was built. It also shows that the land was rented and a sort of mortgage paid. Why has this never been referred to before by other scholars? It does throw an interesting light on the Bristol community, and would alter the numbering of modern-day communities.

The debts Bristol Jews left behind are recorded in the following list:

Bristol Bonds owing in 1290

	MONEY £ s d			CORN £ s d		
Josce of Caerleon		7	0	–	–	–
Aaron, son of Josce of Caerleon	10	0	0	–	–	–
Isaac, son of Josce of Caerleon	4	10	0	20 qrs. = 6	13	4
Cok of Strygyl (Chepstow)	2	10	0	10 qrs. = 3	6	8
Isaac and Cok	1	17	0	20 qrs. = 6	13	4
Cok and Sarah, widow	4	6	8	–	–	–
Solomon, son of Hagin	2	0	0	60 qrs. = 20	0	0

[89] JHSE *Trans.* XXV, 1977, P.44.

	MONEY			CORN		
	£	s	d	£	s	d
Sarah, daughter of Benedict	1	17	0	12 qrs. = 4	0	0
Jacob, son of Jacob	–	–	–	18 bush. =	9	0
Sampson of Winchester	–	–	–	10 qrs. = 4	0	0
TOTAL	£27	7	8	£45	2	4[90]

From the total of £72.10s.0d in money and corn it can be seen that the business affairs of the Bristol Jews were at a very low ebb compared with those of two other western centres which are recorded. Hereford, to which several of the Gloucester Jews migrated after 1275 and including Jose, son of Aaron of Caerleon, was reported to have possessed money debts to the value of £1,479.5s.4d., corn bonds £458, and wool bonds of £169.13s.4d; total £2,106.18s.8d.[91] Exeter's return gives £1,058.4s.2d in money (of which the Bristol Aaron of Caerleon claimed £27.6s.) and £180.13s.4d. in bonds for corn; total of £1,238.17s.6d. Against these impressive figures, the total for Bristol of £72.10s looks very small indeed.

Of the seven houses listed earlier, which were ordered to be sold, not one had found a purchaser in the following year. No houses of the old Jewry by the river are mentioned. There is no further record of what became of these houses and land, unlike the other towns were Jews lived. The Jewry of old Bristol ceased to exist until a new community arose in the eighteenth century in a considerably easier political climate, though being a port, particularly of the Hanseatic League, it is likely that Bristol's Jews passed through the city at various times.

NAMES OF JEWS IN MEDIEVAL BRISTOL

1154–1196

Samuel
Moses, son of Rabbi Isaac
Rabbi Yom Tov, son of Moses
Isaac, son of Moses
Simon, son of Moses
Benedict
His wife, Leah
Moses, son of Benedict
Joseph, son of Benedict
Sturmis (?)
Isaac, son of Judah
Benlivinger

Preciosa
Isaac Furmager
Deulacresse Furmager
Abraham, son of Vives
Isaac Episcopus (le Veske)
Manasser
Solomon, son of Isaac
Jacob, son of Jose
Judah Gabbay
Abraham Gabbay
Samuel le Pointur
Amiot [*Chancellor's Roll (1196 p.187)*]

---

[90] qrs. = quarters, bush. = bushel, old measurements of corn.
[91] JHSE *Trans.* II, 1894–1895, p.92.

1221–1250

Jacob, son of Samuel of Oxford
His daughter, Antera
Joseph Furmager
Bonefey Furmager
Isaac, son of Bonefey Furmager
Moses, son of Bonefey Furmager
Dulce Furmager
Vives le Pointur
Michael, his son-in-law
Leo, nephew of Abraham Gabbay
Solomon, son of Abraham
Milo Episcopus (le Veske)
Lumbard of Cricklade
Episcopus (le Veske)
Their mother, Saphira
Abraham Folet and his sister
Vives, son of Abraham
Bonefey Michael
Solomon le Turk
Michael le Veske
Levi, son of Dieubenie
Aaron (Adrian)

His wife, Rachel (Richolda)
Lumbard (chirographer)
John ⎫
His sister, Joan ⎬ converts
Christina ⎭
Solomon, son of Aaron (chirographer)
Solomon of Ilchester
Isaac of Bath
Isaac, son of Jurnet (Jacob)
Cresse, son of Milo le Veske
(chirographer)
Jacob of Coutances
His wife, Pimenta
Jacob, son of Jacob of Coutances
His wife, Belecote
Isaac, son of Jacob of Coutances
Filee
Jacob, son of Filee
Bella, wife of Jacob Filee

1253–1290

Elias of Chippenham
Joseph of Caerleon
Isaac, son of Joseph of Caerleon
(chirographer)
Aaron, son of Jose of Caerleon
Abraham, son of Joseph of Caerleon
Cresse, son of Joseph of Caerleon
Samuel, son of Joseph of Caerleon
Henne, wife of Joseph of Caerleon
Joseph, son of Isaac
Isaac, son of Isaac
Dieulebenie, son of Samuel
Samuel, son of Samuel of Wilton
(chirographer)
Solomon, son of Samuel of Wilton
Belasez (murdered 1266)
Cressaunt, son of Pictavin (chirographer)
Hak (Isaac) le Prestre (chirographer)
Solomon, son of Isaac of Wilton
Isaac Hariprud of Wilton (Isaac of
Marlborough)
Abraham Honiprud or Hariprud
Manser, son of Solomon of Calais

Mendaunt, son of Isaac
Deulegard, son of Vives
Preciosa
Aaron, son of Aaron
Isaac of Sodbury
Saphira, daughter of Selke
Bonamy, son of Jose
Hak (Isaac), son of Meirot
Swetman, son of Meirot
Aaron of Ireland, son of Benjamin of
Colchester
Saffre, son of Deulecresse
Moses of Kent
His wife, Gyna
Aaron (murdered 1287)
Cok (Isaac) of Strygyl
Sarah, the widow
Solomon, son of Hagin
Sarah, daughter of Benedict
Jacob, son of Jacob
Sampson, son of Isaac of Winchester

TOTAL: 104

Post-Expulsion Anglo-Jewry: 1492–1697

Since the expulsion of the Jews from Spain in 1492 and from Portugal in 1497, there was the occasional notable visitor. Dr. Rodrigo Lopez (c.1525–1594) left Portugal and lived for a time in Antwerp, before coming to England in 1559, in the reign of Queen Elizabeth I. He was living in the parish of St. Peter le Poer in London by 1571. His medical knowledge came from the ancient East, unknown at that time in the rest of Europe. He was elected to the College of Physicians and in 1571 was chosen to give an anatomy lecture, but he declined this honour. Before 1584 he was appointed house physician to Robert, Earl of Leicester, favourite of Queen Elizabeth I. He was accused of helping Leicester to remove his enemies by poison. Later he became the Queen's trusted physician and she granted him the monopoly of importing aniseed and sumac in 1589.

Meanwhile Philip II of Spain conquered Portugal and the deposed pretender to the throne of Portugal, Don Antonio, came to England in 1581. Lopez was involved in the subsequent intrigue. He dealt with spies travelling between Spain and England. Negotiations for peace with Spain were the background to much of the plotting. However Spain was no more interested in peace than England. Ferrara, an accomplice of Lopez, was arrested. Shortly afterwards another go-between returning to England was captured and incriminated Lopez, suggesting he might poison the Queen. Lopez was arrested, tried, found guilty and sentenced to be hung, drawn and quartered at Tyburn in 1594.[1]

It is possible that the lurid romances told as a result of this case gave rise in part to the character of Shylock in the *Merchant of Venice*. Dr. Lopez made Elizabethan society aware of the existence of Jews in both good and bad ways.[2]

---

[1] Martin Hume, M.A., 'The So-Called Conspiracy of Dr. Ruy Lopez', JHSE *Trans.* VI, 1908–1910, pp.32-55, and John Gwyer, 'The Cause of Dr. Lopez', JHSE *Trans.* XVI, 1945–1951, pp.183–184. For a very full account of his life, see Joseph Jacobs, *Jewish Encyclopædia*, 1925, VIII, pp.181–182.

[2] Heinrich Grätz, *Shylock in der sage im drama, und in der gsecuicute*, Krotoschin, 1880, and Sidney Lee, *Gentleman's Magazine*, February, 1880.

Also in the reign of Elizabeth I, mining was a growing and important skill. The operators were usually German and kept their methods a closely guarded secret. Mining for copper was profitable for Daniel Hochstetter in Keswick. Joachim Gaunze was born in Prague. In 1581 he appears on the scene to investigate the smelting methods practised in Keswick, which he found to be most unsatisfactory and unnecessarily expensive. His expertise was later utilized at Neath, where the industry was founded during Gaunze's stay. He must have travelled from Cumberland to Neath regularly. He introduced a new process for the:

> makeing of copper, vitriall, and coppris and smeltinge of copper and leade ures.[3]

His usual residence was in Blackfriars, London. He reappears in 1589 in Bristol, perhaps after a visit to the Cornwall tin or copper mines where his knowledge was also valuable. On Friday, 12th September in that year, the Minister, Richard Curteys, planned to engage him in a 'conference in the Hebrew Tongue' and therefore visited the house of Richard Meyes, innholder. When the miner came in, the conversation started and Curteys asked Gaunze some test questions about the divinity of Jesus, to which Gaunze replied that 'he is not the Sonne of God', which Curteys found 'odious'. Thereafter they spoke in English so that the bystanders could understand what went on. When brought before the Mayor and Aldermen of Bristol, Gaunze openly said he was a Jew, born in Prague in Bohemia, adding that he had never been baptized and did not believe any Article of Christian faith as he was not brought up in them. On 17th September he was sent to appear before the Privy Council.[4]

The men who signed these charges were all solid citizens of Bristol. Robert Hitchen, Mayor, had played his part against the Spanish Armada the previous year. Aldworth had been Mayor in 1583 and assisted Walsingham in his colonisation of Newfoundland. Much later, Edward Colston became famous in Bristol for creating schools and almshouses. Richard Cole was said to be 'active, far-sighted, prudent and benevolent'. All have left a mark on the charities of the town. Yet the public prejudices of their time persuaded them to arrest a man who had rendered real service to England, simply because, when challenged, he proclaimed himself to be a Jew. It may be that no action was taken because he was employed by Walsingham. Both he and Burghley knew him well. The Privy Council did protect foreign

---

[3] Full details in English State Papers, Domestic Series, Elizabeth, vol.152, No.88.
[4] Full details in English State Papers, Domestic Series, Elizabeth, vol.226, No.46.

miners against pains and penalties which they incurred. Sadly there is no more information about Joachim Gaunze. Neither is his death recorded on a known tombstone in England or in his home town of Prague, although Cecil Roth states that Joachim (Zalman) Gaunze was buried in 1619 at Prague where his tombstone states he was a son of Rabbi Seligman Gans.[5]

In a case covering the period from 1545 to 1555 before the Inquisition in Portugal from November 1557 to September 1558, Thomas Fernandez said he was a native of Lisbon, and an orphan. He and his sister Branca Fernandes went to live with their uncle and aunt, Hector Nuñes and Beatrice Fernandez in Bristol.[6] He said that they kept the Sabbaths, the Festival of Passover and the fast of Yom Kippur. Hector Nuñes, physician, and Simão Roiz, surgeon, living in London sent them information each year of the days of the Jewish festivals. Other Jews living in Bristol at this time include Antonio Dias, merchant, aged about sixty, Jafor Dias, Jorge Dias, Jurdão Vaz, a seaman, Pero Vaz, surgeon. He remembered seeing Beatrice Fernandez teaching Jorge Dias various prayers. She is elsewhere reported, when travelling to London, to have been provided with new cooking utensils which had not been used for preparing non-Kosher food, at the inns where she stayed. Nuñes was invaluable to the English Government in 1587 when he provided the information that Philip II was gathering the Armada for the invasion of England. It is known that Hector Nuñes did not stay long in Bristol but when or why he left is not known.[7]

But the official resettlement came later. The Jews who had left Spain in 1492 or Portugal in 1497, settled in the Netherlands, which, though a Spanish possession at the time, was much more open-minded about the religion of its citizens. In the seventeenth century, a group of Sephardim (Spanish Jews) settled in London, living as Maranos, that is to say they worshipped as Protestants in public, and privately kept the Jewish laws and festivals. In 1655 representations were made to Oliver Cromwell to permit Jews to live openly in England but the Committee was not in favour of the idea. Further applications were made and in 1658 Menasseh ben Israel came from

5 Israel Abrahams, *Joachim Gaunse – A Mining Incident in the Reign of Queen Elizabeth*, JHSE *Trans.* IV, 1899-1901, pp.83-101. His tomb from Cecil Roth, *The Middle Period in Anglo-Jewish History*, JHSE *Trans.* XIX, 1960, p.11.
6 From the 1986 exhibition *200 Years of Bristol Jewry*, discussing Thomas and Branca Fernandez. 'The small community of *marranos* or clandestine Jews sought refuge in Bristol due to their connections with the cloth trade for which the city was an important centre'.
7 Lucien Wolf, 'The Case of Thomas Fernandez before the Lisbon Inquisition' found among his unpublished papers, printed in JHSE *Miscellanies* II, 1935.

Amsterdam to discuss this subject with Cromwell. By June of that year it was agreed that Jews could live and worship freely and buy land for a cemetery in England. It is not necessary to discuss the resettlement, other than to remark that in the end it took place for economic, rather than any other reasons.

The Sephardim were followed by Ashkenazim (in the early 1670s) from Germany and Eastern Europe who came to better themselves. They emigrated with support from early Hanoverian Kings. Their first cemetery was founded in 1697.[8]

---

[8] It is worth noting that a new congregation requires consecrated ground to bury their dead before going to the expense of buying a house for a synagogue. One can, after all, worship anywhere.

The Modern Community Established: 1740–1876

A bout 1740 a number of Jewish pedlars arrived in the provinces and set up communities. In 1753, one Henry Simons stated in a legal deposition that he had intended to visit the synagogue in Bristol two years earlier. From this we can deduce that a small community with a reader already existed in the city.[1] *Felix Farley's Journal* for 24th November, 1753 carries the following report:

> Bristol, December 1st: whereas Jonas Levy, a travelling Jew, on Sunday 25th was found murdered between Abergavenny and Crickhowel.

He had been strangled and his brains were 'beat-out'. He was interred in the Jews' burying ground at St. Philips. Goods valued at £100 had been stolen and his pockets had been turned out. The report concludes:

> The Jews residing in this city do hereby promise a reward of twenty pounds to any person that shall apprehend the murderer, to be convicted of the same, to be paid by the Clerk of our Synagogue.[2]

It is not know whether anyone claimed the reward but the *Manchester Mercury* for 1st January, 1754, reported the escape from Salford gaol at the end of 1753 of a man suspected of robbing and murdering a Jewish pedlar in Wales.[3]

The foundation of the first three synagogues between 1756 and 1842 is described in Chapter 5. Possibly the first wedding in the new building consecrated on 15th September, 1786 was held on Wednesday, 27th December, 1786, between Mr. Israel Cohen of Virginia (probably not U.S.A.) to Miss Solomon, daughter of Mr. Solomon of Exeter.[4]

---

[1] Noted in the 1986 exhibition '200 Years of Bristol Jewry'.
[2] This offer of a reward in the South-West seems to be unique in Bristol.
[3] Above details from R.R. Emanuel 'The History of Bristol Jewry' in the Newsletter, No. 4/88 of Temple Local History Group, Bristol.
[4] *Sarah Farley's Bristol Journal*, 30th December 1786. Unfortunately there is no marriage register to provide further information.

In an attempt to determine the size of the Bristol community in the late seventeenth- and much of the eighteenth-century the rate books were combed for information.[5] Searching for likely Jewish names threw up many that were possible and more that were probable. Then, as now, not everyone was sufficiently prosperous to pay rates. Though the numbers found were insufficient to make any appreciable analysis, a summary appears below. There was clear growth from 1761 to 1800. Most of the community lived in the Parishes of Temple, St. Mary Redcliffe and St. Thomas throughout the period. By the 1790s many had moved across the river to the area near Broadmead and Castle Street. These were tradesmen who lived above their shops. By 1810 they were found in St. Paul's Parish, once rather grand, but now deserted by people moving to Clifton. Meanwhile the middle-class members lived in St. James' Square and Brunswick Square. By the 1830s there were more Jews living in the Parishes of St. Paul, St. Augustine and St. James. Moving across the river was a definite improvement. Ill. 2 shows some of the churches as they are today.

RATE BOOK SUMMARY

TEMPLE PARISH:	1750–1760:	6 names
	1770–1780:	14 names
	1790–1800:	21 names
	1810–1820:	11 names
	1830–1840:	17 names
	1850–1860:	20 names
	1870:	5 names
St. THOMAS PARISH:	1750–1760:	–
	1770–1780:	3 names
	1790–1800:	7 names
	1810–1820:	5 names
	1830–1840:	17 names
	1850–1860:	18 names
	1870:	6 names
St. MARY REDCLIFFE:	1750–1760:	5 names
	1770–1780:	2 names
	1790–1800:	4 names
	1810–1820:	2 names
	1830–1840:	9 names
	1850–1860:	11 names
	1870:	4 names
St. NICHOLAS PARISH:	1750–1760:	3 names
	1770–1780:	1 name

---

[5] Rate books are further discussed at the beginning of Chapter 5.

	1790–1800:	–
	1810–1820:	4 names
	1830–1840:	9 names
	1850–1860:	12 names
	1870:	4 names
CASTLE PARISH:	1750–1760:	–
	1770–1780:	–
	1790–1800:	4 names
	1810–1820:	2 names
	1830–1840:	7 names
	1850–1860:	13 names
	1870:	3 names
St. PETER PARISH:	1750–1760:	–
	1770–1780:	–
	1790–1800:	–
	1810–1820:	1 name
	1830–1840:	7 names
	1850–1860:	9 names
	1870:	8 names
St. STEPHEN PARISH	1750–1760:	3 names
	1770–1780:	7 names
	1790–1800:	5 names
	1810–1820:	4 names
	1830–1840:	5 names
	1850–1860:	2 names
	1870:	1 name
CHRISTCHURCH:	1750–1760:	–
	1770–1780:	–
	1790–1800:	–
	1810–1820:	1 name
	1830–1840:	11 names
	1850–1860:	6 names
	1870:	3 names
St. PAUL PARISH:	1750–1760:	–
	1770–1780:	–
	1790–1800:	–
	1810–1820:	3 names
	1830–1840:	13 names
	1850–1860:	17 names
	1870:	2 names
St. JAMES PARISH:	1750–1760:	3 names
	1770–1780:	4 names
	1790–1800:	3 names
	1810–1820:	9 names
	1830–1840:	32 names
	1850–1860:	20 names
	1870:	4 names

St. MICHAEL PARISH:	1750-1760:	–
	1770-1780:	5 names
	1790-1800:	–
	1810-1820:	1 name
	1830-1840:	11 names
	1850-1860:	4 names
	1870:	3 names
St. AUGUSTINE PARISH:	1750-1760:	–
	1770-1780:	–
	1790-1800:	–
	1810-1820:	9 names
	1830-1840:	26 names
	1850-1860:	21 names
	1870:	9 names

In 1845, the Chief Rabbi sent a questionnaire to all congregations. The Bristol reply states that they have 36 Baalei Batim (householders), 40 seatholders, about 150 individual adult members (male). So it was not a large community, though it may well have grown as the century wore on. There is no way of knowing. The only other comment on the size of the Bristol congregation was in a report by Julius Jung, author of the *Small Communities Report* for the Jewish Memorial Council written on 9th April, 1962. He stated that the congregation:

> is at the moment composed of fifty families or about 120 individuals, whilst thirty children attend the Hebrew Classes.[6]

To give these numbers some meaning, several people have been listed with their trades and addresses and, where available, any other information about them.[7] The list shows the wide range of occupations which is still as evident in the community up to the present time.

Use has also been made of the one record book of Bristol Hebrew Congregation that survived from the nineteenth century. It is a register of births with a few entries for the years 1829–1830 and continuous entries from 1849 to November 1893 and deaths from 1828–1829 and 1848–1862.

Samuel Isaacs lived in Counterslip, from 1837 to 1852 dealing in diamonds and plate. His daughter, Gertrude, reappears in Chapter 8,

---

[6] From the papers of the Office of the Chief Rabbi, now housed at the Greater London Record Office. This is confirmed in testimony to the Bristol Jewish History Group, see chapter 14, p. 185.

[7] Information collected from rate books 1750–1878 and street directories backing up the rate book information. Rate books are kept at Bristol City Record Office. There are no books after 1878 until the twentieth century.

JOS. ROTHCHILD, WATCH & CLOCK
MAKER, JEWELLER and SILVERSMITH
Of Nos. 17, BROADMEAD, and 37, HIGH STREET,
In returning thanks to his Friends and the Public generally for their
kind support at the above Establishments, begs to announce that, in
consequence of the expiration of the Lease at 37, High Street, on and
after the 29th instant the BUSINESS will be entirely carried on at 17,
BROADMEAD, where he hopes to receive a continuance of that
patronage which it will be his constant study to merit.
N.B. In order to effect a clearance, the remainder of the Stock at
37, High Street is now selling off at a considerable reduction.

Bristol Mercury and Western Counties Advertiser, 23rd September, 1848.

page 120. Isaac Rothschild was in Redcliffe Street, from 1831–1846 as a jeweller and silversmith.

A rather better address was that of Moses Blanckensee, a jeweller who owned a 'Birmingham warehouse' at 7, Bath Street from 1843 to 1868. From the Census of 1851 Moses and his wife, Mary Ann, were married in London, where they had two children, Henrietta born in 1844 and Rosa in 1850. At Bath Street, they had four more children, Rachel born in 1850, Lazarus in 1854, Leah in 1855 and Louis in 1857. Two years later he had moved up the social ladder to Pritchard Street in St. Paul's Parish where two more children were born, Betsy in 1859 and Myer in 1863.

Joseph Rothschild was living at various times at the Upper and Lower Arcades, St. James Parish, later moving to Broadmead and Stokes Croft from 1834 to 1864, as a jeweller. His naturalization dated 1853 states that he arrived in England in 1822 and that he was married and had ten children, all of whom were born in Bristol. Only four of them appear in the birth register: John born in 1829 at Bridewell Street, who cannot have survived long since he is not recorded in the 1841 Census, Moses born in 1830 at Redcliffe Street, Isaac in 1849 and Selina in 1851, both born at Broadmead. From 1848 (as above) he advertised occasionally as a watch and clock maker, jeweller and silversmith, at Broadmead and also at High Street, Bristol.

In 1857 his advertisement is for a:

Wholesale and Retail CIGAR and FANCY TRADE, selling every description of pipes, cigar cases, snuff-boxes, purses, pocket-books, sticks at his premises 22 Union Street.

Matilda Rothschild died on 22nd July, 1878, and her death was remembered on a tombstone at Barton Road Cemetery, together with her husband, Joseph Rothschild, who died on 4th January, 1881.

Barnett and Maria Lazarus lived in Bristol from 1855 when they were recorded in the rate books at 98 Redcliffe Street. In Barnett Lazarus' naturalization certificate dated December, 1864, he is quoted as a silversmith and pawnbroker from Poland. The births of his children, Samuel (1858), Selina (1863) and Dinah (1866), appear in the birth register.[8]

The Platnauer family set up in business as jewellers in Bath Street. In 1844, Joseph Platnauer and his family had a business as watchmakers in Temple Street, while from 1851 Joseph and his second oldest son, Samuel Platnauer, were described in the Directories for 1854–1866 as 'clock and clock case manufacturers, watchmakers, dealers in English and Geneva watches, importers of French and American clocks, wholesale warehouse for Lancashire tools and materials'.

His brothers joined them, Louis in 1861 and George in 1862. When sites in Victoria Street were being sold they took one. Their name can still be seen on that building which they left only in the 1940s. Michael Joseph Platnauer appears again in Chapter 5, p. 72 and the family in Chapter 10, p. 144. (See also ill. 23.)

Samuel and Fanny Platnauer had eight children recorded in the birth register between 1857 and 1872, all but the eldest born at No. 1 Cave Street. Michael Joseph and Sophia Platnauer had eleven children between 1858 and 1876, all born in Clifton. At least three of them did not live for long. George and Julia Platnauer had five children between 1859 and 1867, mostly at a number of addresses in St. Pauls. Their youngest was born at Whiteladies Road, Clifton.

Simon and Joel Solomon were also in Temple Street from 1840 to 1868, trading as pawnbrokers and salesmen. Simon and his son, Joel, came from Falmouth. From 1830 to 1855 Simon Solomon also had a business in Castle Street as a pawnbroker and salesman on the other side of the river. Joel Solomon was living in Stokes Croft, St. James, from 1867.

The division between jewellers, watchmakers and pawnbrokers is often narrow and, now, impossible to judge whether someone who said he was a jeweller might also be lending money. One person to make this abundantly clear was Maurice Michael, pawnbroker, jeweller and silversmith, who appeared in Bath Street in 1841 and

[8] Barnett Lazarus' naturalisation papers are at the Public Record Office, Kew, ref. Close Rolls C54/16467, p.29. Samuel Lazarus appears in Chapter 13, page 176.

remained there until his premises were demolished in 1870. His story is completed in Chapter 9, pages 136–137. In a similar line of business, Lewis Solomon was running a loan and discount office from 1854 to at least 1878 in Bridge Street.

Moses Alman appears as an appraiser and auctioneer from 1781 to 1783 in St. Thomas Street; from 1786 to 1812, Jacob Moses Alman was shown at the same address. From 1825 to 1832 M. and J. Alman were proprietors and occupants of 10 Thomas Street. Moses Mosely Alman (or Mosely Moses Alman) was at the same address from 1833 to 1851 and described himself as an appraiser and auctioneer in the 1836 Directory. From 1821 to 1854 they lived in Wells Street and later Orchard Street, in St. Augustine's Parish, where the directory states they were brokers and commission agents.

Lazarus Alman was at 27, Bath Street from 1835 to 1838, where the street directory of 1837 described him as having a musical instrument warehouse. He moved to 9, Thomas Street in 1845, returning to 29, Bath Street from 1849 to 1851, where the 1850 directory states he was an accountant. Finally he lived at 9, Thomas Street from 1852 to 1870 when 1 to 9, Thomas Street were demolished to make way for Victoria Street.[9]

Abraham Levy was in Temple Street from 1838 to 1848, as a wholesale boot and shoe maker and Noah Solomon in Bath Street from 1840 to 1847, was a hardwareman.

Solomon Levy ran a Bazaar at Union Street from 1833 to 1841, the year of his death. His widow, Arabella Levy was in Wine Street in 1843, but soon moved to College Green. Solomon Levy and Arabella Joseph were born in Falmouth and married there, where it is probable that their first child, Sophie was born. Their second daughter was born in Exeter and all subsequent children in Bristol, but too early to appear in the birth register. They lived in Bristol from 1830 and Solomon Levy appears in the rate books in Union Street from 1833. He had been proprietor of the Bristol Bazaar in Union Street for some fourteen years. About a year earlier he had decided to move his business to 39 College Green. He embarked on extensive alterations to the building, which were expected to take three months. However the inevitable building delays meant that his investment in new goods was not being turned into profit. He became depressed, and on Thursday, 14th January, 1841, he took his own life[10]. His widow, Arabella Levy, with eight children to support, the youngest not yet a

---

[9] The variety of information about the Alman family in particular shows the different requirements of both rate books and street directories.
[10] Inquest reported in the *Bristol Mercury*, 16th January, 1841.

NEW YEAR'S GIFTS

BRISTOL  BAZAAR,
39 COLLEGE GREEN.

MESSRS. LEVY, JOSEPH, AND CO., respectfully announce their return from the Home and Continental Markets, with a large and elegant Stock of NOVELTIES, adapted for Presents, &c., and to which at this season of the year they particularly invite the public attention. Their Establishment will be found rich in splendid specimens of papier machée, in desks, portfolios, card baskets, screens, inkstands, card cases, &c.; the much admired Frankfort blue and white enamelled work; elegant illuminated and gilt leather desks, blotters, knitting boxes, carriage companions, &c.; reticules, purses and bags, worked with beads, &c.; Bohemian glass vases and toilet bottles, Dresden and other ornamental China; alabaster, rosewood, mahogany, coromandel, and other desks; workboxes and dressing-cases, gold, steel and electro-gold bracelets, chains, brooches and every other description of jewellery; and an endless variety of fancy articles adapted for luxury ornament.

Closed from Friday sunset until Saturday dusk.

Felix Farley's Bristol Journal, 17th January, 1846.

year old, opened the Bristol Bazaar in College Green on Tuesday, 26th January. The *Bristol Mercury* of the previous Saturday stated:

> We were favoured with a view of the premises in the early part of the week . . . and we have no hesitation in saying that it is one of the most magnificent shops of the kind in the kingdom. The extent of the bazaar is 88 feet by 37 feet and it is fitted up in such a manner as to admit of the fullest display of the beautiful and varied stock. . . . The establishment will be quite an ornament to our city, as we trust, it will be a lasting source of profit to the widow and family of its spirited but ill-fated projector.

Arabella Levy advertised regularly in all the Bristol papers. The advertisement above is typical of her business. Her advertisements always included the notice that they closed from Friday sunset to Saturday dusk and also for Jewish festivals as and when appropriate. She was trading as Levy, Joseph, and Company, from January 1846 until, in May 1849, Mr. H. Joseph, almost certainly a relation, had moved to Birmingham. See advertisement below.

SELLING OFF ! SELLING OFF ! !
IMMENSE REDUCTION AT THE BRISTOL BAZAAR
COLLEGE GREEN
In consequence of one of the Proprietors removing to Birmingham,
whither the Wholesale Business will be Removed, Messrs. LEVY,
JOSEPH & CO. beg to announce that the *whole* of their immense stock
must be Sold. An opportunity is, therefore, offered to the public in
general to supply themselves with articles of general use, as well as of
vertû and taste, at prices a third less than those usually charged.
The Stock consists of gold and silver watches, best town-made solid
gold jewellery, best Sheffield plated wares, in cruets, candlesticks,
urns, epergnes, vegetable dishes and covers, dish covers, &c.; richly-
cut and plain glass decanters, wine glasses, tumblers, dishes, sugar
basins, butter coolers, &c; best Sheffield ivory and black handle knives
and forks. Elkington's electro plate, in cruets, tea and coffee services,
side dishes and covers, spoons, forks, &c.; solid mahogany and rosewood desks, dressing cases, bagatelle boards, &c.; Bohemian glass in
great variety, elegant ormolu, marble and bronze clocks, going 14 to
21 days, warranted correct timekeepers; papier maché tables, desks,
pole screens, inkstands, envelope cases, portfolios, pen cases, card
cases, &c.; papier maché and japan tea trays, in endless variety; russian
and morocco leather desks, papetries, portfolios, &c.; china ornaments
and lustres in great variety, an excellent assortment of superior pistols,
mathematical instruments, measuring tapes, accordions, barometers,
thermometers; and a variety of articles too numerous to mention.
Messrs. L.J. & Co., beg to recommend an early call, as the whole stock
must be positively sold.
N.B. Closed from Friday, sunset, till Saturday, dusk.

Bristol Mercury, 23rd September, 1848.

He continued to be one of her suppliers, not only from Birmingham,
but also London, Paris and Sheffield. Finally, she advertised as A. Levy
and Company from January 1852, when she ceased dealing in glass
and therefore had a sale lasting for several weeks ending on 19th June,
1858, when she let the premises to Mr. Ring. She ceased advertising in
October and went to live in London with her daughter, Esther Cohen,
at whose home she died aged 94 on 14th June, 1897.[11]

---

[11] Advertisements quoted on 10th January, 1846 in *Felix Farley's Bristol Journal* as Levy
Joseph & Co., 12th May, 1849 in *Bristol Mercury*, 31st January, 1852 in *Felix Farley's
Bristol Journal* but now A. Levy & Co. and finally on 16th October, 1858 in the
Bristol Mercury.

MESSRS. LEVY, JOSEPH, AND CO.
beg to call the attention of their Friends and Public to their extensive
Assortment of ELECTRO PLATE, an Article which, besides being the
very best substitute for Silver, is calculated to endure, in constant wear,
for 20 years.
The following list is respectfully submitted:–

	£ s. d.		£ s. d.
Table-Spoons (per doz.)	1 8 0	Salt, Mustard and Egg	
Table-Forks "	1 6 0	Spoons (per pair)	0 16 0
Dessert-Spoons "	1 10 0	Gravy-Spoons "	0 16 0
Dessert-Forks "	1 7 0	Soup-Ladles (each)	0 16 0
Sugar-Tongs (per pair)	0 4 0	Sauce-Ladles (per pair)	0 16 0
Splendidly-pierced		Candlesticks "	0 16 0
Sugar-Basins, with		Handsomely-chased Set,	
Ruby Glass (each)	1 4 0	containing Coffee-Pot, Tea-	
Splendidly-pierced		Pot, Sugar-Basin, and Cream-	
Salt-Sellers (each)	0 4 3	Jug, with Gilt Inside	6 0 0

Bristol Mercury, 18th August, 1849.

Across the river, in All Saints' Parish there was Samuel Solomon at Broadmead from 1832–1844 running a wholesale clothes warehouse. He moved to Corn Street from 1844 to 1848, where he had an outfitting establishment, later run by Lewis Solomon (who retired in July 1853 in favour of his wife Catherine Solomon) until 1856.

Mr. Abraham Mosely, surgeon dentist of 30, Park Street advertised:

. . . His newly perfected INCORRUPTIBLE ARTIFICIAL TEETH . . . he can ensure the most correct articulation and perfect comfort in mastication. . . . His charges are on the most moderate scale EQUALLY SO WITH ANY OTHER DENTIST whilst his materials and workmanship of the finest description. *Consultations free of charge.*[12]

Some of his verbiage must have been true, for he continued in business until the 1870s when he was joined by his son, Louis. His name appears in the *Jewish Chronicle* in 1873 as Treasurer of the Congregation distributing the prizes at the Sabbath School[13].

Abraham Mosely died aged 72 years, on 27th November, 1889, in London at the home of his son, Alfred. On 21st December the same year the Bristol Hebrew Congregation met and:

[12] *Felix Farley's Bristol Journal*, Saturday, 3rd January, 1846.
[13] *Jewish Chronicle*, 31st October, 1873.

Unanimously resolved that, in consideration of the many valuable services rendered to the Congregation by the late Abraham Mosely, formerly of Bristol, a perpetual 'yizkor' be inscribed in its books.[14]

One can only guess what 'the many valuable services' he performed were since they were not reported and we have no minute books.

It was Alfred Mosely, C.M.G., Abraham's youngest son, who proposed to donate 'an obelisk to the city of Bristol as a memorial of the War in South Africa to be erected in College Green'.[15] However, for reasons of their own, Bristol City Council suggested alternative sites which were unacceptable to Mr. Mosely and it was erected in Plymouth.[16]

Joseph Cohen was at 45, or 49, Wine Street from 1833, as a straw hat maker and wholesale straw plait dealer, where he was joined by Isaac Ballin in 1841, who occupied the premises on his own from 1847 to 1878. Joseph Cohen continued as a straw hat maker and wholesale straw plait dealer at 31 or 41 Wine Street from 1846–1870.

Isaac Ballin's early advertisements show that he sold furs at 49 Wine Street. See example of his advertisement on next page. In 1850 he branched out to sell millinery and straw bonnets in Park Street. But this was not a success and a year later he closed the Park Street premises and announced he was 'entering more extensively into the wholesale trade'.[17] Like Arabella Levy, Isaac Ballin announced that he always closed his shop from Friday evening to Saturday evening.

He disposed of his business to Messrs. Lodge & Company and moved to London in 1858.[18] Neither the notice of his death in London, nor his obituary on 1st December, 1897, mentioned his residence in Bristol.

David Hyam created a thriving outfitters' emporium in Wine Street, Bristol, which traded there for many years. His grandfather,

---

[14] *Jewish Chronicle*, 27th December, 1889.
[15] *Jewish Chronicle*, 15th November 1901.
[16] Alfred Mosely, C.M.G., Ll.D., Knight of Grace of the Order of Jerusalem, was educated privately and at Bristol Grammar School, served with the Princess Christian Hospital, South Africa, educationalist and philanthropist, died 22nd July 1917. Alfred's elder brother, Gerald, lived in Bristol, where he was a solicitor. His son, Archie Gerald, was educated at Polack's House, Clifton College, and Wadham College, Oxford, at both of which he obtained scholarships, he became a barrister and later a judge. Sir A.G. Mosely, Kt, died 21st January, 1951 *Who Was Who*, 1921–1930 and 1951–1960.
[17] *Bristol Mercury*, 5th July and *Bristol Mirror*, 12th July, 1851.
[18] His advertisements appear in the *Bristol Mercury*, 22nd June, 1850, 6th April, 1850, 5th July, 1851 (and the *Bristol Mirror*), and 17th April, 1858.

MOURNING BONNETS,

EXTRAORDINARILY LOW PRICES,

AT I. BALLIN'S, 49, WINE-STREET.

WHOLESALE ENTRANCE – CHEESE MARKET.

ELEGANTLY TRIMMED.

Ladies' Silk and Crape	..	2s 11d	..	5s 6d	..	7s 6d	..	8s 9d
Ladies' Satin and Crape	..	3s 11d	..	5s 9d	..	8s 6d	..	9s 6d
Ladies' Plain Crape	..	3s 11d	..	5s 9d	..	9s 6d	..	10s 9d
Ladies' Chip	..	3s 11d	..	5s 6d	..	6s 6d	..	9s 6d
Ladies' Black Straw and								
Willow	..	2s 11d	..	4s 6d	..	5s 3d	..	7s 6d
Ladies' Half Mourning	..	3s 11d	..	4s 9d	..	6s 3d	..	8s 6d

Closed from Half-past Six on Friday Evenings, and re-opens
at Dusk on Saurdays.

Bristol Mercury, 20th September, 1856.

Simon Ipswich, came from the Rhineland to live in Ipswich. Simon's son, Hyam Hyam, started a tailoring business. Hyam had six sons and three daughters. Benjamin Hyam (the second son) lived in Manchester and is recorded as starting a firm named Hyam and Co., selling ready-made gentlemen's clothing with branches in many cities.[19] David Hyam (the third son) came from Manchester and set up as a tailor and outfitter at 42 Wine Street from 1839, where his shop remained until 1884.

At first his home was at 6, Bridge Street; later he moved to Clifton. From September, 1848 he advertised regularly as D. Hyam in the most glowing terms. In 1859 he was trading as D. Hyam & Co., but in the 1870s changed the name to Hyam and Co. until 1884 when he retired from business.[20]

It is probable that David's Bristol firm was part of the business in Manchester although it advertised as D. Hyam & Co. Like Arabella Levy's business, they were closed on Friday at dusk until Saturday at dusk and for all Jewish festivals, as quoted below for New Year and the Day of Atonement. David Hyam moved to Bedford Villa, Clifton, in 1847 where he remained until 1852, when he left to join his

---

[19] From Malcolm Brown, 'The Jews of Norfolk and Suffolk before 1840', JHSE *Trans.* XXXII, 1990–1992, pp.229–230.

[20] In the *Bristol Mercury and Western Counties Advertiser* of 9th October, 1858, he advertises as D. Hyam, in the same paper of 18th June, 1859, he appears as D. Hyam & Co., in the *Bristol Times and Mirror* of 31st July, 1869, the advertisement is for Hyam & Co.

D. HYAM,

42,

WINE- STREET,

IS MAKING VERY EXTENSIVE PREPARATIONS
FOR THE ENSUING
AUTUMN AND WINTER TRADE,
AND WILL BE ABLE
TO SHOW HIS FRIENDS
VARIOUS ENTIRELY
NEW IMPROVEMENTS
IN OVER-COATS, &c.,
DIFFERENT TO ANY PREVIOUS SEASON.

TO MAKE ROOM
FOR THE WINTER STOCK,
D. HYAM
IS SELLING,
AT VERY REDUCED PRICES,
EVERY VARIETY OF DRESS ADAPTED FOR PRESENT
WEAR.

JACKETS FOR SHOOTING,
TROUSERS FOR SHOOTING,
WAISTCOATS FOR SHOOTING,
WITH THE EXTRA POCKETS IN, &c.,
OF VERY STRONG
MATERIALS OF VARIOUS DESCRIPTIONS
THAT WILL
RESIST THE THORN,
HAVE BEEN SHRUNK
AND MADE WATERPROOF.

HYAM,
42,
WINE-STREET,
CLOSED EVERY SATURDAY UNTIL DUSK.

NOTICE TO THE PUBLIC.
This ESTABLISHMENT will be CLOSED from MONDAY
EVENING, 29th September, until WEDNESDAY EVENING,
1st October, at Half-past Six o'clock; and on THURSDAY,
October 9th, until Half-past Six in the Evening.

Bristol Mercury, 20th September, 1856.

brothers, all now living in Bayswater, London. His manager, left in charge, was Abraham Benjamin, eldest son of Joseph Benjamin, second Reader to the Congregation. The *Western Daily Press* of 19th February 1872 reported:

AMUSEMENT IN WINE STREET: On Saturday a most amusing and exciting scene was witnessed. For several previous evenings one of the tradesmen had attracted large crowds. The neighbours, particularly across the street, considered the obstruction an impediment and tried to defeat the show by strong lights and a Punch and Judy show.

RETIRING FROM BUSINESS.

HYAM & CO., 42 WINE ST.,

SATURDAY, MARCH 22ND

LAST DAY OF THE

IMPORTANT SALE

OF
MEN'S CLOTHING
YOUTH'S CLOTHING
BOY'S CLOTHING
WOOLLENS Sold in any Lengths
Or GARMENTS made to Order
HOSIERY
HATS
MACKINTOSHES
UMBRELLAS
Various little Lots, &c.

FURTHER REDUCTIONS.

FURTHER REDUCTIONS.

FURTHER REDUCTIONS.

FURTHER REDUCTIONS.

FURTHER REDUCTIONS.

FURTHER REDUCTIONS.

SATURDAY, MARCH 22ND.

LAST DAY OF SALE.

HYAM & CO., 42, WINE STREET,
BRISTOL.

(*Bristol*) *Observer* of 22nd March, 1884.

On 21st February in the local magistrates court a case was brought by the police against Mr. Hyam for an obstruction caused by a magic lantern show and against Mr. Weston for a Punch and Judy show. Mr. Hyam's manager appeared before the court and stated that he could do nothing without his employer's express instruction. However it was noted that there had been no exhibition outside his shop the night before, i.e. 20th February. The manager stated they had commenced

58

PHOTOGRAPHY
CARTES DE VISITES AT SIX SHILLINGS PER DOZEN.
MONS. GUTTENBERG respectfully informs the Inhabitants of Clifton and the vicinity that he has opened Business at 29, TRIANGLE, and that he has made great Alterations and Improvements as regards the light, &c. M.G. is now in full practice, and guarantees to produce Portraits the same as his Specimens, at the above price, and large ones equally cheap in proportion. None but First Class Portraits delivered. Satisfaction in every branch of the art guaranteed, as M.G. has practised the Art of Photography above 20 years, and as he manufactures his own chemicals he is able to produce Portraits of every size and style, from the very smallest to the very largest, in very superior style. Visitors treated with the greatest civility and punctuality.
29, TRIANGLE, CLIFTON.

Bristol Times and Mirror, 11th November, 1865.

simply with a trade advertisement but it had become more interesting as the crowds increased. Mr. Hyam was sent a letter and agreed to discontinue the exhibition.

It may have been due to hard times that the Bristol firm closed in 1884, while the main business of Hyam & Co. went bankrupt in 1887.[21]

Marcus Guttenberg arrived in England from Poland in 1849. He was naturalized in 1864 when he was living at Horlton, County Durham, with his wife and two children. They moved to Bristol about a year later and had seven more children at 29, The Triangle, and 17, Royal Promenade, Queen's Road. By the time of his removal to Manchester in about 1878, he had five children remaining alive. He was a photographer who advertised regularly in the local press until September 1871. He appeared to be a Frenchman, 'Mons. Guttenberg', but his advertisement above makes this improbable, for the word 'Visites' should not have an 's'.

It seems that Guttenberg ran a successful if unadventurous business:

> Photography attracted some of the brightest and most ambitious young men of the 1860s and 1870s. One of them was William

---

[21] Closure had been advertised consistently from January, 1884. See, on page 58, the advertisement of 22nd March that year. Timothy Halford, a descendant of the Hyam family, told the author about the bankruptcy.

Green, born in Bristol in September 1855, who became apprenticed to an established Bristol photographer named Maurice
Guttenberg. The young Green showed immediate signs of talent
behind the camera and wanted to improvise and experiment, but
his employer was more interested in safe and solid society portraits. Green resigned and moved to Bath.[22]

Maurice Guttenberg was in no mind to take on the new ideas of his
ambitious apprentice. By April 1880 he was living in Manchester
where he died on 11th June, 1891.

From 1845 to 1858 David Nyman, late of Bath, had a business in
St. James' Barton. He had been President of Bath Hebrew Congregation and Trustee of the lease for their synagogue with St. John's
Hospital. In his will he left a sum to cover the annual rent for the term
of the lease until 1890. He traded as a furrier in Bath from 1834 to
1840, but he moved to Bristol following his bankruptcy where he
manufactured fur and velvet hats.[23] His business was seldom advertised in the Bristol press but this news item is worth noting:

> A HATTER'S TEETOTAL PARTY – The journeyman hatters in the
> employ of Mr. David Nyman, cap and hat manufacturer of this
> city, on Monday last partook of a splendid tea, purchased by the
> proceeds of the fines, &c. This is a step in the right direction, and
> offers an example worthy of imitation to the trade in general.[24]

Whether it occurred again was not reported. In 1852 David Nyman
contributed £5 to rebuilding the Bristol Athenaeum. But his membership was not an unalloyed triumph.

> ROBBERY FROM THE ATHENAEUM – On Monday evening a grey
> greatcoat, the property of Mr. David Nyman, St. James' Barton,
> was stolen from where it had been hung up. The coat was one
> with large bell sleeves, silk velvet collar, lined throughout with
> black silk, and trimmed with braid. In the pockets were a Free-
> mason's apron, a pair of gloves and a pocket book containing

---

[22] From Adrian Bell, *Yesterday in Bath*, Pitman Press, Bath, 1972. William Green is
better known as William Friese-Greene. He was born in Bristol in 1855, and
educated at Queen Elizabeth's Hospital School, Clifton. He later trained with
William Fox Talbot, an early experimenter in photography. He took out the first
patent for moving pictures. He died in London in 1921. *Dictionary of National
Biography*, 1912–1921.

[23] People have enquired if there was a connection between Bath and Bristol. Bath, at
one time, employed poor men from Bristol to make a minyan. There were only
two people who moved from Bath to Bristol, David Nyman and later on A.J.
Goldsmid. See chapter 13, p. 162.

[24] *Bristol Mercury*, 18th January, 1851. There is no connection with Lewis Carroll's
Mad Hatter!

two bills of exchange, one for £28.10s. the other for £21.9s. and sundry other papers, the property of the owner of the coat.[25]

Sadly, there was no report of the coat and its contents being found, but there were more agreeable press reports:

> Mr. D. Nyman, hat and cap manufacturer, St. James' Barton, on Wednesday, 13th instant, gave a dinner to all the men employed on the premises on the occasion of his retiring from business. His successor, Mr. Henry Simmons, gave a most feeling address to the men and the evening was one of enjoyment.[26]

David Nyman and later Henry Simmons' place of business was, as has been noted, at No. 12 St. James' Barton, earlier owned by Sir Abraham Isaac Elton of Clevedon (1718–1790), fourth of that name – lawyer and Town Clerk to the City of Bristol – a great builder and modernizer. The house was originally built by John Strahan in 1728. Sir Abraham's architect, William Paty, designer of Arnos Court, redesigned the house for him. In 1778, Sir Abraham offered to let the Town Council have the building as its new Mansion House for £1,500, a tidy sum in those days. The offer was considered but declined.[27] (See ill. 3.)

What happened to the house between 1778 and 1840, when David Nyman moved in, is not known. Some time after Henry Simmons left it was taken over by Colonel Harrison, who reinstated the living quarters as they would have been in the eighteenth century. But they were ultimately doomed as the City Council in its wisdom created the ring road in 1956, the work continuing into the early 1960s. It demolished Sir Abraham Elton's house and the rest of St. James' Barton, together with so much else in that area of Bristol. Today that splendour has gone, in favour of a roundabout called St. James' Barton bounded on one side by Debenhams, on the other by Avon House and the Sun Life Group building opposite Bristol Bus Station. The house in question would have been at or near the entrance to the bus station.[28]

Henry Simmons occupied the premises as hat and cap manufacturer from 1859 to 1878 if not longer (rate book evidence ceasing in 1879) and was a notable figure in both Jewish and local affairs for many years. See Chapter 7, pages 113–115, for more about Henry Simmons.

---

[25] *Bristol Mercury*, 15th March, 1856.
[26] *Bristol Mercury*, 16th January 1858.
[27] Andor Gomme, Michael Jenner and Bryan Little, *Bristol, an Architectural History*, Lund Humphries, London, 1979, pp.127–128.
[28] The house was featured in the *Western Daily Press*, 19th January 1956. The City Council's decision to demolish the area was reported in the *Bristol Mirror* with photographs of work on the new road layout in progress on 24th May 1956.

In the great tradition of Bristol glassmakers, Montague Durlacher in Bridge Street, St. Mary le Port, from 1856–1857, manufactured drinking glasses and sold glass chandeliers. Levy Levy was at two different addresses in Upper Arcade from 1827 to 1851 trading as a glass dealer and engraver.

John Solomon lived and worked as an optician at Cheltenham Square, Bath Parade, Cathay, and finally Thomas Street, St. Mary Redcliffe Parish, from 1837 to 1878. John Braham, also an optician, was at St. Augustine's Back from 1831 to 1863 and he owned a building in Hanover Street variously described as a tenement and a workshop from 1832 to 1839. By virtue of this property he was recorded as an elector in the 1850 register, and presumably others. John Braham and his family is discussed more fully in Chapter 7, pages 104–111. His sister, Esther Braham was at Lower Arcade from 1845 to 1849 and with her sister, Julia, in 1850 to 1851 at Haberfield Crescent trading as milliners.[29]

Joseph Frankel Alexander and his brothers were in Bath Street from 1825 to 1863 as commission merchants and ship agents. Their main business as ship brokers was on the Quay from 1825 to 1878. By the end of the period they were living in Park Street, on the other side of the river.

Joseph owned four houses in Great George Street. These were inherited by his brothers, Abraham and William Wolfe on his death and held by them at least until 1878. One of these was probably the home of William Wolfe Alexander from 1841 to 1849. Later, he lived in Great George Street from 1832 to 1840, moving to 26, Berkeley Square where he remained until his death in 1878.

Abraham Alexander lived in Queen Square from 1817–1830. According to the rate books, Joseph Frankel Alexander had lived at 41, Park Street from 1823–1850 although he died on 23rd November, 1848. This is one occasion when it took the rate books a little while to notice a death. After his brother's death, Abraham lived there until 1865.

John and Joseph Abraham carried on a business as wine merchants in King Street from 1830 to 1861, when Joseph, being too busy on City Council business, put in a manager. The affairs of John and Joseph Abraham, Abraham Alexander and William Wolfe Alexander are dealt with further in Chapter 9, pages 129–132 and Chapter 10, pages 139–144.

---

[29] Esther Braham also appears in chapter 6, page 86, chapter 7, page 104.

Religious Buildings: 1756–1871

SYNAGOGUE BUILDINGS

T he rate books[1] on pages 64 and 65 in Temple Parish show an entry for 'The Jews' Synagogue' from 1756. This is the house pictured in a watercolour drawing by Hugh O'Neill dated 1819 in the Braikenridge Collection in Bristol City Museum and Art Gallery. It shows some picturesque timber-framed houses in Temple Street. One of these is:

> a noted Ale House . . . now frequently known by the name of the Stone Kitchen in which the great Ale Drinkers of the city spend most of their evenings.
> This old House is said to have been the residence of Sir John Knight, mayor in 1663, & some years ago was used by the Jews as a Synagogue, until in 1786 they removed to the building formerly the Weavers Hall in this street which they fitted up for their own accommodation & for which they still continue to pay a rent.[2]

The move to the Weavers' Hall was probably due to a need for larger premises which suggests more Jews were finding Bristol a profitable place to set up in business permanently. The only evidence to confirm this supposition is the story of Lazarus and Isaac Jacobs[3] but there must have been others of whom no records exist at this early period except for the Jessel family, who were also involved. It is known that Lazarus Jacobs, glass-maker, financed the redecorations and paid the minister's salary. The Weavers' Hall[4] was in Temple Street,

---

[1] Collectors visited all the houses in their parish every six months for the various rates, Land tax, Poor rate, Cleansing, etc., and many of these records still exist. They provide the modern researcher with an accurate guide to residence in the eighteenth century, always provided the person one is researching was wealthy enough to pay rates.

[2] The rent was eight guineas a year, paid in advance. This note is written on the back of the drawing.

[3] Chapter 7, pages 101–103.

[4] The Weavers' Company in 1786 had become so diminished in numbers that they ceased to maintain a hall. The building was transferred to the Jews, who decorated it in what Mr. Barrett terms 'a neat expensive manner' and opened it on the 15th September as a Synagogue. John Latimer, *Annals of Bristol*, vol. 2, facsimile reprint Bristol, 1970, p.475.

An Assessment on the Parish of Temple (alias Holy Cross) in the City of Bristol for Defraying the Charges of Cleaning The Streets of the said Parish for one whole Year Commencing At Christmass 1754 and Ending at Christmass 1755

	Rents £	S	D
Tho.ˢ Witchurches Sen.ᵗ or Occupier			
Susanna Sylivan	4	1	
Widow Poole	4	1	
Tho.ˢ Willmott	8	2	
Long Row			
Chip	7	1	9
Widow Richardson	7	1	9
Paul Baker	10	2	6
Hill	4	1	
Tho.ˢ Bevan	10	2	6
Hurfords Warehouse Pvid			
John Burt poor			
William Willmott	6	1	6
Temple Street			
Tho.ˢ Browning	14	3	6
Abra.ᵐ Mansell	7	1	9
Sarah Clifshold	12	3	
John Badcock & Sen.ᵗ or Occupier	16	4	
Kennedy poor			

64

An Assesment on the Parish of Temple alias Holy Cross in the City of Bristol for Defraying the Charges of Cleaning the Streets of the said Parish for one whole Year Commencing at Christmas 1756 and Ending at Christmas 1757.

@ 3½ @ pound

(2)	Yr. Rent			
William Willmott	16	0	4	8
Mr. Williams	10	0	2	11
Richard Sloper	14	0	4	1
Bilby Bedford	8	0	2	4
Susa: Sylvan	5	0	1	5½
Widdow Pol	4	0	1	2
Thomas Willmott	10	0	2	11
Jews Synagogue	8	0	2	4
Long Row.				
Henry White	7	0	2	0½
Widdow Richardson	8	0	2	4
Thomas Bowen	10	0	2	11
Richard Hill	6	0	1	9
Thomas Bevan	10	0	2	11
Harford Warehouse void				
John Birt Poor				
James Burch	6	0	1	9
Temple Street				
Thomas Browning	15	0	4	4½
Abraham Mansil				

65

opposite Temple Church, one of the few buildings remaining from that era. (See ills 4 and 5.)

The letter reprinted below from *Sarah Farley's Bristol Journal*, commemorates the consecration that took place on the 22nd September, 1786, a week after the opening. The evening of this day was the beginning of Rosh Hashanah. The writer gives an idea of the general attitude to Jews at the time. His spelling has been retained:

SIR, I AM now in my little retreat, have plenty of leisure for writing, and am glad of an opportunity of compleating my promise of describing to you the ceremonies of consecrating the new Synagogue lately founded and built by Mr. Jacobs of Temple Street. – I gained admission into that place of worship just at the time the founder of it was reading part of the 8th chapter of the first book of Kings, which I have since perused in our English bible, and find to be as applicable as any part that could be selected for that purpose, it containing Solomon's prayer that the petitions of all people offered in his Temple should be heard and accepted. I need not say that their whole service was performed in Hebrew, a language I am entirely unacquainted with; but as I got a seat next to a very ingenious and communicative Jew, I gained such explanation as agreeably astonished and surprized me. – The Laws of Moses, which are held most sacred by the Israelites, were taken out of the Ark, and carried seven times round a high seat in the centre of the Synagogue; where their Priests usually read service; at each time was chaunted by the congregation a psalm well suited to the solemn occasion; and every time the laws were brought near the Ark, slow music, in divine harmony, seemed to lift up each heart to the Supreme Author of their wise commandments; with every mark of profound reverence the Laws were returned to the Ark: The Priest then ascended the centre seat, when in an audible and affecting voice he most earnestly prayed. I heartily wished to be informed what that prayer meant; my instructive neighbour, who procured me the seat next him, pointed to a large square frame, and gave me to understand that that was the translation; I was delighted to find it a well wrote prayer for the King and Royal Family. By the time I had concluded reading it, my ears were struck with the words 'Our gracious King George the Third,' admirably set to such music as filled the soul with awful devotion. – The Queen's name was delivered with the same form and respect; then 'His Royal Highness, George, Prince of Wales and all the Royal Family'. – At the conclusion of each Name the congregation with uplifted hands and eyes chaunted Amen! – That prayer ended with the music of 'God save the King'. – If I was surprized at the prayer for the King you can readily believe I was also astonished and pleased at hearing the music of 'The Right Worshipful, the Mayor, and his Brethren the Aldermen and Council of this city'. – My intelligent friend perceived my thoughts in my countenance, and pointed over his head, where I again beheld another square frame, similar to that for the King containing a pathetic entreaty for the prosperity of the Mayor, Aldermen, Council and Trade of Bristol. – I say astonished and delighted, to find so undeniable proof of their liberal and charitable wishes for those who differ with them in religious sentiments. – The whole was concluded with their usual evening service, which was conducted with equal order and solemnity. I have been taught to believe that their worship was without form or order; but I now imagine our natural prejudice to what we do not comprehend makes us misconstruct their whole religion. – I am informed the plan, founding, and advancing all the expenses to the building and ornamention of this Synagogue is intirely Mr. Jacob's; who, from a public spirit to serve his brethren, has taken this uncommon share of trouble and cost upon himself.

Their public prayers for our King and country, offered up with the most decent fervency; the solemn order with which their whole service must be distinguished, (even by those who are unacquainted with their language) the laudable spirit that so strikingly exists among them to worship the Supreme Creator with reverence and awful piety, makes me now esteem them very different from the usual prejudice I once harboured against them, and has been the means of lengthening this epistle more than I intended.

I am, Sir, your most faithful friend and servant,

CANDIDUS

The Order of Service survives and shows that after the afternoon service in the building known as the Stone Kitchen, Lazarus Jacobs annulled the sanctity of that synagogue and the whole congregation proceeded, two by two, to the Weavers' Hall. The service included two hymns specially composed for the occasion. These are in acrostic form, each line of the first beginning with the Hebrew initial letters BRISTOL and of the second ELIEZER-BEN-JAKOV, the Hebrew name of Lazarus Jacobs. Copies of pages from the Order of Service appear below.

The ceremonial silver hallmarked 1786, the splendid curved mahogany ark doors, the wrought ironwork which surrounds the Ten Commandments above them and the four brass pillar-candelabra at the corners of the bimah are now in the synagogue in Park Row. Those at Plymouth (1762) and Exeter (1764) are identical. Bristol also had two matching smaller brass candlesticks on the reading desk itself but these did not survive rewiring some years ago.

סֵדֶר חֲנוּכַת הַבַּיִת

דבית הכנסת החדשה

שנבנה פה בְּרִיסְטָאל ע"י האלוף והקצין הנעלה · ראש הקהלה · כה"ר אֶלִיעֶזֶר מר יצחק י"ו
בחפצו ונתקדם ביום הפטי כ"ג אלול לסדר ולפרט אַתֶּם נִצָּבִים הַיּוֹם כֻּלְּכֶם לפ"ק

נדפס בדפוס החדש והמשובח אשר הוקם

ע"י כה"ר לֵיבּ זוּסְמַנּש וחבירו י"ו

פ"ה ק"ק

לְרֵגִין

בנת אם אבא באהל ביתי אם אולה
לפ"ק

חֲנוּכַת בֵּית הַכְּנֶסֶת

ונכנסים והולכים כל אחד ואחד על מקומו הקבוע לו בכבוד · והש"ץ שלה על הבימה ומברך על הטלית ומתעטף ומתחיל לומר

יי בָּרוּךְ הַסֶּרֶךְ אַבָּא בֵּיתֶךָ · עַם קְהַל עֲדָתֶךָ · לְרַגֵּן וּלְסַפֵּר תְּהִלָּתֶךָ :
יי בָּאוֹר פָּנֶיךָ · שָׁכוֹן בְּבֵית מְכוֹנֶךָ · וְקַבֵּל תְּפִלּוֹת בָּנֶיךָ :
קהל שְׁמַע יי קוֹלֵינוּ · אֵלֶיךָ נִקְרָא וְתַעֲנֵנוּ · וּשְׁלַח לָנוּ גוֹאֲלֵנוּ ·
לַהֲבִיאֵנוּ אֶל הַר קָדְשֵׁנוּ · וְלִבְנוֹת בֵּית תִּפְאַרְתֵּינוּ :

ואחר כן אומרים החזן והקהל כפסוק אחר פסוק אַתָּה הָרְאֵתָ לָדַעַת כּיֵּו שֶׁאוֹמְרִים בשמחת תורה ובסיומים לֵוִיהִי בנסוע
כותבין הׄחזן ואומרים עד גמירה .

ואחר כן יאמר החזן עם הקהל שבקהל בתולבים כ' קפיטל מ' פסוק י"ב התחיל לא אחר בליית ב' אחר לסבון בערצל עד פסוק ם' המסייס כי זהו הללויה אין עד .

ואח"ך יוליאו כל ספרי התורה מן ההיכל והחזן מתחיל

יי הָשִׁיר נָשִׁיר לֵאלֹהֵינוּ ·

רָון וְשֶׁבַח לְמַלְכֵּנוּ :

קהל וִיהִי נֹעַם יי אֱלֹהֵינוּ עָלֵינוּ :

חי יְהִי יי עִמָּנוּ ·

קֶעֹוֹד וּסְמוֹךְ מִשְׁכְּנֵנוּ :

קהל וּמַעֲשֵׂה יָדֵינוּ כּוֹנְנָה עָלֵינוּ :

יי קֶוֹב לָנוּ תּוֹרַת פִּיהוּ ·

אֲשֶׁר צִוָּה בְּיַד מֹשֶׁה נְבִיאֵהוּ ·

לֹא נִשְׁכַּח דְּבָרֵיהוּ :

קהל וּמַעֲשֵׂה יָדֵינוּ כּוֹנְנֵהוּ :

68

הנה אל ישועתי · בו אבטח ולא אפחד · כי עזי וזמרת יה · ויהי לי לישועה ‏יי ‏:
קל הנה אל ישועתי וכו'

אמונים עם נשאו · ידיכם קדש שאו · יחד לפני אל באו · נשתחוה ונבריעה ‏יי ‏:
קל הנה אל ישועתי וכו'

לאל תהלות עוטה · נזמר שיר ונכטה · רב מחולל צור נוטה · השמים כיריעה ‏יי ‏:
קל הנה אל ישועתי וכו'

יה כל בחכמה יוצר · חסד לאלפים נוצר · עיר מבצרי תבצר ואסוף הצולעה ‏יי ‏:
קל הנה אל ישועתי וכו'

עוז ידו יסדה ארץ · וגם טפחה ערץ · סובב סובב במרץ · בלי לאות ויגיעה ‏יי ‏:
קל הנה אל ישועתי וכו'

זמרה ותהלה · לאל מאד נעלה · אתה שומע תפלה · עדי כל בשר יבואו לברכה ‏יי ‏:
קל הנה אל ישועתי וכו'

רעה צאן מגורשי · לביתך יובילון שי · ושלח מהר בן ישי · לבת מחלה ונועה ‏יי ‏:
קל הנה אל ישועתי וכו'

בשלום תשוב לבת אהובה · זכור לכתה באהבה · במדבר בערבה · בארץ לא זרועה ‏יי ‏:
קל הנה אל ישועתי וכו'

רציים להשלים רצוני · ודורשים איה מעוני · ישוב כלאיש על כנו · ועל משמרתו ‏יי ‏:
קל הנה אל ישועתי וכו'

תנדל שמך פודה וגואל · קבץ נדחי ישראל · וקהלות יעקב יקהל · ולכו גרוגה ‏יי ‏:
קל הנה אל ישועתי וכו'

עזי ומגיני · ישור לשיר מעני · תטיב לך הגיוני · ובחסדך תצילני מטיב ‏יי ‏:
קל הנה אל ישועתי וכו'

קדוש ונורא אל · גאה גאה · בידך נוראה · חדש עלינו שנה הבאה שנת גאולה ‏יי ‏:
קל הנה אל ישועתי וכו'

בנה לציון עירך · ותשיב שכינתך לבית מקדשך · ותשבר עול קמיך · וכל עושי רשעה ‏יי ‏:
קל הנה אל ישועתי וכו'

חון על שאריתנו · ובטובך שמחנו · כימות עניתנו · שנות ראינו רעה ‏:
קל הנה אל ישועתי וכו'

זכור צדקת אב המון · היה אצלך אמון · ולבניו חיש אל קדמון · והקם את השביעה ‏יי ‏:
קל הנה אל ישועתי וכו'

קרב לנו שנת ברכה וישע · אל חי ועובר על פשע · שיחנו כזבחי תישע ‏יי ‏
ובטוב בירתך נשבעה ‏:
קל הנה אל ישועתי · בו אבטח ולא אפחד · כי עזי וזמרת יה · ויהי לי לישועה ‏:

וחם'ג מקבל הבבת ומתפללין הערבית כנהוג

The *Bristol and Hotwell Guide* of 1789 by Shiercliffe mentions the 'Jews' Synagogue, lately erected in Temple Street, said to be the neatest belonging to that people in England'.

Matthews' Guide of 1794 describes the building as:

> very well fitted-up, painted, and furnished with altar piece [ark doors?] branches, candlesticks, &c., in such a stile, that though it is not one of the largest, it is one of the handsomest places of worship in Bristol.

The 'branches' referred to must be the still-surviving brass Chanukah candelabra, part seventeenth-century Dutch, part eighteenth-century English, probably made in Bristol.

According to Ashmead's maps of Bristol dated 1828, there were two synagogues between 1825 and 1835. One is at the building that had earlier been known as the Weavers' Hall, the second was in a court just south of Counterslip, half way between Temple Street and Temple Back. It has been suggested that something similar occurred in Manchester where the rift lasted from 1826 to 1834. That was ascribed to the older entrenched members of the congregation holding on to key positions and not allowing newcomers to be similarly treated. The response of those who were excluded was to form a breakaway community.[5] The rift was healed in both towns and each celebrated by building a new, larger synagogue as the existing buildings were not large enough for the combined congregations.[6] (See ill. 19.)

In 1840 Bristol Hebrew Congregation bought the Quakers' Meeting House in a court to the west of Temple Street. By 1842 the refitting (almost a complete rebuilding) was effected. The new synagogue was consecrated on 23rd August. All four papers, *Felix Farley's Bristol Journal*, The *Bristol Mercury*, *Bristol Mirror* and *Bristol Gazette*, (the last three of which were identical) of the time reported the event:

> . . . It is almost a new construction. . . . The edifice is approached by a colonnade, which leads to the vestibule communicating with the principal hall. On entering the latter, the visitor is struck with its beauty and the taste with which it has been finished. Directly facing him, at the eastern end, is a portico, in the Grecian style of

---

[5] This situation was typical in Anglo-Jewry. For example a schism took place at the same period because only founder-members of Seel Street Synagogue, Liverpool, had a vote. C.P. Hershon kindly provided this confirmation.

[6] Much of this story of the early Synagogues appeared in an article by R.R. Emanuel 'The History of Bristol Jewry' in the Newsletter, No. 4/88 of Temple Local History Group, Bristol.

architecture, supported by marble columns, with their capitals
and entablature highly finished and ornamented with gold. . . .
The building is lighted chiefly, by day, by a magnificent cupola,
which occupies a considerable portion of the roof, the interior of
which, below the glass, is divided into panels ornamented with
bosses. There is also a window of ground stained glass on either
side of the portico, and in the centre, immediately over the Ark
one of purple glass with the Ten Commandments in Hebrew
characters, in amber, the effect of which is very beautiful. . . . On
the same bench might be seem some of the strictest communicants
of the established church with independants, methodists, quakers
and baptists, and all in immediate contact with the descendants of
Abraham.[7]

The service was chanted by Mr. Abraham Barnett of London
late of this city, assisted by Mr. Green and a number of chor-
isters, Mr. M. Moss presiding at the pianoforte.[8]

Interestingly both the Weavers' Hall and the Quaker Meeting
House, after vacation by their original occupants, were used by the
Methodists before being used as synagogues.

There are few reports specifically about the synagogue in Temple
Street but it is mentioned in the *Jewish Chronicle* of 25th September,
1857:

The Bristol congregation has renovated its synagogue and large
rooms by an outlay of £320. The building was erected fifteen
years since together with a large room used as a committee room
and a sukkah[9] at a cost of £2,600; it owes but a small debt
thereon, and for a small congregation there are few more
prosperous. The officers, Mr. Levy Levy and Mr. John Braham,
were re-elected for the present year, the former for the seventh
time, parnas of this congregation, the latter has filled the office of
gabbai several times, and under their management the
congregation will, no doubt, continue to be prosperous. Great
credit, we are assured, is due to the former of these zealous
officers for the sacrifices and exertions made by him for the
welfare of the congregation.

In October 1865, a New Streets Committee (part of the Local
Board of Health) was formed and work began on the new street to be
called Victoria Street. The case for the synagogue in Temple Street

---

[7] *Bristol Mercury*, 20th August, and *Bristol Gazette*, 25th August, 1842.
[8] *Felix Farley's Bristol Journal*, 20th August, 1842.
[9] This sukkah in the Temple Street Synagogue is not mentioned in any other
newspaper reports, although one was built at Park Row in the twentieth century.

71

was easier to settle than the argument with Maurice Michael.[10] It is a matter of conjecture whether they would have had a better deal if Joseph Abraham (whose untimely death occurred on 30th January, 1867) had been spared long enough to assist them. In May, 1868, the surveyors received a claim for £5,500. The President of the Hebrew Congregation, Samuel Platnauer,[11] said they wanted to obtain similar accommodation elsewhere but were having difficulty in finding a suitable piece of ground. The surveyors suggested a site in Lower Maudlin Street. This property was not suitable, nor was one at 47, Park Row (later the Prince's Theatre, destroyed in a bombing raid). By September the sale price with the Hebrew Congregation for £3,950 plus £50 for their tenant, Joseph Benjamin, the reader, and preliminary costs of £25.4s.0d. had been agreed. The indenture was signed for the Synagogue by Abraham Alexander, William Wolfe Alexander, Levy Levy, Joseph Michael, Michael Joseph Platnauer, John Solomon the younger, Philip Douglas Alexander, Abraham Mosely, Moses Blankensee, Henry Simmons, Moss Cohen and Jonas Rousseau.

Also at this time, in Park Row, the Little Sisters of the Poor were required to demolish the porch of their building for road widening. But this would mean they would have to rebuild the whole of the front wall, a very expensive operation. They would prefer to sell and move to alternative accommodation. For this sale they required £2,500, which the Committee accepted, maybe because there was a Councillor assisting them. In May, 1869, Samuel Platnauer wrote to the Committee proposing to purchase the site lately occupied by the Little Sisters of the Poor for £550, raised to £800 by the surveyors.[12] (See ills 7–9.)

To excavate the ground and build the new synagogue cost more than the amount received for the building in Temple Street. The community was in debt for many years until Moses Blanckensee helped out by paying off the balance of £392 in 1883, thirteen years after the work was completed. This was to be the first purpose-built synagogue of the Bristol Congregation, but it was some time before it was decorated. The architect was Hyman H. Collins of London, a descendant of Isaac Collish, Jew Preacher of Bristol in the 1700s. The architect in charge of the work was S.C. Fripp, the city surveyor

---

[10] Further details of the work of the New Streets Committee and Maurice Michael's sale appears in the Chapter 9, Reform of National and Local Government. pp. 135–138.

[11] Samuel Platnauer also appears in Chapter 4, page 50, and Chapter 10, page 144.

[12] The sale of the premises of the Little Sisters of the Poor appeared in Bristol Town Council's New Streets Committee minutes from 18th February, 1868, to 9th February, 1969.

THE NEW JEWISH SYNAGOGUE IN PARK ROW. – The new Synagogue which has been erected in Park-row for the Jews resident in this city was consecrated on Tusday, on which occasion Dr. Adler, of London, was present. The building, as most of our readers are aware, occupies the site on which formerly stood the asylum of the little Sisters of the Poor. The exterior is unusually plain, and what little architectural taste has been displayed upon the principal entrance has been to a considerable extent marred by the undue prominence given to the reader's house. The interior of the Synagogue is in accord with its external appearance; it is an oblong building, with a gallery running round three of its sides, and having the customary reading desk in the centre. The sanctuary at the eastern end was specially designed by Mr. Collins, architect, of London .... The carving represents the foliage of eastern plants, all of which have an allegorical meaning. The floor of the Synagogue is twelve feet above the level of the road, and the vestibule at the western end is approached by a broad flight of steps. As is customary with the Hebrew persuasion the galleries are reserved for women and children. The cost of the site and building has been upwards of £4000, more than one-third of which amount was expended in excavation, occasioned by the inequality of the land at this point, which is about 30 feet above the level of the roadway. The architect was Mr. Fripp, one of the city surveyors ....

The Bristol Mercury and Western Counties Advertiser, Saturday, 9th September, 1871.

responsible for the design and work on the new Victoria Street,[13] the cause of this expensive removal.

Of necessity it was a simple building, the only luxury (which they could ill afford) was the stone-arched baldachino over the ark, similar to the Grecian portico in the Temple Street building. The Ten Commandments over the Ark, the Ner Tamid, and the brass candlesticks all came from the old synagogue, as much due to the need for economy as of sentiment. In 1879 the interior was lavishly painted and stencilled at the expense of Henry Simmons, President, which decorations have long since been obliterated.[14]

At this time much of the community that had lived in Temple Street and neighbouring areas had moved to St. Pauls, which at this period had declined and was inhabited by the poorer section of the community. Middle income families were living in King Square while the better off lived in Clifton. The choice of site for the Synagogue of the Bristol Hebrew Congregation bore little or no relation to the place of residence of the community, but more to the need to make a quick decision.

---

[13] The sale of the synagogue in Temple Street and the purchase of the site in Park Row appeared in Bristol Town Council's New Streets Committee minutes from 19th May, 1868, to 24th August, 1869.

[14] Much information for this paragraph appeared in the article by R.R. Emanuel, 'The History of Bristol Jewry', in the Newsletter, No. 4/88, of Temple Local History Group.

CEMETERIES

In Bristol the next event after the consecration of the Stone Kitchen is a note about their newly-erected burial ground. *Felix Farley's Bristol Journal*, 31st March, 1759, contains the following advertisement:

> ## To be Sold in fee,
> ### A handsome Dwelling-House and Garden
> ### With a BRICK-YARD,
> Situate in the Parish of St. PHILIP and JACOB;
> The *Jews'* Burying Ground and some Buildings are
> in said YARD.
> Also, *To be sold in Fee Farm*,
> ### Five DWELLING-HOUSES,
> Situate in the Parish of St. JAMES,
> Near the BOWLING-GREEN.
> Enquire of Mr. Thomas Iles, Mason, at the Brick-Yard, aforesaid.

The deeds of the disused but still surviving Barton Road Cemetery show that on 9th November, 1759, the property was inherited by Thomas Trout, junior, on the death of his father. The area referred to was in the middle of the brickfields marked on Roque's map of 1750. Ashmead's map of 1828 shows it marked with the cross symbol of a burying ground. That the cemetery could only be leased was against Jewish law, which states that a burial ground must be an eternal possession.[15]

Part of Great Gardens (where the glassmaker, Lazarus Jacobs once lived, see pp. 101–103) was, in 1811, designated a private burial ground. This was purchased from the estate of Isaac Jacobs (son of Lazarus Jacobs) by Moses Abraham in 1830. Isaac Jacobs and members of the Abraham families were buried here.

The reason for this new cemetery was, no doubt, that the freehold of the St. Philips cemetery in Barton Road (described above) was not acquired until 8th August, 1859, for £210, also purchased by Moses

---

[15] The early part of the cemetery story appeared in the article by R.R. Emanuel, 'The History of Bristol Jewry', in the Newsletter, No. 4/88, pp. 14–31, of Temple Local History Group.

Abraham. Both are shown as burial grounds on Ashmead's maps of 1828.

The old cemetery of Bristol Hebrew Congregation in Barton Road, St. Philips was in an area described in recent correspondence with Benjamin Price, a life-time resident of St. Philip's Parish, as:

> the largest Parish in England until 1756. The main population was in Old Market whose members belonging to St. Philip's Church were buried in its Churchyard until 1854. But non-members of St. Philips (paupers, suicides, itinerants, people found dead, nonconformists, etc.) were buried in unhallowed ground, that is to say in the old Brickfields. Until the 1930s 'to be buried in the Potter's Field' meaning a pauper's funeral, was a prospect which horrified even the poorest.

Mr. Price remembers as a child that streets built over the Brickfields (to the east of Barton Road) had a ghostly air and the children avoided playing there. He went on to describe the state of the cemetery when he was a boy in the 1920s which, as will be seen, bears out Mr. Simmons' arrangements for a caretaker:

> Every morning on my way to school I passed the cemetery on the corner. It was interesting when a Jewish family came to visit. They would arrive, usually by car, and the caretaker, a Mrs. Bellringer, who lived in a house opposite, would unlock the gate. Immediately inside the door was a glass covered porch with wooden sides up to about three feet six inches, glass windows and a glass roof, just like a long summerhouse. The burial area was an absolute picture with flowers and plants growing, all beautifully tended and immaculately kept. We also had glimpses into the cemetery when Mrs. Bellringer was tidying up and left the outer door open to Barton Road and we would look in on our way to school. The surrounding walls were always maintained in good condition and about nine to ten feet high.[16]

On 1st December 1901, Henry Simmons wrote to Samuel Lazarus, President of the Congregation. A fire at Mr. John Mardon's premises adjoining the old burial ground at St. Philips, had made the wall dangerous. It was pulled down by the firemen breaking tombstones and levelling graves to the ground, thus making restoration of the Burial Ground necessary at very great expense. Mr. Simmons was organizing the restoration with the help of a small committee including

---

[16] Benjamin Price's oral testimony to the author. As a boy he attended St. Philips's Church. He is amicably aware of the presence of Jews in the neighbourhood where he grew up. Other memories of his appear in chapter 13. pp. 166-167.

Morris Nathan and Samuel Lazarus, president of the Congregation. The caretaker's house which had been for a long time in a dilapidated and insanitary condition had either to be rebuilt or pulled down. They had failed to obtain compensation from the City Council but Simmons had sufficient funds promised to restore the Ground and to pull down the house. To have it re-built and make it habitable would require a larger sum of money and he therefore asked the President to call a meeting to ascertain the Congregation's wishes. If Council decided to rebuild it, he would accept their decision but they would have to provide the funds. Alternatively, he could easily make arrangements for someone close by to keep the ground in order and hold the keys. The General Meeting agreed that the house be pulled down and that the spare ground be made available for more graves.[17]

Nearly a year later Henry Simmons wrote to the President again. Mr. Mardon had rebuilt the wall and instead of two small windows, he had four large ones overlooking the Burial Ground. The deeds of the cemetery between Mr. Mardon's business and the Bristol Hebrew Congregation gave the Congregation the right to close the windows or to enforce the owner do so. Henry Simmons thought John Mardon, as owner of the property, ought to be asked for compensation. Had the fire not taken place and caused so much damage, Mr. Simmons would have advised that Mr. Mardon be left alone. Since he had received the insurance money, there seemed no reason why they should not ask for compensation. After a meeting of the Congregation to discuss the matter, it was proposed that a letter be written to Mr. Mardon informing him that the Congregation would accept an annual rental of four guineas for the windows. Since the minutes at this stage are only of general meetings and the Treasurer's record do not go back prior to the Second World War, it is not possible to tell if such rental was ever received. One would like to think that it was.

Finally, the cemetery was reconsecrated on Sunday, 26th July, 1903:

> . . . The Committee decided to pull down the house and put right the insanitary situation. A sum of over £200 was raised, the contributors including Lord Rothschild, and the work was carried out.
>
> The reconsecration took place on Sunday, when there was a large assembly, with many gentile friends among the congregation. The service was conducted by the Rev. J. Abelson, who said that when they looked at the ground that day and contrasted it

---

[17] From Bristol Hebrew Congregation Minutes of General Meetings of the community, which commence in December 1901 with this correspondence.

with what had formerly been there they ought to offer a prayer of the deepest thanksgiving to the Almighty Father who had privileged the congregation to enter into the enjoyment of so goodly a heritage. A choir of boys, conducted by Mr. Simmons, took part in the service. At the close a vote of thanks to Mr. Simmons for his untiring efforts in connection with the restoration was moved by Mr. Lazarus, seconded by Mr. N.P. Tanchan.[18]

The work celebrated on that day lasted into the 1920s and 1930s and probably ceased with the death of Mrs. Bellringer who, given the state of the cemetery after the Second World War, cannot have been replaced. (See ill. 10.) Another quotation from Benjamin Price will explain:

In January 1942, I went into the services and did not return to Bristol until May 1964. My subsequent visits to St. Philips were short. I knew the area was being vandalised by the planners, so I did not stay long. When I became interested in local history this changed. On 15th May 1986 I went to the Jews' Burial Ground (its 1859 title) and was appalled at the dereliction. The gate (which had once been a door) was kept open permanently by rubbish fallen from the walls and industrial rubbish dumped on the path leading from the gate where the glass covered porch once stood. Looking up to the top of the wall to the left of the gate it was obvious not only had stone fallen from the walls, but they had been reduced in height. The side wall had been lowered considerably. There were electrical cables and, I think, a washing machine. The rubbish extended towards the graves, in fact some graves were partly covered with stones. Some tombstones and grave surrounds were damaged. Some tombs towards the back of the cemetery were choked up with bracken, also gravestones were flattened, broken, stones had fallen from the wall and partially covering the graves.

With regard to the condition of the cemetery: very few people lived in the area, the damage, I think, was not attributable to them. The industrial rubbish could have been dumped by any one of the several local businesses. It is highly unlikely that children would go near the place to do other more wanton damage. But cider drinkers, dossers or vagrants, etc. would not have been averse to dossing down out of the wind and weather and out of sight of the Police, particularly during the day when the construction acts as a sun trap. I wrote to the Evening Post, who passed the message on and action was taken to repair the walls and the gates and to tidy the whole place up. It looked much better the next time I saw it.

---

[18] *Jewish World* and *Jewish Chronicle*, 31st July 1903.

In the 1990s the Chevra Kadisha (Burial Society) of the Bristol Hebrew Congregation ensured that the gate was properly locked with a padlock and the grass and weeds cut from time to time. One hopes it will never return to the state in which Benjamin Price found it in 1986.

At a General Meeting on 1st June, 1913, the old cemetery in Rose Street (referred to in the minutes as Brook Court Cemetery) was compulsorily purchased by the Great Western Railway for a new goods yard. Ground for a new cemetery was bought in the Fishponds area of Bristol. The remains of those buried at Rose Street together with their tombstones were removed to Fishponds in the late 1920s.

The photograph (ill. 11) shows all that was left of Rose Street in the 1980s. This area has since been totally changed and even these buildings no longer exist.

COMMUNAL EDUCATION

Bristol's early-Victorian Jewish population of three hundred made it one of the five largest communities outside London. In reply to the Chief Rabbi's questionnaire of 1845 the Congregation reported that there were 36 Baalei Batim (house-holders), 40 seatholders, about 150 adult members. There was no mikveh (ritual bath) but it was hoped to erect one. It is believed this was in Rose Street, which was closed in the 1920s.[19] There was no Hebrew school but the children of the more affluent went to Hebrew Boarding Schools and the others were taught Hebrew by the Shammas (Aaron Levy Green) and Chazzan (Joseph Benjamin). For other subjects they attended local schools or specialist teachers.

The Bristol Hebrew Ladies' Benevolent Society was founded in 1845 and greeted effusively by the *Voice of Jacob*. The objects of the Society were the education and improvement of the moral, religious and social condition of the resident Jewish poor. The report in the *Jewish Chronicle* dated 22nd Tammuz, A.M. 5612 – 9th July, 1852, appears opposite.

The syllabus included Hebrew and translation, English reading, writing, spelling and grammar, geography, history and sewing. At this point the lack of further reports in the press means that judgement on their future progress cannot be ascertained. However a letter to the *Jewish Chronicle* on 27th March, 1862, reports on the seventeenth anniversary meeting of the Society and desires:

---

[19] The Chief Rabbi's questionnaire was briefly mentioned in chapter 5, p. 48.

BRISTOL.—We have before us the sixth report of the Bristol Hebrew Ladies' Benevolent and Educational Society, of which Mrs. Adler is patroness, and Mrs. D. Hyam president and treasurer, which was founded January 1st, 5605, and shews what can be done with even limited means, if we go but to work with earnestness and determination.

"The close of the year induces the committee of the Hebrew Ladies' Benevolent Society to offer to their subscribers a report of their proceedings, and of its present state. The committee are happy to report the favourable progress of the society. At its commencement, the limited state of their funds prevented them from establishing a regularly organised school; but they are happy to say, that, through the zealous co-operation of several gentlemen, who have kindly promised to assist them with annual subscriptions, they are enabled to carry out effectually the primary object of the society — the education of the children. To the benevolent supporters of the society, who feel an interest in rescuing the young from ignorance, imbuing their minds with the love and fear of God, and bestowing on them the rudiments of useful knowledge, this must afford great gratification ; and every effort will be made to maintain the efficiency of the school.

" The school has now been established six months, and the average attendance of children has been fourteen. The committee are happy in recording, at the examination of the children at the last half-yearly meeting, an obvious improvement in their English education; and that the diligence and interest evinced by the teacher, augur well for future success. They cannot close this report, without thanking Mr. Benjamin for his zealous and strict attention as Hebrew instructor to the children.

" The committee beg to tender their acknowledgments to A. Abraham, Esq., of Liverpool, for the handsome donation of eighteen copies of his valuable work, ' Moral and Religious Tales, for the Young of the Hebrew Faith,' and would take the opportunity of suggesting to other friends who may have it in their power, this mode of assisting the objects of the institution.

" The usual relief has been bestowed at the festivals, during sickness, confinements, etc., in provisions and money."

From March, 1850, to March, 1852, the balance shews that the donations amounted to £26, and the subscriptions to £98 11s. 6d.

Report on the Bristol Hebrew Ladies' Benevolent Society, *Jewish Chronicle*, 9th July, 1852.

79

... to vindicate our Hebrew women from the stigma of being uncharitable and irreligious. The children, fourteen in number, dressed in their new attire (given them annually for the approaching Passover), were examined in Hebrew and English and acquitted themselves to the satisfaction of all present. The writer regrets that fourteen subscribers have withdrawn, but hopes the good work will continue in spite of this loss.

To give some idea of the situation nationally:

... there were six Jewish day schools outside London. Three flourished, those in Birmingham, Liverpool and Manchester, and are well-developed today, while the three smaller schools eventually vanished or were absorbed into some kind of Talmud Torah, the reverse of the problem at the Jewish Free School.[20]

However, as the community had only about 260 Jews in 1850[21] it could hardly support a full-blown school. In the Census of 1853, the Board of Deputies *Return of Schools*, showed Bristol Hebrew Schools having three teachers and fourteen pupils, which gives one some idea of the size of the community.

In 1858 the *Jewish Chronicle* advertised a private Boarding and Day School for Jewish Young Ladies in Bristol.

Jewish children also attended secular schools and in 1859 the newspaper proudly reported a list of prize winners at Bristol Grammar School:

At the Midsummer examination, recently held, the following young co-religionists gained prizes, viz: Masters Braham for writing; Ballin, French beyond competition; Charles Solomon, modern languages; S. Solomon, modern languages, history and geography; L. Mozeley, drawing and mathematics. The last named young gentleman likewise gained a government prize for drawing at the Fine Arts Academy. It may be interesting to the friends of education to know that the above school contains about two hundred pupils, nine of them being of the Jewish persuasion.[22]

---

[20] C.P. Hershon, *Hebrews, to Make Them English*, Bristol, 1983, p.3.

[21] Margoliouth, *Jews of Great Britain*, vol. III, 1851, p.133, and V.D. Lipman, *Social History of the Jews in England, 1850–1950*, 1954, p.300.

[22] *Jewish Chronicle*, 1st July, 1859. James Braham attended the school from March, 1841 to June, 1855. Samuel Ballin was there from November, 1847 to December, 1859. Charles and S. Solomon attended respectively from October, 1846 and April 1848, both leaving in December, 1860. L. Mozeley refers to Louis, son of Abraham Mosely, see Chapter 4, pp. 54–55. He was at the school from July, 1848 to December, 1861. His older brother, Alfred, was there from October 1855 to December, 1870. A later report of the Grammar School dated 1882 appears in Chapter 6, pp. 91–92.

1 Jacob's Well, Clifton. (photo: Simon Ferguson, 1996)

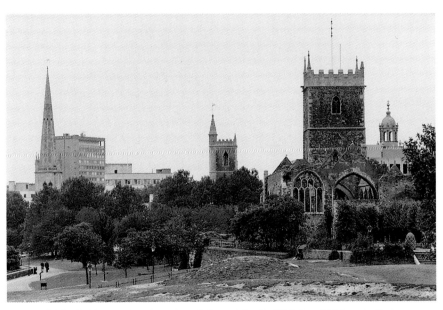

2 Castle Green: churches, from left to right, St Nicholas, St Mary le Port, St Peter and All Saints. (photo: Simon Ferguson, 1996)

3 Number 12 St James' Barton: place of business for David Nyman and later Henry Simmons. Destroyed for a new road. (Western Daily Press 19.1.56)

PLEAS TO SAVE from demolition this lovely house in St. James's Barton failed in Bristol today. The Planning and Public Works Committee decided to ask for permission to pull it down to make way for an entrance to a new bus station. The house was owned by the late Col. R. N. Harrison.

4 Temple Church. (Bristol Reference Library, photo: John Adler, c.1990)

5 Shakespeare Inn and Temple Church. (Bristol Reference Library,
photo: John Adler c. 1990)

6 Old house in Temple Street, known as the Stone Kitchen, which housed the Synagogue from 1756 to 1786. (drawing by H O'Neill, 1819, collection: Bristol City Museums and Art Gallery)

7 Park Row Synagogue. (drawing by Samuel Loxton, for article 'The Bristol
Synagogue and Jewish Worship', *Bristol Observer* 4.1.1896)

8 Park Row and Lodge Street. (Bristol Reference Library, photo: John Adler c. 1990)

9 Park Row Synagogue interior (drawing by Samuel Loxton, *Bristol Observer* 4.1.1896) and, below, photograph by Michæl Wagen, 1997.

10 Barton Road cemetery in dereliction, as seen by Benjamin Price on May 15th, 1986.

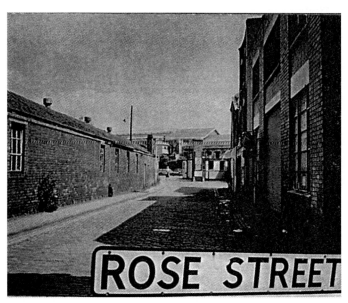

11 Site of the Rose Street cemetery: remains of the street in 1992. All these buildings have since been demolished. (photo: Simon Ferguson)

12 Rev. Levy Green. The original of this portrait was said to be at Jews' College, London. (*Transactions* XXV, plate XII)

moved to Liverpool.[8] Recently Rabbi Jonathan Romain suggested in an article in the *Jewish Chronicle* that nineteenth century ministers took more trouble over their sermons than their flock, but it may well have had more to do with the nature of the reports that are sent to the newspapers which concentrate on the excellent sermons preached by the ministers of the time.

The congregation's next minister was Aaron Levy Green (August, 1821–11th March, 1883) from London. (See ill. 12.) He was remarkably precocious, first appointed as Reader to the Great Synagogue aged only fourteen, and to Bristol in 1838 aged seventeen years. He was a man of outstanding ability who was to leave his mark on Anglo-Jewry. At this time the Bristol community:

> was relatively of far greater importance than it is today when its Jewish population is put at 400. . . . In 1850 the Bristol congregation was among the five largest outside London, its 300 inhabitants making it the equal of Portsmouth and smaller only than Liverpool, Manchester and Birmingham. . . . His first concern must, of course, have been the synagogue services and in this connection a problem arose from his desire to introduce regular sermons. . . . The Bristol authorities seem to have feared that sermons would disturb the morning service; but a compromise was reached and sermons were permitted on Saturday afternoons.[9]

On 31st July, 1844, he married a Bristol girl, Phoebe Levy (daughter of Joseph Levy, a native of Hanover) and they had thirteen children. The couple moved to 1, Pritchard Street near Brunswick

---

[8] Professor Isaacs (1810–1879) joined the Liverpool Old Hebrew Congregation in 1836 and served the New Hebrew Congregation from 1849. He was appointed to the Chair of Hebrew at Queen's College, Liverpool, but was tempted to Manchester in 1862, having divided his services for some time between the two cities. He was probably the most remarkable preacher in the ministry, even though English was not his first language. He had great ability to move congregations, and the famous funeral oration that he preached in 1837 for William IV – who was hardly well-disposed towards Jews – filled the synagogue to overflowing and the mighty 'amen' was heard streets away. (B.L. Benas, *Transactions of the Society of Lancashire and Cheshire*, LI, Liverpool, 1899, p.64). These sermons were often printed verbatim in the *Kos Yeshuos* (Cup of Salvation), the Liverpool Yiddish newspaper, and the local press. He was a very active honorary manager of the Liverpool Hebrew Schools (1843–63) and preached regularly on their behalf from 1842. He acted as Hebrew Master to the Schools from 1849–56, having had practice as a teacher in Bristol. The West Country can claim, therefore, to have incubated, if not hatched, at least one, if not more, of the country's most distinguished ministers.

[9] Alex M. Jacob, 'Aaron Levy Green 1821–1883', JHSE *Trans.* XXV, 1977, p.90.

Square in St. Pauls. On his marriage Aaron Levy Green's salary was raised from twenty-seven to thirty shillings. In 1849 the Bristol Hebrew Ladies' Benevolent Society paid tribute to his 'continued and unwearied efforts in religious instruction of the children'.[10]

He was a perpetual student in Jewish law and, once in London, wrote regularly for the *Jewish Chronicle* signing his articles with the pseudonym 'Nemo' ('No-one'). One of his first compositions was 'Dr. Croly, Ll.D., versus Civil and Religious Liberty', 1850, an attack on Croly who opposed Jewish entry to Parliament. His interest in education (or maybe the need for extra finance) started early and is shown in his work for the Bristol Hebrew Ladies' Benevolent Society quoted above and his advertisement:

> The Rev. A.L. Green will be happy to divert a few spare hours to GIVE LESSONS in the Hebrew language, Grammar and Literature, to prepare gentlemen for the Church or University. First-rate references can be given as to proficiency, &c., . . .[11]

During his fourteen years in Bristol he led '. . . a useful and unostentatious life, discharging the duties of his office with a zeal and intelligence which won for him the affection and esteem of his congregation.'[12]

He left for London in 1851 to serve the Great Synagogue as second Chazzan and assistant secretary. In 1855 the same synagogue opened a branch in Great Portland Street (later to be known as the Central Synagogue) and appointed Aaron Levy Green as its First Reader, a post he held until his death on 10th March, 1883. Ever forward-looking, he promoted London and Anglo-Jewry, in his work on the Anglo-Jewish Association. He also initiated the Mansion House Relief Fund after the Russian massacres of 1881.

At a General Meeting of the Bristol Hebrew Congregation on 13th December, 1908, a letter was received from the Rev. A.A. Green, offering the community a portrait of the late A.L. Green, for the Committee Room. The offer was accepted. One wonders what happened to this generous gift. Green's valuable library of Judaica and Hebraica is kept in Jews' College, which he helped to found. In religion, he was liberal-minded and aroused much opposition, especially his sermons and his series on 'miracles'.

---

[10] *Jewish Chronicle*, 4th May, 1849.
[11] The *Bristol Mercury*, 24th August, 1850. The '&c.' in this notice and elsewhere is the way they printed 'etc.' in the Bristol newspapers of the time.
[12] Obituary in *Jewish Chronicle* and *Jewish World*, 16th March, 1883.

Joseph Benjamin Theomin came to England from Franstadt in Prussia to serve as Chazzan and Shochet at Sheerness in 1837:

> . . . His departure from Sheerness is deeply regretted; as consequent upon our inability to support him and his family adequately to his merits and abilities. The confidence that our brethren in Bristol will appreciate him as he deserves consoles us for the loss of his services.[13]

While he served the Jewish community in Sheerness he dropped the name 'Theomin' as his surname for everyday use. It only remained on his naturalization certificate and his will since he had not gone to the trouble of changing his name by deed poll. His eldest son was also naturalized as Abraham Benjamin Joseph Theomin, which confirms this supposition.[14] Joseph Benjamin was appointed as Second Reader to Aaron Levy Green at Bristol in September, 1844, where he remained until his death, in February, 1880.

Joseph Benjamin's first wife died (probably in Sheerness since there is no tombstone for her in the Barton Road cemetery) leaving him with two sons, Abraham and Lewis. Abraham worked for D. Hyam and Company, as manager of their ready-made clothing store in Wine Street. Joseph Benjamin married again. His second wife was Esther, sister of John Braham, optician, of Bristol.[15] They had one son and two daughters. The son, David Ezekiel Benjamin, attended Bristol Grammar School and was then apprenticed in the hardware trade. In 1874, David emigrated to Melbourne, Australia, and by 1879 was living in Dunedin, New Zealand. He was successful in business and became wealthy. He built himself a house modelled on a Gloucestershire manor house, in remembrance of childhood holidays in the village of Olveston, the name he gave his new home.[16] Miss Stella Fitchett came to Bristol to enquire about David Edward Theomin's background. He must have adopted 'Theomin' as his surname once he was well established.[17]

---

[13] *Jewish Chronicle*, 6th September, 1844.

[14] Joseph Benjamin's will is at Somerset House, London. His naturalization papers are at the Public Record Office, Kew, ref. *Close Rolls*, C54/15281, p.28. Those of his son, Abraham Benjamin are also at Kew, ref. *Close Rolls*, C54/15272, p.39.

[15] Esther Braham also appeared in chapter 4, page 62, and chapter 7, page 104.

[16] Mrs. Nancy Burton told me this story before we met Miss Fitchett.

[17] David Benjamin attended Bristol Grammar School from April, 1852 to December, 1864. This was researched by Miss Stella Fitchett, the archivist of the Dunedin Museum situated at Olveston, given to the city by David's daughter after his death. She first contacted Mr. M.L. Booker, then archivist of the school, who contacted the writer. It was a very satisfying research task.

After Aaron Levy Green had left for London in 1851, he was replaced by Jacob Lindiner:

On Shabbat Hagadol, Mr. Lindiner, the candidate for Chazzan to the Bristol Congregation, gave an excellent discourse on the precepts of Pesach, which was listened to with great attention; we also learn that this gentleman's mode of reading has given such satisfaction as is likely to lead to a permanent engagement.[18]

In the Census of that year, Mr. Linder was a visitor in the home of Joseph Benjamin, 103, Temple Street. He was 25 years old, born in Hungary. He described himself as officiating minister at the Synagogue. However, he may not have been so satisfactory, for in January, 1855, the Congregation advertised for a Chazzan and a month later in the *Jewish Chronicle*, Samuel Landeshut addressed the:

Wardens and Seatholders of the Bristol Congregation: Gentlemen, I beg hereby to tender to you my sincerest thanks for the honour you have conferred on me by electing me Reader of your Congregation; and trust by due attention to the duties of that office, to continue to gain that approbation and merit your esteem for many years. I have the honour to be, Gentlemen, Your obedient Servant,

SAMUEL LANDESHUT.
London, 26 Shebat, 5615

He was naturalized in February, 1859, and his certificate shows that he was born in Sifra in Prussia, came to England in 1846 and already had three children.[19] He arrived in Bristol in 1855. He lived with his wife at 18, Phippen Street and, according to the birth register of Bristol Hebrew Congregation, they had two more children, Annie in 1856 and J. in 1858, while living there. He conducted services with ability and gave interesting sermons, all reported in the *Jewish Chronicle*. He advertised as a teacher of Hebrew in the *Bristol Mercury*. In 1859, he was elected Reader to the Manchester Hebrew Congregation.[20]

---

[18] *Jewish Chronicle*, 16th April, 1851. His Census entry later that year gives his name as Linder, but it does seem to refer to the same person.
[19] Naturalization papers at Public Record Office, Kew, ref. *Close Rolls*, C54/15344, p.55.
[20] In 1876 he was appointed as the first minister at St. John's Wood Synagogue. Then he became Secretary of the London Jewish Board of Guardians, whom he served diligently until his early death in 1877, aged only 59. His eloquence and erudition while at Manchester were still remembered with pride in 1907. From Rev. J. Abelson, 'Some Reminiscences of Bristol Jewry' in the *Jewish Chronicle*, 5th April, 1907.

After Samuel Landeshut left Bristol advertisements for a replacement appear in the *Jewish Chronicle* in July, 1859. The Rev. Isaac Samuel was chosen and served the community as Minister until his election to the Central Synagogue in 1864. His most notable achievement seems to have been the creation of a choir:

> A considerable improvement to the great satisfaction of the worshippers has just been introduced in the performance of divine service in the Synagogue at Bristol. An efficient choir, well-trained and organised by the minister, the Rev. I. Samuel, officiated for the first time on Pentecost last. The choir is composed of boys and young men, most of them sons of members of the congregation. We learn that they acquitted themselves admirably and are considered a very valuable acquisition. We may mention that the reverend gentleman is well qualified for this task by his large experience learned in the metropolitan synagogues.[21]

The choir does not re-appear in reports of Bristol Synagogue events in the *Jewish Chronicle* until 1879, for the consecration of the Synagogue after redecoration:

> The officiating Minister was the Rev. G.J. Emanuel of Birmingham. Mr. D.M. Davis of the New West End Synagogue attended specially to conduct the local choir.[22]

This choir had been started by Henry Simmons but may not have lasted for more than a year or so. Another was reported in 1886, again trained and led by Henry Simmons when:

> . . . the best thanks of the Congregation are especially due to Mr. Henry Simmons who, besides undertaking the laborious office of President, has also instituted a choir for the Synagogue at his private expense and constantly displays the greatest zeal and active interest in the welfare of the schools.[23]

According to later reports he led the choir until 1903 and may well have continued helping it thereafter. The choir seats behind the Bimah were probably put in during the improvements made at his expense in 1879. The choir continued in existence until all its members volunteered for war service in 1914 and none returned from the front.[24] Subsequent attempts to recreate a choir were made in the inter-war years but were less successful.

---

21 *Jewish Chronicle*, 29th May, 1863.
22 *Jewish Chronicle*, 14th February, 1879.
23 *Jewish Chronicle*, 27th August, 1886.
24 R.R. Emanuel kindly provided this information. A photograph of their memorial is in ill.32.

In Jewish worship choirs are not accompanied. Musical instruments were included in the ritual of the Temple in Jerusalem but in remembrance of its destruction in 70 C.E., are not used in Sabbath worship in synagogues. They may be used on other days of the week.[25] The concept was introduced into this country at Seel Street Synagogue, Liverpool, in the first half of the nineteenth century, long before London took up the idea. Bristol was among the first to copy Liverpool.

The Rev. Meyer Mendelssohn was naturalized in 1863 when he was Minister to the Exeter Congregation. He was born in Prussia and had lived in England since 1850. His appointment to Bristol Hebrew Congregation was not recorded in the Jewish press but he must have arrived some time in 1867, for he is mentioned as officiating with the Rev. Joseph Benjamin at a wedding on 4th June in that year. He offered lessons in German to residents of Bristol. He remained until some time after 2nd August, 1878 when the *Jewish Chronicle* reported that 'The Rev. M. Mendelssohn of Bristol has been appointed Minister of the Grigualand West Congregation and will shortly proceed to the Cape to enter his duties.'

That must have been where he died, as on 17th June, 1898, the *Jewish Chronicle* printed the following notice:

> On 8th June at the residence of the bride's sister, Beech Hurst, Portland-road, Edgbaston, Birmingham, by the Rev. G.J. Emanuel assisted by the Revs. I. Fink and B. Wolff, Sidney Mendelssohn of Kimberley, South Africa, son of the late Rev. M. Mendelssohn of Kimberley, formerly of Bristol, married Emma, youngest daughter of the late Moses Blanckensee of Clifton, Bristol.

In March, 1871, the Rev. Berman Berliner,[26] headmaster of the Borough Jewish Schools, was elected minister of the Bristol Synagogue in place of the Rev. Meyer Mendelssohn. A year later the *Jewish Chronicle* reported that he had established a Sabbath school where the average attendance was thirty-five.[27] In June, 1875, he married Helen Benjamin, the youngest daughter of Joseph Benjamin. He remained in Bristol until called to St. John's Wood Synagogue in August, 1878.

---

[25] A feature of Jewish religious life is that choirs, as many other organizations, come and go. My thanks to Rabbi Bernard Susser for this background information and C.P. Hershon for the rest of the paragraph.
[26] The Rev. Berliner appears briefly in Chapter, 5, page 81.
[27] It will be recalled that Sabbath Schools were introduced by the Hebrew Ladies' Benevolent Society but appear to have ceased without remark; see Chapter 5. They clearly have a similarly sketchy existence to choirs.

Helen Berliner died at their London home on 15th May, 1893. An intimate friend of hers wrote of her on this occasion:

> If ever a woman in Israel died as an angel on earth it was this good, dear soul, so quiet and unassuming, doing good without show, indeed more than her strength permitted. Last February, I accompanied Helen Berliner part of the way to take a poor girl a pair of spectacles which she had procured for her. On returning home she was much exhausted and mentioned that a bad smell in the neighbourhood she had visited had much affected her, and characteristically added that she was glad she had gone alone. Thus her last act and thought was charity and consideration for others.[28]

Rev. Berman Berliner served St. John's Wood Synagogue till his retirement in December, 1912, when he received a testimonial.[29] A year later he died.[30]

The nineteenth-century register of births and deaths, records that Joseph Benjamin performed circumcisions from 1849 to 1877, with help from Abraham Muller between 1872 to 1879. Muller's next post was at Exeter.[31]

Joseph Benjamin had lived in the house next to the synagogue in Temple Street as tenant of Bristol Hebrew Congregation until their move to Park Row. Thereafter he lived at 9, Queen's Parade, just across Brandon Hill from the synagogue in Park Row. He died on 11th February, 1880, after which a tombstone (ill. 13), probably set up by the Congregation, carried the following message:

> for nearly 40 years 2nd Reader and Faithful Servant of the Bristol Congregation, he earned the love and commanded the respect of all who knew him.

He had been their longest serving minister providing help and assistance to many Ministers as Chazzan and Shochet since his arrival in Bristol in 1844. His wife, Esther Benjamin, née Braham, died on 19th February, 1891, in St. John's Wood at the home of their son-in-law.

---

[28] *Jewish Chronicle*, 19th May, 1893. She was the youngest daughter of the Rev. Joseph Benjamin

[29] *Jewish Chronicle*, 13th December 1912.

[30] 'The scholarly, spiritual head of St. John's Wood Synagogue' was the Rev. Joseph Abelson's description of him in 'Some Reminiscences of Bristol Jewry', in the *Jewish Chronicle*, 5th April, 1907.

[31] In a list of Ministers leading services on the Day of Atonement, the Rev. A. Muller was at Exeter, *Jewish Chronicle*, 29th September, 1882.

The Rev. David Fay was educated at the Jews' Free School and started his ministry as Preacher and Headmaster at Hull. He was appointed Minister and First Reader at Bristol in May, 1880 and received complimentary remarks for sermons rendered on High Festivals in the *Jewish Chronicle*:

> . . . The Rev. David Fay delivered two impressive sermons in the course of the Day of Atonement. . . . he preached on the first day of New Year on 'Retrospect and Prospect', taking his text from Ecclesiastes, XI.9.
> On the Day of Atonement he delivered a sermon describing the day as one of spiritual joy and reconciliation and drew a parallel between the false atonement of those who were satisfied with merely observing the day as one of abstinence and the true atonement of others who regarded it as a medium for making their peace with God, adding the determination to stem the tide of evil and strengthen the current of good.[32]

He opened a house for Jewish pupils of Bristol Grammar School and his students' results were reported in the *Jewish Chronicle*:

> BRISTOL GRAMMAR SCHOOL: At the recent distribution of prizes, Leslie Jacobs gained the Class prize for Arithmetic, First Certificate for Latin and Certificate for the solution of Arithmetical problems; Arthur G. Morse gained the Class Prize for Latin and First Certificate for Arithmetic.

> BRISTOL GRAMMAR SCHOOL: At a recent examination at the above school, Leslie Jacobs came first in his class in Arithmetic and received honourable mentions in Latin, French and English; A.G. Morse was mentioned in his class for Latin, French, Arithmetic and English and A. Jacobs came first in his class in Latin, English, Arithmetic and Botany.

> BRISTOL GRAMMAR SCHOOL: Mr. S. Morley, M.P., distributed prizes and certificates to the successful pupils of the above school on Tuesday last. The following Jewish boys, all pupil boarders at the Rev. D. Fay's house, distinguished themselves:– Second Form: Leslie Jacobs – prizes for Latin and Writing, certificates for the solution of Arithmetical problems and Mathematics; A.G. Morse – certificates for Latin and Arithmetical problems. First Form: A.J. Jacobs – special prize for Physical Science, prize for Modern History, certificate for the solution of Arithmetical problems, Latin, Arithmetic, English and French; A.J. Goldsmid

---

[32] *Jewish Chronicle*, 1st October, 1880, and 7th October, 1881.

91

– certificate for Divinity and solution of Arithmetical problems, second class; J. Follick, certificates for Divinity, Arithmetic and English; E.A. Goldsmid – certificate for Latin.[33]

In July, 1884, he was the successful candidate for the office of Preacher at the Central Synagogue, London in place of Aaron Levy Green who had died suddenly the year before.[34]
In April, 1880:

> By invitation of the Wardens of the Bristol Hebrew Congregation, the Rev. A.H. Eisenberg of Canterbury Congregation, conducted the services and lectured in the Synagogue on Friday evening and Sabbath last.

By October:

> The Services on the Day of Atonement were efficiently conducted by Mr. M. Lorie of Pentre, Rhondda Valley (who gratuitously volunteered to officiate) assisted by the Second Reader, Mr. Eisenberg.[35]

The Rev. A.H. Eisenberg appears as the last keeper of the register of births and deaths that survived from the nineteenth century. He performed circumcisions from 1880 to 1893 when the book closes, leaving a number of unused pages. Clearly he ceased using it when he moved to Bridge Street, though it may well have remained in his possession until he left Bristol for London.

The Rev. Eisenberg was in Bristol at the time of the 1881 Census which showed that he and his wife, Rebecca, were both 39 years of age, and they had five children, Leah aged 22, Miriam aged 15, Golda aged 13, Katie aged 9 and Hyman aged 7, all of whom were born in Poland.[36]
On 26th April, 1885:

> At a meeting of members of the Bristol congregation on Sunday last, Mr. Joseph Levy, a student of Jews' College, was unanimously

---

[33] *Jewish Chronicle*, 4th August, 22nd December, 1882, and 3rd August, 1883. An earlier report of the Grammar School dated 1859 appeared in Chapter 5, pages 80–81.

[34] Other candidates were the Rev. Joseph Polack and the Rev. Moses Hyamson, both of whom came to Bristol later. The Rev. David Fay resigned from the Central Synagogue in July, 1902, owing to ill health and died in March, 1907. The *Jewish Chronicle* carried a long and detailed obituary.

[35] The invitation to Rev. Eisenberg appeared in the *Jewish Chronicle*, 23rd April and the report of the Day of Atonement service on 1st October, 1880.

[36] His later contribution to the Bristol Congregation appears in chapter 12, pp. 157 and 159–160.

elected Minister to the congregation in succession to the Rev. D. Fay, of the Central Synagogue.[37]

He wrote a powerful protest against the Conversionist Societies in the local press (see Chapter 8, pages 122–123). His commitment to the religious education of the children was high. When the children of the Hebrew and Religion Classes were examined:

> The examiner in his report considers that 'the results of the examination are in every respect satisfactory, that the task undertaken by the teachers has been performed exceedingly well and that they have done their work conscientiously, especially the principal teacher, the Rev. Joseph Levy, B.A., Minister of the Congregation.'[38]

He started a fund to obtain a small organ which was well used both in the schoolroom and the synagogue on Sundays. He also appears to be the first Minister to speak to non-Jewish groups in Bristol about Judaism:

> On Thursday, 10th May, the Rev. Joseph Levy, B.A., delivered a lecture in the Unitarian schoolroom on the 'Jewish Idea of God'. The treatment of the subject called forth a healthy display of enthusiasm from a very large audience. In his vote of thanks, the Rev. A.N. Blatchford, B.A., spoke in favourable terms of all that had been said, which statement met with prolonged applause. The local papers remarked 'the subject was treated in a very able and instructive manner'.[39]

Joseph Leonard Levy, (born London, 24th November, 1865, died Pittsburg, 26th April, 1917), was educated at Jews' College and took his B.A. at University College, London, at Bristol University and at the Western University of Pennsylvania (D.D.). He was the Minister to Bristol from 1885 to 1889.[40]

In 1889, he married Henrietta Platnauer, third daughter of Michael J. Platnauer, when 'a festive gathering of Jews and Christians came

---

[37] *Jewish Chronicle*, 1st May, 1885.

[38] *Jewish Chronicle*, 27th August, 1886.

[39] *Jewish Chronicle*, 18th May, 1888.

[40] He later served B'nei Israel, Sacramento, Philadelphia (1893–1901) and from then until he died, the Rodeph Shalom Congregation, Pittsburg. He was a considerable scholar and translated the Tractate 'Rosh Ha-Shanah' of the Babylonian Talmud (1895). Other books included *The Greater Lights* (1895), *Home Service for Passover* (1896), *The Nineteenth Century* (1901), *A Book of Prayer* (1902), *The Jews' Beliefs* (1903), *The Children's Service and Hymnal* (1903), *Text-Book of Religion and Ethics for Jewish Children* (1903), *Sabbath Readings* (1904) and eight volumes of Sunday lectures. He edited the *Jewish Criterion* published in Pittsburg. (See the *American Jewish Year Book*, 1904.)

together to witness the event. The choral portions of the service were sung by the choir . . . and Mr. D.M. Davis of the New West End Synagogue presided at the harmonium.[41]

He was said to have ranked among the foremost leaders of advanced Jewish thought in America by the Rev. Joseph Abelson in 'Some Reminiscences of Bristol Jewry' in the *Jewish Chronicle* of 5th April, 1907.

The Rev. Moses Hyamson was elected in his place and commenced his duties on Saturday, 8th March, 1890. With Henry Simmons he founded the local branch of Chovevei Zion (an organization set up to foster the national idea of Israel and to establish agricultural colonies in the Holy Land)[42] in 1890, but it seems to have disappeared (or not been reported) by the end of the following year. Zionism as an interest of Bristol Congregation had to wait until the dawn of the next century and the Rev. Joseph Abelson as minister.

At the examination of the children of the congregational classes a cordial vote of thanks was accorded to the teachers, the Rev. Moses Hyamson and Abraham H. Eisenberg. In September, 1892, the Rev. Hyamson married Miss Sara Gordon, daughter of one of the Ministers at the Great Synagogue. In October that year he was elected to Dalston Synagogue and delivered his farewell sermon at Bristol in December that year. He was elected Dayan in January, 1902. In 1906 the Rev. Abelson remarks in 'Some Reminiscences of Bristol Jewry' that Hyamson's versatility in English and Rabbinic jurisprudence had secured him a well-earned place in the Beth Din. The death of the Very Rev. Hermann Adler, Chief Rabbi of the United Congregations of the British Empire, in July, 1911, made an election necessary and it took place the following year between Rabbi Dr. J.H. Hertz, Dayan Hyamson, Rabbi Dr. Bernard Drachman (Hertz's teacher), Rabbi Prof. (later Sir) Herman Gollancz and Samuel Daiches.[43] In the interregnum Dayan Hyamson was virtually acting as Chief Rabbi. Dr. Hertz was elected.[44]

In August, 1893, the Bristol Hebrew Congregation advertised for

---

[41] *Jewish Chronicle*, 4th January, 1889.

[42] See David Feldman, *Englishmen and Jews*, Yale University Press, New Haven and London, 1994, pp.343–344.

[43] For a full report of the campaign, see Chaim Bermant, *Troubled Eden*, London, 1969, pp.187–189.

[44] Dayan Hyamson went to New York where he served the Orach Chayim Congregation and later the Jewish Theosophical Seminary where he became Professor of Codes in 1915, *Jewish Chronicle* and *Jewish World*, 9th May, 1913. In 1940 he became Emeritus Professor, *Jewish Chronicle*, 7th July, 1915, and he died on 9th June, 1949, *Who Was Who*.

'. . . a gentleman as Baal Korah, Chazzan and Lecturer. Salary £150 per annum. Apply to Henry Simmons, Kingsland House, Clifton, Bristol'.[45]

It would appear that this advertisement was seeking a replacement for the Rev. A.H. Eisenberg who is not mentioned in the Jewish press after September, 1893, in notices from the Congregation in Park Row. In fact he had moved to Bridge Street.[46] On 25th February, 1894:

> at a general meeting of the congregation held last Sunday, Mr. Henry Simmons, President in the chair, the Rev. L. Mendelssohn, B.A., minister of the Newcastle Congregation was unanimously elected minister of this congregation.[47]

The Rev. Lewis Mendelssohn, B.A.,[48] spent only a short time in Bristol and, like so many other Ministers of his day, the only reports are of his sermons on the first and last days of Festivals, and:

> THE OBSERVANCE OF THE FAST OF AV: For some years it has been thought that the Ninth of Av ought to be observed in a more impressive way than it usually has been. Although many religious persons attend Synagogue in the evening and morning to read the Book of Lamentations and chant solemn dirges, to the women and young there is no inducement to spend several hours in the synagogue nor any opportunity to understand the solemnity of the occasion. As a step in the right direction, Mr. Henry Simmons, President of the Bristol Congregation, arranged that the Minister, the Rev. L. Mendelssohn, should deliver a sermon on Sunday afternoon before the commencement of Minchah. The sermon, an impressive one, was on the destruction of the Temple dwelling on the questions: 'Why is Zion dear to every Israelite?' and 'What was it that brought about the destruction of the Temple?' In spite of unusually bad weather there was a very good attendance.

On 1st February, 1895, he preached his farewell sermon before leaving for Dublin. Rev. J. Abelson, in his 'Some Reminscences of Bristol Jewry', said that:

---

[45] *Jewish Chronicle*, 11th and 25th August, 8th September, 1893.
[46] See Chapter 12 for his story.
[47] *Jewish Chronicle*, 2nd March, 1894.
[48] Previously the Rev. Lewis Mendelssohn had studied at Jews' and University Colleges in London. His first appointment was to the Hebrew Schools in Melbourne, Australia. Then he returned to England to be minister of the Newcastle-on-Tyne Congregation.

95

Lewis Mendelssohn's attachment to orthodox Judaism of an enlightened and scholarly type stood him in good stead once he was Burial Rabbi to the United Synagogue.

Clearly the congregation that worshipped at Bridge Street had a big effect on that at Park Row; for example, before their existence a special service for the Ninth of Av would certainly not have been announced with such solemnity, if one had been held at all.

Rev. A. Levinson first appears in October, 1894, taking the High Festival services with Lewis Mendelssohn. His ministry in Bristol covered the amalgamation between the Bristol Hebrew Congregation and the small community at Bridge Street which meant that Rev. Ritblatt joined and Rev. Eisenberg returned to the Bristol Hebrew Congregation. Rev. Eisenberg stayed in Bristol until his retirement in 1902. Then he went to live in London, where he both organised and taught the Kilburn, Brondesbury and Hampstead Talmud Torah Schools. His obituary in 1920 tells us that:

> He was a native of Warsaw and descended from a family of great learning and piety. He was a great Talmudist whose delight was to impart knowledge to others.[49]

In March, 1899, the Rev. Joseph Abelson was elected to Bristol:

> Happily the difficulty in the Cardiff Congregation which has been the subject of some correspondence in our columns, has been solved, as far as regards the Rev. Mr. Abelson, by the election of that gentleman to the post of minister at Bristol. . . .[50]

There must have been a good correspondent (who may well have been the Rev. Abelson) to the Jewish press at this period for the amount of news about Bristol increased dramatically.

> Services on the Day of Atonement were conducted by the Rev. J. Abelson, B.A., and the Rev. J. Polack, B.A., of Clifton College, who kindly volunteered his services. . . . Before Neilah, the sermon was preached by Mr. Abelson, from the text 'Woe is unto us, for the day is going away, for the shades of evening are spreading themselves out'. The sermon concluded with a prayer. Overflow services were held in the schoolroom adjoining the Synagogue. Messrs. Rosenthal, Fox, Harrisberg and I. Belcher were the officiants.

---

[49] *Jewish Chronicle*, 21st May 1920. The Rev. A.H. Eisenberg died on Sunday, 16th May 1920.

[50] *Jewish Chronicle*, 24th March, 1899, under 'Notes' not 'Provincial News' where most information quoted here was found.

The services on the First Day of Tabernacles were conducted by the Rev. J. Abelson assisted by the Rev. Mr. Ritblatt. Mr. Abelson preached on the moral and religious significance of the Rabbinic laws concerning the Succah. . . .[51]

Rev. Joseph Abelson was moving on. According to an article in the *Jewish World*:

At a meeting of the Trustees of Aria College, held at the Town Hall, Portsmouth, yesterday week, Mr. Claude G. Montefiore in the chair, the Rev. J. Abelson, B.A., was unanimously appointed Principal of the College. The College was temporarily closed last year, but is now to continue (under the foundation of the late Lewis Aria) to educate candidates for the Jewish ministry, preferentially those born in the County of Hampshire.[52]

His farewell sermon on 11th January, 1907, and his article 'Some Reminiscences of Bristol Jewry' in the *Jewish Chronicle* of 5th April that year have provided much useful information. He returned from Portsmouth to lecture to the Jewish Literary and Debating Society in 1909 and 1914 and to take High Festival services in 1918. Sometime afterwards he served the Leeds Hebrew Congregation and later returned to Cardiff for a while.

After Joseph Abelson left Bristol, the Rev. Hyman Goodman, was elected as minister, teacher and Chazzan in 1907. (See ills 14 and 15.) He was a native of Portsmouth, had attended Aria and Jews' Colleges, and served the congregation in Hanley, before coming to Bristol. On 24th May, 1907 the *Jewish Chronicle* announced that:

a special children's service was conducted by the Rev. H. Goodman in the Synagogue on Sabbath afternoon, upwards of 150 children attending. It is proposed to conduct these services on the first Saturday in each month.

Sadly they are not mentioned again, and this may have been a single event. Rev. Goodman took part in outings and treats to the children and appeared to have been popular. From the minutes of the Congregation, however, he seems to have suffered from poor communication with its officers and had considerable difficulty in improving his salary. He resigned in 1916 to become officiating clergyman to the troops in the London area.

---

[51] *Jewish Chronicle*, 22nd September, 1899.
[52] *Jewish World*, 2nd November, 1906.

At the same time as Rev. Goodman was appointed, Rev. B. Paletz was elected to serve as assistant teacher and porger to help Mr. Ritblatt. In addition, he served the Chevra Kadisha from 1909 and became its secretary in 1918. He is remembered for his good singing voice by many of those to whom the Bristol Jewish History Group spoke. He resigned in 1919, having been appointed to Hammersmith Synagogue in London, although returning from time to time to officiate at special services in Bristol. He remained at Hammersmith, becoming its Emeritus Minister in 1955. In that year, also, he returned to Bristol to lead the High Festivals in the autumn.

A notable Minister, in much the same way as those praised in the nineteenth century by the *Jewish Chronicle*, was the Rev. Arthur Barnett. He was elected in November, 1920, but his time in Bristol had its problems:

> . . . I am most anxious to obtain a qualification but demands upon my time here leaves precious little time for serious study. As Reader I have to preach every week (which involves much preparation time). I am practically single-handed in the religion class. I am expected to do visitation work at the institutions and investigate for the Board of Guardians, collect all manner of funds, take the lead in all branches of activities of the community and visit my flock also.
>
> When I arrived, Bristol was suffering from a lack of guidance and initiative from its previous Ministers and I have had to do much work which should not have been left to me. . . . Bristol had too many bookworms for ministers and has suffered in consequence.[53]

He resigned in February, 1924, having received a call to the Western Synagogue. Once in London he became a member and sometime President of the Jewish Historical Society of England. He returned to lecture to the Jewish Literary Society in March, 1926.

Rabbi Harry Swift, the first Minister to be known by that title, was elected on 31st January, 1926. In September of that year he received his Rabbinical Diploma and the congregation duly congratulated him. From 1929 to 1932 he served as Hon. Secretary to the Board of Guardians. In 1931, he acted as Shochet in the absence of that functionary. During his time in Bristol, he lectured to a number of non-Jewish groups such as members of the Cathedral College and the

---

[53] From a letter from the Rev. Arthur Barnett to the Chief Rabbi dated 22nd March, 1922, among papers of the Chief Rabbi's Office, file on Smaller Communities, kept at the Greater London Record Office.

Theosophical College. He received a call to Shepherd's Bush Synagogue in September, 1932, and his letter of resignation was accepted on 26th June, 1934.[54] He was well remembered by many of those interviewed by the Bristol Jewish History Group.

The Rev. Simon Sussman from Darlington was elected in February, 1934, as second Reader, Shochet and assistant Teacher in place of Rabbi Swift. The Congregation encouraged him to train as a Mohel, which he did. He and his family lived in Synagogue House until the damp and rat menace persuaded them to complain to the Synagogue Council. The repair bill of £250 was more than the Council could afford. It was not surprising that Rev. Sussman found another post in Plymouth in 1944.

The Rev. Louis Sanker had been elected in 1935 and, in spite of one complaint, seems to have served the community well. However, in 1944 he chose to join the R.A.F. as a chaplain. The Congregation wanted him to return but his failure to answer letters led in due course to his resignation in June, 1947.

Up to the outbreak of the Second World War in 1939 Bristol Hebrew Congregation employed two ministers. Membership declined owing to the war and by 1959 it was so bad that one minister could not be replaced because of the deplorably low attendance at services.

Since there were so few members, between 1944 and 1962 the Congregation employed five ministers for varying lengths of time. In the gaps when one had left and another had not been appointed they relied on knowledgeable members to lead services. When the Rev. Max Modell was elected in 1962 things began to look up. As an article in the *Recorder*, the magazine of the Bristol Hebrew Congregation, put it:

> ... he came to a community that had been in decline for decades. Attendance at services had diminished to a point where a minyan was a luxury. The social fabric of the community was becoming as frail as the very shul itself. The old hall had become unusable and although the shul was able to struggle through its centenary year in 1971, it was closed shortly afterwards as a dangerous structure. ... In 1973 the community determined its desire to continue to exist. The 'Save Our Shul' group began fund-raising and a generous bequest focused and encouraged the collective drive to renovate the buildings and revive the spirit of

---

[54] Minutes of Bristol Hebrew Congregation, 1901–1971, and *Jewish Chronicle* 1925–1934. He later served St. John's Wood Synagogue and the United Hebrew Congregation in Durban.

Bristol. Throughout these times Max Modell continued to serve. Without him, the story might have been a sadder, more final account of dissolution.[55]

Rev. Modell retired to Bournemouth because of failing health in 1990 and died there in 1992. His career has yet to be fully chronicled.

---

[55] Alex Schlesinger, 'A Tribute to Rev. Max Modell', April, 1992, *Recorder*, magazine of Bristol Hebrew Congregation.

Lay Leadership: 1760–1904

L azarus Jacob, patron of the Synagogue, came from Frankfort-am-Main around 1760 to become one of Bristol's best-known glassmakers.[1] It was never easy for a foreigner to establish himself in business and even in Bristol if you came from Clifton you were an interloper. To start trading if you were not a burgess was an offence for which one could be prosecuted. It may be that he started out by peddling glassware around the countryside, engraving it to order. That he started in a humble way can be gathered from the advertisement in *Felix Farley's Bristol Journal* of 23rd February, 1771:

February 23, 1771
BROAD-CLOTH
At LAZARUS JACOB's, Glass-Cutter, nearly opposite
Temple-Church, Bristol, during the ensuing Fair,
Will be sold by Auction or Otherwise,
A Very large, good, and fresh Assortment of super fine,
best Seconds, and Livery BROAD-CLOTH. – They will be
sold at Prime Cost, the Maker of them being about to decline
Trade.

In 1774, Perrot's, one of Bristol's main glass-houses, went bankrupt and their property at 108, Temple Street, consisting of two houses with adjoining fine gardens and orchards, was bought by Lazarus Jacob. He set up as a flint glass (precursor of lead glass) cutter and engraver together with his sixteen-year old son, Isaac, and they soon took their place in the front rank of glass-makers, manufacturing much of the blue glass which was becoming very fashionable. About 1750, Michael Edkins, artist, came to Bristol probably from Birmingham. His ledger is preserved in the City Library, where work he did for glass firms including Lazarus Jacob is recorded. In 1763 he painted a board and back shed for Lazarus; 86 gold letters and two gold decanters and glasses all for £1.16s.6d. From 1785 to 1788 there

---

[1] Lazarus and Isaac Jacobs also appear in Chapter 5, pages 63–67.

follow countless entries in blue and 'enamel' glass, cream jugs, basins, bottles, jars and sugar basins, including the favourite 'setts' or garnitures for the mantelpiece.

The term 'Bristol blue' may have come from the frequent mentions in Edkins' ledger together with Jacobs' habit of signing their pieces, for blue glass was made at many other places besides Bristol and many other types of glass were made in that town. The elegance of shape and depth of colour, particularly the violet shades, make Bristol blue highly collectable, and when signed, fetch very high prices.

In 1787 Lazarus Jacob moved to Avon Street and then to:

> the delightful retreat of Great Gardens, Florio's happy spot, fragrant with jasmine, roses and orange trees, beauteous with fantastically cut yew and holly trees.[2]

Great Gardens was demolished for Temple Meads Station and further damage was caused by the 1960s ring road. On the 21st April, 1796, the *Bristol Gazette* reported:

> Died on Thursday at Great Gardens, after a short illness, Mr. Lazarus Jacobs, a Jew and an eminent glass maker.

He was interred in the Barton Road cemetery. His widow, Mary, née Hiscocks, of Templecombe, Somerset, survived him until 1816, when she died aged 81.[3] Lazarus left £100 per annum to his wife, with his plate and main household property, which after his death were to go to the two sons of his younger daughter Susannah who had married Joseph Moses Alman. His son, Isaac, received £60 per annum and there was provision for the two daughters of his elder girl, Hannah, wife of Hiam Emden. The residue went to the grandsons together with the 'holy utensils', i.e.. Sabbath candlesticks, wine cup and spice box. Both the girls had made good marriages. The wealthy Almans gave money to London charities[4] and Hiam Emden, who came from Amsterdam, is described in the family tree as a gentleman.

Isaac took over the firm and his eldest son, Joseph, born in 1790, was apprenticed to him at the age of 14. Under Isaac's direction the

---

[2] W. Goldwyn, *A Poetical Description of Bristol*, 1712, p.15; quoted by Zoë Josephs in 'Jewish Glassmakers', *JHSE Trans.* XXV, 1977, pp.110–111.

[3] 'It is an odd fact that both Lazarus and Isaac appear to have married out of their faith. Isaac's wife, Mary, née McCreath, of Shrewsbury, died only a fortnight after her mother-in-law, aged 51. Could they have been glassmakers's daughters? . . . Their family tree shows nothing but Jewish names until recent times', Zoë Josephs, 'Jewish Glassmakers', *JHSE Trans.* XXV, 1977, p.111.

[4] The Alman family were described in Chapter 4 above.

business went from strength to strength. In 1799 Great Gardens and Avon Street became purely business premises and he bought a house at 16, Somerset Square, in 1799, in 'a retired situation neatly built of brick'.[5] It was convenient both for work and for synagogue but away from the smoke.

By 1805 the roses and orange blossom of Great Gardens must have disappeared, for in that year Isaac launched out on a new project: the Nonsuch Glass Manufactory. A year later he described himself as 'Glass Manufacturer to His Majesty'. His fame largely rests on the fact that he signed some of his coloured wares, no doubt a form of advertising, examples of which may be seen at the Victoria and Albert Museum, the Jewish Museum, both in London, the Bristol Museum and Art Gallery, the Ashmolean Museum, Oxford, the Cecil Higgins Museum in Bedford, and the Gloucester Museum.

In 1809 Isaac built himself a fine home in Weston-super-Mare which he called Belvedere. In the same year, he was admitted to the liberties of the City by order of the Common Council. Examples of Isaac Jacob's work can be found in ill. 16.

By 1812 his son, Joseph, aged 22, was engaged to be married. Maybe owing to his father's financial worries, he was put in charge of the business. When his engagement was broken off, he demanded to become a partner in the firm. However Isaac would not agree and for a time Joseph left, only to return after ten days, when Isaac offered him an extra £300 a year over and above his board and lodging.

In 1820, Isaac Jacobs was declared bankrupt. He had not been able to sell his magnificent mansion and he was so depressed that he shut himself in his home refusing to see anybody. The former Royal glassmaker and pillar of the Jewish community was nothing but a 'dealer and chapman', an object of public notoriety. He died in 1835 and was buried in the Great Gardens burial ground.

By the middle of the century, Belvedere had been divided in two, one part as a crammer, an Academy where young gentlemen are prepared for University, the other as a dame school. The glasshouse in Great Gardens, apparently next door to Carrington's firm, was probably absorbed by that business and later into the Phoenix glass-works.[6]

Barnet Lyon Joseph was born on 29th June, 1801, in Falmouth. He married Betsy Jacob and they left for Bristol in 1823. He was young and energetic and must have joined in the affairs of the Congregation

---

[5] Zoë Josephs, *op.cit.*, p.111.
[6] Details of the life and times of Lazarus and Isaac Jacobs from Zoë Josephs, 'Jewish Glass-Makers', JHSE *Trans.* XXV, pp.109–113, and discussion with Raphael Emanuel.

with a will. At the tender age of 24 he was elected President of Bristol Hebrew Congregation and is likely to have held the post until he left for Liverpool in 1835 where he was a founder of the Hope Place Synagogue and of the Hebrew Schools. He also took Prof. D.M. Isaacs with him. He died on 26th October, 1880, in Birmingham leaving an estate worth £5,500 and, having fathered fourteen children and educated the eleven who survived.[7] His name appears in the rate books from 1826 to 1832 at 7, Union Street and in the street directories from 1819 at the same address, trading as a silversmith, jeweller and watch-maker, and in 1832 at 1, Catherine Place, Stokes Croft. There are no further entries, confirming that he left Bristol in 1835. He set up as a jeweller and silversmith in the fashionable area of Liverpool at 42, Bold Street.

By the time that Barnet Lyon Joseph had left, the lay leaders of the community were John Braham (briefly mentioned in Chapter 4, page 62) and Levy Levy. John Braham, optician, was born in Plymouth. He must have come to Bristol probably with his mother, certainly with his brothers, James and George, and sisters, Julia and Esther, as a young man. His brother, George Braham, went to Bath where he set up as an optician at 6 George Street.[8] One of their sisters, Esther Braham,[9] had married the Rev. Joseph Benjamin. John Braham was a ratepayer from 1831, and registered as an elector from 1845.

The youngest sister, Julia Braham, appeared as a wool draper in the 1841 Census. On 28th August, 1850, she married Henry Essinger and a year later their daughter, Rosa, was born. In the 1851 Census, Henry Essinger stated he had a business as a straw plait manufacturer employing five milliners, including his wife Julia and her sister Esther Braham. Since he did not advertise in the local press there is no more to add about his business affairs. He died aged thirty in October, 1854.

Meanwhile Henry Moses in August, 1853, advertised a lottery: '£58 worth of property for one shilling'. Tickets were available from 28, Bath Street. By September not enough tickets had been sold, so he postponed drawing the prizes until 20th September, 1853. The paper tells us nothing more of this exploit.[10] On 24th October, 1858, he married Julia Essinger, née Braham, at John Braham's residence in St.

---

[7] Information from Dr. Anthony P. Joseph of Birmingham, a descendant of this family and additions by C.P. Hershon.

[8] Malcolm Brown and Judith Samuel, 'Jews in Bath', Jewish Historical Studies, JHSE, XXIX, 1982–1986, p. 148.

[9] Esther Braham previously appeared in chapter 4, page 62, and chapter 6, page 86.

[10] He advertised in the Bristol Times and Felix Farley's Bristol Journal on 21st May, 20th August and 3rd September 1853.

Augustine's Parade. The 1851 Census shows that there were two children in the household, Rosa Essinger and Henry Moses, both aged 9. Rosie, daughter of the late Henry Essinger, married Paretz Bernstein of Stockton and Darlington on 17th July, 1883, at St. John's Wood Synagogue, London.

John Braham served the Congregation as Gabbai in the 1850s and 1860s and was a tower of strength to the community. He wrote to the *Jewish Chronicle* in support of education for future Rabbis in 1844, long before Jews' College was founded. The then Chief Rabbi, Nathan Adler, wished to establish a college which could produce a corps of teachers able to give instruction in English to children in chederim (Jewish schools). He issued a circular proposing the creation of a college. In January, 1852, a public meeting was held to raise funds for the seminary and day school. Yet, for lack of funds, neither was opened until 1855. Once Jews' College was established, Hebrew was taught to an elementary level and classics and general literature were included in the curriculum.[11]

In business John Braham showed a talent for innovation and an appreciation of publicity. One of his earliest entries in the local press appeared in *Felix Farley's Bristol Journal* of 24th January, 1835:

> Mr. Braham of St. Augustine's Parade, having announced he will certainly close his exhibition on the Hydro-Oxygen Microscope the ensuing week, we strongly recommend all those who are fond of viewing wonders of nature in her minutest and most interesting forms, and have not witnessed the astonishing effects of the microscope, to avail themselves of the opportunity of doing so.

For some years J. Jackson had been an optician at 17, St. Augustine's Parade. In 1839, the local street directory showed that John Braham was trading with Jackson at the same address as 'goldsmiths, jewellers, chronometer, watch and clock makers'.[12] (See ill. 17.)

A year later, the business was taken over by John Braham, who recalled his predecessor in the title of his shop: Braham, late Jackson, established 1797, which suggests that was when J. Jackson started in business. No more is known of their business connection, but it is said that John Braham married Jackson's daughter, Henrietta, which would have taken place in about 1827 (their eldest son, Henry, was

---

[11] David Feldman, *Englishmen and Jews, Social Relations and Political Culture, 1840–1914*, Yale University Press, New Haven & London, 1994, p. 61.

[12] While there was no dominant trade for Jews in Bristol, it is interesting to note that they practised as goldsmiths, silversmiths, jewellers and watch-makers, as in every major British centre.

born in 1829).[13] There are no civil or synagogue records at this time to confirm this. One of John Braham's first advertisements appeared in *Felix Farley's Bristol Journal* of 10th January, 1846 (see opposite) in which he advertised patent spectacles.

Another occasion when he appeared in the local press was an exhibition he arranged with Thomas Mountain at the Victoria Rooms in April, 1850. They put on lectures about the exhibition of the ruins and antiquities at Babylon and Nineveh soon after these cities had been excavated. It appears from the newspaper reports there was not the support expected, so the exhibition was remounted at the Public Rooms in Broadmead at a lower entrance fee, when they were more successful.

In 1851 he exhibited at the Great Exhibition and received much gratuitous publicity in all the Bristol papers:

> *THE GREAT EXHIBITION* of 1851: The list of articles to be sent from Bristol and the neighbourhood to the Exhibition included Mr. John Braham and Company's spectacles showing their improvement from their first introduction in the reign of James I to the present time and some optical instruments.[14]

In a review of the Exhibition, the *Illustrated London News* in May, 1851, noted:

> In spectacles adapted for use, Mr. Braham's case is the most interesting. He has exhibited specimens of spectacles from their earliest invention, and has illustrated the various modes adopted by Sir Isaac Newton, Doctors Kitchiner, Wollaston and Herschell. We have the highest opinion of the Pantoscopic spectacles which are menisci lenses, as recommend by the great Wollaston, so ground and fixed in frames, that the eye can look at near objects through the glass, but at distant objects over the frame. This form should be adopted by all who first take to glasses, as it allows the use of these adjuncts to vision without injuring the eye by straining it when the glass is not required. In Mr. Braham's case of spectacles the visitor will have an opportunity of examining the mode in which 'pebbles' are made from blocks of quartz. Slices of

---

[13] Max Dunscombe in 'Established 1797' in *The Bristol Templar*, Spring 1989, pp. 16-19, told the story of his grandfather, Matthew William. John Braham, a Jew and an optician, took over from J. Jackson, and was succeeded by Matthew William Dunscombe, both non-Jews, in what was clearly a very successful enterprise.

[14] *Felix Farley's Bristol Journal*, 4th January, 1851. The underlining is copied from the advertisement.

BRAHAM'S PATENT SPECTACLES.

The efficacy of BRAHAM'S IMPROVED PATENT PANTOSCOPIC SPECTACLES AND EYE PRE-SERVERS, and the *superiority over all others is fully confirmed* by the numerous testimonials the Patentee has received from those who now wear them. The advantage of these spectacles consists in their being the perfect shape of the eye, and placed at the correct angles, so that the rays of light from every object of vision passes in a direct line to the organ of sight; thus rendering them preferable to all others for needlework or reading by candle light, and they do not require to be removed from the head when the eye is directed to distant objects. The following have been received from highly respectable gentlemen:-

"3, Great Queen's-street, Lincoln's-inn-fields,

January 7, 1846.

"SIR, – The two pairs of your patent spectacles, for which Mr. Guthrie requested me to send to you, he approves of very much, and it is evident the principle upon which they are constructed meets his entire approbation, as he himself uses the first pair which he had of you. The Duke of Wellington also continues to use those you furnished him with. Mrs. Wright and myself find great comfort in wearing them; and I think it will be very desirable that the valuable improvement you have made in this important article should be generally known, it being of great advantage to all persons requiring the aid of glasses.

"I am, Sir, your obedient servant,

"W. WRIGHT, Surgeon Aurist."

"To Mr. John Braham, Optician, Bristol.

"I have been enabled to recommend Mr. Braham's improve-ment in Spectacles, from a conviction of their being so very superior to those in common use.   J.G. LANSDOWN.

"St. James-Square, Oct. 7, 1845."

J.B. has just completed and adapted his patented principle to concave Spectacles, and to persons who are short sighted they are far more agreeable and advantageous than those of the old kind.

To ensure a perfect article, purchasers should observe than on every pair is stamped – "BRAHAM, Patentee, Bristol."

∵ An extensive assortment of all kinds of Optical and Mathe-matical Instruments, Rules, Scales, Globes, Thermometers, &c.

17, ST. AUGUSTINE'S PARADE,

Near the Drawbridge.

Felix Farley's Bristol Journal, 10th January, 1846.

transparent stone are first cut, these are ground to the requisite curve and then polished, when they are ready to be inserted in the frame.[15]

In spite of his advertisement alleging a patent in 1846 above, the only one found at the Patent Office is dated 16th February, 1861.[16] This refers to the ability to hang a separate lens over the spectacle frame for other purposes. The one quoted is for rifle shooting, when longer sight would be required than, say, for reading. From the written patent it is clear that John Braham made his own spectacles for sale and must have been very proficient at this useful art. In November of that year the local press gave it further, free publicity:

> With the limited knowledge we possess of the nature of the eye and the construction of spectacles for assisting impaired vision, we cannot follow the description or use of the variety of spectacles and eye glasses which have been show to us by Mr. John Braham, who has contrived and patented what appears to us some very ingenious and useful assistants for all who may require the aid of spectacles. . . . The helical spring eye glass is really unique, and the rifle spectacles must prove highly useful, and initiate those who use the rifle to become good shots. . . . The spectacles . . . assist the eye of persons who read much by candle or gas light and whose sight is impaired by natural decay or other causes. They will prove very useful to those who earn their livelihood by needlework, and will, doubtless, be of particular benefit to shoemakers, tailors, sempstresses, who work for the most part on black materials. . . . Mr. Braham has obtained Letters patent from His Imperial Majesty, the Emperor of the French, for his newly improved inventions in spectacles as exclusively secured to him in this country by patent from Her Majesty.[17]

John Braham died by his own hand on 14th August, 1864, at his new home 17, Doughty Street, London. He had retired from business and was to have visited Bristol that Sunday morning. The inquest, held two days later, showed that he believed he did not have sufficient money to live on and that he would die in the workhouse. Lewis Braham, physician, his son, said his father had been subject to despondency, which had continued for some months. There was a

---

[15] Quoted identically in the *Bristol Mercury*, *Felix Farley's Bristol Journal* and the *Bristol Mirror* of 24th May, 1851.

[16] The advertisement in *Felix Farley's Bristol Journal*, 10th January, 1846, quoted above, stated that John Braham was a 'patentee'. However, his entry at the Patent Office is dated A.D. 1861, 16th February, No. 389, a copy of which was sent to the author by Mr. Terence J. Bryant, following his enquiry about John Braham.

[17] *Bristol Times*, 2nd and 23rd November, 21st and 28th December, 1861.

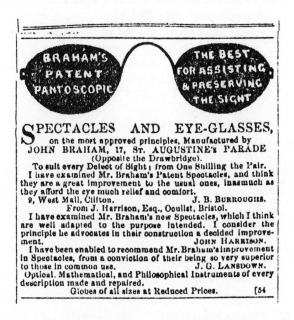

SPECTACLES AND EYE-GLASSES,
on the most approved principles, Manufactured by
JOHN BRAHAM, 17, St. AUGUSTINE's PARADE
(Opposite the Drawbridge).
To suit every Defect of Sight; from One Shilling the Pair.
I have examined Mr. Braham's Patent Spectacles, and think
they are a great improvement to the usual ones, inasmuch as
they afford the eye much relief and comfort.
9, West Mall, Clifton.   J. B. BURROUGHS.
    From J. Harrison, Esq., Oculist, Bristol.
I have examined Mr. Braham's new Spectacles, which I think
are well adapted to the purpose intended. I consider the
principle he advocates in their construction a decided improvement.   JOHN HARRISON.
    I have been enabled to recommend Mr. Braham's improvement
in Spectacles, from a conviction of their being so very superior
to those in common use.   J. G. LANSDOWN.
Optical, Mathematical, and Philosophical Instruments of every
description made and repaired.
    Globes of all sizes at Reduced Prices.   [54

Bristol Mercury supplement, 31st March, 1855.

tendency to suicide in his family, for the deceased's mother had destroyed herself. The jury returned a verdict of 'Suicide under temporary insanity'.[18] He was buried at Barton Road Cemetery.[19]

After John Braham had left Bristol for London, his sons, Frederick Joseph and Joseph carried on the business and advertised regularly from June, 1863 to May, 1864. Then Joseph and another brother, James D. Braham, traded in opposition in Bristol, advertising from October, 1865 to March 1866. Joseph's lack of success can be seen by the fact that he was judged bankrupt on 9th May, 1866, promising to pay his creditors five shillings in the pound by two equal instalments

---

[18] The report of the death of Rosa Braham, mother of John, James and George appeared in the *Bristol Mercury*, 24th December, 1842. That for John Braham appeared in the *Standard* and *Daily News* (both of London) of 16th August, 1864.

[19] The most successful of the three brothers, John, James and George Braham, was James. He lived in Liverpool, married Henrietta Jackson, of a well-known Liverpool Jewish family. (They are unlikely to be related to J. Jackson, John Braham's predecessor in business.) In his will, James left an annual prize to poor girls at the School in Hope Place, Liverpool. He died on 5th February, 1873, and Henrietta died on 24th February, 1890. In her will, she left generous sums to family, including George's son, James, and many friends.

109

NOTICE OF REMOVAL.

FROM 17, ST. AUGUSTINE'S PARADE,
TO 24, COLLEGE-GREEN, (Corner of Unity-street), BRISTOL.
ESTABLISHED 1797.
PATENT SPECTACLE MANUFACTURY.

J. BRAHAM, OPTICIAN,

Respectfully announces that he will remove on the 20th November to the above address, where he trusts to receive a continuance of the patronage of the Nobility, Gentry, Residents and Visitors of Bristol, Clifton and Suburbs bestowed upon this establishment for nearly three-quarters of a Century.

Prior to the date of removal a reduction in price will be allowed off OPERA & RACE GLASSES, TELESCOPES, BAROMETERS, THERMOMETERS, &c., &c.

NOTE THE ADDRESS!

Removal on the 20th Instant.

Joseph Braham's advertisement on 11th November, 1865. *Saturday Bristol Times and Mirror.*

secured by his elder brother Lewis and Michael Aaron Jessel, his father-in-law.

From the article by Max Dunscombe already mentioned, it appears that Max's grandfather had met John Braham on a London omnibus and they had taken a liking to each other. Dunscombe's studies gained him certificates in optics and kindred subjects from the London College of Science. He then returned to Bristol and by 1874 was able to purchase the Braham business, together with Braham's large collection of spectacles which probably went back to his earlier association with Jackson. The shop had moved from No. 17 to No. 10, St. Augustine's Parade (where the Hippodrome is situated today). Dunscombe, in his turn, continued to advertise that the business was founded in 1797.

After the bankruptcy, Joseph Braham moved to 45 Leamington Street, Westbourne Park, London, living with Catherine, his wife, whom he had married on 26th August, 1863, and their two children, Florence and Sidney. His brother, Henry, was in the rag and jute trade. Joseph joined him, investing money in the business. He died by his own hand on 5th November, 1866, in their warehouse in St.-George-in-the-East. An inquest was held on 9th November at which Henry said there was a suicidal tendency in the family. His father had hanged himself

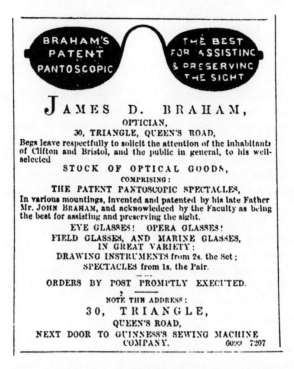

James D. Braham in the Saturday *Bristol Times and Mirror*,
13th January, 1866.

four years ago, and his grandmother had drowned herself. After
reading a letter left by Joseph, Henry said that the deceased had a
delusion about the way in which his money had been invested that was
a mistake and he imagined that he was in pecuniary difficulties.[20]

Michael Jessel had a shop (ill.18) on the corner of St. Augustine's
Parade and Colston Street from at least 1862 when he first advertised.
One of his daughters, Catherine, had married Joseph Braham. After
Joseph's sad demise, she and their children lived with the Jessels. In
the Census of 1871, Florence Braham, aged 6, was living with them
and in 1881, she and her brother, Sidney aged 15, were there.
Catherine died in Glasgow on 4th April, 1897.

In 1879, Michael Jessel was elected Vice-President, and in 1880,

---

[20] The inquest on Joseph Braham's death appeared in the (London) *Express* of 10th
November, 1868.

Warden of the Bristol Hebrew Congregation. Whether he remained on the Council is unknown as the newspaper reports fail us yet again, but they do relate that he was elected to its Council again in April, 1891. Michael Jessel died at the home of his son, John, in Bristol on 7th February, 1896, in his 88th year. His cousin, Sir George Jessel, was a Member of Parliament from 1868 and the first Jewish Master of the Rolls from August, 1873.

Levy Levy was born in Barton Regis, Gloucestershire.[21] He appears in rate books from 1802 at various addresses in St. James' Parish and also for a house and shop in Temple Street. His first advertisement in the local street directory of 1806 states he was an optician. By 1814 he also had a glass warehouse and by 1819 he ceased advertising as an optician, but had become a glass dealer and engraver. In 1832 he was selling lamps and in 1837 his shop was described as: '. . . a rich cut glass manufactory and lamp wholesaler and the only French shade warehouse in Bristol'.[22]

This must have been a successful concern, for in 1854 he handed over the business to his sons, Abraham and Frederick Levy. In 1858, Frederick Levy had moved to Leamington Spa to take the waters where he died after a long and painful illness in July, 1865.[23]

From 1858 Abraham Levy was trading on his own. He appeared in the local press in 1868 when he was involved in a legal dispute. He had received an order for two chandeliers but the purchaser did not specify how many lights they should have. At that time it was customary to deliver three-light chandeliers unless otherwise stated. In this case the plaintiff had required two-light chandeliers, for which reason he did not pay for them. Abraham Levy took him to court for payment and obtained his money.[24]

In December, 1850, Levy Levy, President of the Bristol Hebrew Congregation, signed the letter to the *Jewish Chronicle* advertising for a minister to replace Aaron Levy Green. His service to the community continued for many years and on his retirement as Warden in 1862, he was given a testimonial:

> Mr. Levy Levy, being about to retire from the office of President of the Hebrew Society in this city, it is intended to present him

---

[21] Barton Regis was outside the City of Bristol. That area is now known as Clifton. The census of 1851 shows that Levy Levy, aged 63, was living with his wife, Elizabeth, aged 54, born in Plymouth; three sons, aged 14, 17 and 19, and a daughter, aged 12, all born in Bristol.
[22] Rate books from 1802 to 1849 and street directories from 1806 to 1850.
[23] *Jewish Chronicle*, 28th July 1865.
[24] *Western Daily Press*, 17th July, 1868.

with a silver salver in recognition of his past services. The salver, which has been manufactured by Messrs. Williams at the Drawbridge, is a very handsome piece of plate and does great credit to the makers.[25]

A report of the ceremony appeared in the *Jewish Chronicle* on 21st November, 1862:

> . . . In acknowledgement of the great services rendered by this gentleman to his community. The testimonial was presented, with a few appropriate remarks, by the senior member, Mr. Abraham Alexander. Mr. J. Abraham then . . . commented on the part the worthy warden had acted in fulfilling the office of Parnas for the last twelve years, stating that during that period he had advanced nearly £1,000 to his congregation accepting instalments in receipt, payable entirely at the convenience of the congregation; that by his strenuous exertions the balance of the old debt of the synagogue had been cancelled; that he had been the promoter and active agent, both in purse and person, in acquiring for congregational purposes a free burial ground, and all necessary buildings and was now enabled to come before them and announce that the congregation was free from debt. . . . The testimonial was then presented to Mr. Levy. It was a handsome silver salver bearing the inscription:- 'Presented to Levy Levy, Esq., by the Bristol Hebrew Congregation on his retiring from the office of President, and as an acknowledgement for his zeal and valuable services during a series of years, ten of which he was chief warden. – Bristol, 9th November, 1862–5623.

He died in 1876 and was buried at the Barton Road Cemetery in St. Philips.

Henry Simmons was born in Posen, Prussia, and lived in Bristol from sometime in the early the 1850s, as previously cited on p. 61. He did much for the local community in St. James' Parish among whom he lived as well as for the Jewish congregation. For example:

> he acted as Charity Treasurer, familiarised himself with the woes of the poor, he loved to represent a poor co-religionist in the local Police Court. He gloried in representing Judaism under its brightest colours to the townsfolk.[26]

In March, 1862, the city was exercised as to an appropriate

---

[25] *Bristol Times*, 15th November, 1862.

[26] The Rev. Joseph Abelson, 'Reminiscences of Bristol', from *Jewish Chronicle*, 5th April 1907. On 19th September 1902, Henry Simmons was quoted in the *Jewish World* as having presented a Jewish Bible to the Bristol Police Court for the use of any Jewish prisoners who might come before them.

memorial to the late Prince Albert. Henry Simmons supported the resolution in favour of a memorial and in doing so argued that the most appropriate one would be the foundation of a Hospital for Incurables. In the event, insufficient money was donated to complete any of the ambitious projects.

The *Bristol Times* of 21st March, 1863 reported:

> A handsome silver gilt tankard, value twenty guineas, has been presented to Mr. H. Simmons who acted as hon. secretary to the St. James' parochial committee, for his zeal in reference to the arrangements for giving the poor of the parish a treat on the 10th March last.

His business continued in St. James' Barton probably into the 1880s or 1890s, but he had moved to Kingsland House, Whiteladies Road, Clifton by the time he married Selina Marks of London on 24th January, 1866. They had no children. His care for those less well off in the community is apparent from this notice in October, 1864, when he:

> . . . gave to all the Jewish poor a tea and supper. The evening was enlivened by a magic lantern show kindly lent and displayed by Messrs. Braham. It was most gratifying to witness the enjoyment of the recipients, who did not fail to do ample justice to the profusion of eatables, &c., provided. Before departing, Mr. Simmons gave each person, including children, a present of money. The liberal donor, the lady waitresses, wardens, &c., were most enthusiastically cheered by the grateful and joyous assembly.[27]

This was repeated the next year but if it continued thereafter, it was no longer reported. However this was something in which the Hebrew Ladies' Benevolent Society took considerable interest although, again, they receive scant record in the *Jewish Chronicle* and their extant minute books start only in 1909. Selina Simmons took part in the society's work. From 1913, she is reported in the *Jewish Chronicle* as having treated the children of the Congregational Hebrew School to seats at the pantomime and refreshments were included. This was repeated for at least another two years. Henry Simmons died on 16th January 1904 aged 77. (See ill. 20.)

His obituary in the *Jewish Chronicle* for 22nd January states:

> He spent practically the whole of his life in Bristol. A man of the most estimable qualities, he won the esteem not only of the

---

[27] *Jewish Chronicle*, 28th October, 1864.

members of the Jewish community, but of other citizens with whom he came in contact in business, social and freemasonry circles. He was a man of rare benevolence and amiability and will be much missed, especially by the poor of his community. For a period of about half a century he identified himself most closely with the interests of the Jews in Bristol and for about twenty-five years he was President of the Congregation. He was one of the chief promoters of a scheme for erecting the present synagogue in Park Row, a building which was consecrated in 1871 by the late Chief Rabbi; and he was instrumental in carrying out later improvements, as well as arranging for the reconstruction of the old Jewish cemetery at Barton Road, St. Philips.

The Local Press: 1752–1893

T his chapter begins with two events which give some idea of the changing view of the Bristol press and therefore the public between the middle of the eighteenth and the end of the nineteenth centuries.

In 1752 the Government's proposed Aliens' Act to facilitate the naturalization of Jews in the United Kingdom was met with violent opposition and was repealed shortly afterwards. In his history of the Merchant Venturers, Patrick McGrath recorded that:

> There was an outburst of anti-Jewish feeling in the country. In Bristol, the corporation did not join in, but most of the Bristol press was hostile to the act, the Steadfast Society helped whip up popular feeling and the Society petitioned for the repeal of the act.[1]

The *Annals of Bristol* provide additional information:

> In November 1752, the Merchants' Society unanimously resolved to address the members of Parliament for the city, requesting their aid in procuring the repeal of an Act passed during the previous session permitting English-born Jews to enjoy the privileges of British citizens.

The Duke of Newcastle, fearful of losing his majority in the coming elections, panicked. Mr. Nugent, soon to be M.P. for Bristol, was asked to pilot the Bill through Parliament:

> Nugent cynically admitted that he believed the National Act to be a wise and just measure, and that he was acting against his conviction in proposing its repeal . . . the passion of the lower set ought to be humoured.

The repeal Act was passed.[2] But the attitude of the Bristol press would change within the next hundred years or so.

The Age of Enlightenment, as described in the writings of Voltaire and Jean-Jacques Rousseau, created a desire for freedom not only in England but also in the Jewish world of Europe of the late-eighteenth

---

[1] Patrick McGrath, *The Merchant Venturers of Bristol*, Bristol, 1975, p.234. The Steadfast Society was a Tory Club.
[2] John Latimer, *The Annals of Bristol*, Vol. 2, Bristol, facsimile edition 1970, p.299.

century. Life for most Englishmen of the time was short, brutal and insanitary. Few of the poor attended church or were visited by their local clergy, most of whom were non-resident. The rise of the Evangelicals in Anglican Church circles put the social ideas of Voltaire and Rousseau into practice. They had an intense belief in God and the saving power of the Gospel. Conversion was a vital part of their inheritance. Sunday was strictly observed and their hymns made services more lively. They were not accepted as a valuable part of the Church but, in spite of this, their influence was strong.

One of these Evangelicals was William Wilberforce, whose efforts to free the slaves is famous. With the battle to abolish slavery came the realization that the African tribes to whom the slaves belonged were ignorant of Christianity, and many Societies were founded to remedy this, working in England and India as well as in Africa. But for the purposes of this chapter the most important group was the London Society for Promoting Christianity among the Jews, founded in 1809. The Society started work with the East London Jewish community but they were often hoodwinked by their cleverer prey.[3] After some time the Society overcame this and met with greater success. Later they deleted 'London' from their title as their interests covered not only London but the whole of England and as far afield as Eastern Europe and Palestine.

In December, 1848, the *Bristol Mercury* gave:

An account of the labours of the Society's agent in Bristol, Mr. Pieritz. During the past year he had continued his efforts to bring before his Jewish brethren the claims of Christianity and the doctrines of the Gospel with much zeal. He reports that more permanently resident Jews were to be met with than formerly have been found during the past years and that the number of travelling Jews also appears to have diminished. Mr. Pieritz has sought and found many opportunities of conversing with Jews on Christian topics at their own houses and lodging-houses and his visits have often been well received. About 190 have visited him at his own abode, many several times and showed much anxiety on religious questions. As a result several have proceeded to London to the Operative Jewish Convert's Institute. It is impossible to estimate the amount of good that may accrue from the humblest Christian endeavour . . .

---

[3] This still happened in the 1930s. The mother of a member of the Bristol Hebrew Congregation, who came from Hamburg, said that, when she was pregnant with his elder sister, she sought the help of the Society. Treatment was free or at a nominal cost, as the Society hoped for a baptism and a new soul to send to their Hebrew School. Only the Jewish mother got the help she needed.

On 16th July, 1853, the *Bristol Times* and the *Bristol Mercury* observed that:

> the Society attached to the Nonconformist Churches (having no resident missionary in the town) sent tracts periodically to all those Jews whose residence could be discovered. The results of these little messengers might never be known but they were willing to cast their bread upon the waters in hope. The Jews of Bristol had the unenviable notoriety of being pre-eminent in their unwillingness to listen to the word of God, elsewhere success was more marked.

They may have listened politely but were not persuaded. The influence of their minister, the Rev. Isaac Samuel, and their second reader, Joseph Benjamin, at this time, like Solomon Wolfe in Bath,[4] are likely to have prevented most conversions.

In June, 1854, the *Bristol Mercury* ran a leading article on 'The Jews in the Holy Land'. Sir Moses Montefiore had addressed a letter to the Chief Rabbi describing the terrible conditions resulting from drought, together with the fact that Jews were not allowed to own land, and therefore could not grow crops. The Jews were living in villages and towns and begging for a crust of bread to keep alive. Sir Moses' appeal was, of course, to the Jewish communities in England, but here:

> An application having been made to the Israelite Inhabitants of Bristol to assist the Famishing Jews of Palestine in their present state of destitution, they appeal to their Christian Brethren and fellow citizens for aid towards a subscription to relieve those resident in the Holy Land from their present calamitous situation. . . . Subscriptions will be thankfully received by the President, JOSEPH ABRAHAM, Coopers' Hall, King Street; JONAS ROUSSEAU, Broad Street; JOHN BRAHAM, St. Augustine's Back; and at the several Bristol Banks.[5]

Reports naming donors and the amounts given appeared regularly for eight weeks, making a total of nearly £800. Of the donors, 596 were non-Jews, among whom were known city councillors, bankers and businessmen, and 63 Jews whose names mostly appeared in the first

---

[4] In 1829, the Bath Auxiliary of the London Society for the Promotion of Christian Knowledge among the Jews complained that its operations in Bath had failed completely, owing to the great influence of the Rabbi, who would not suffer any tracts to be accepted by his people. *Bath Chronicle*, 15th January, 1829.

[5] *The British Mercury and Western Counties Advertiser*, 10th, 17th, 24th, June, 1st, 8th, 15th, 22nd July and 9th September, 1854.

two weeks. Unexpected names were Isaac Isaacs of Abergavenny who could have been a Jew or a Christian. There was 'a poor needlewoman' and, of course, several 'friends to the Jews'. On 9th September, 1854:

> the President of the Bristol Hebrew Congregation begs to acknowledge donations to the total of £818.7s.2d.[6]

In September that year the same papers reported that the Society for the Promotion of Christianity among the Jews no longer had a resident missionary in Bristol, but two unordained missionaries visited the town. During their visit they had opportunities of conversing with resident Jews. They were encouraged by their reception and considered there was an interesting, though not extensive, field for missionary agency. They suggested the Society might employ a permanent missionary agent in Bristol again.

On 6th May, 1859, John Braham wrote to the *Jewish Chronicle*, part of which was copied by the local papers to the effect that:

> The Hebrews of Bristol recorded by their votes their grateful acknowledgement to the Liberal cause, by voting 26 to 5, while at Cheltenham, where the polling took place on the Sunday, the majority for the Liberal candidate was mainly indebted to the Jews in the recent general election. The public opinion of our land has been for years against us; it is to be hoped a better feeling will largely increase. Our Christian brethren need not fear that the power conceded to us will ever be exerted against sound principles, whether Conservative or Liberal, for we shall ever be found supporting the Throne, the British constitution, and the true liberties of the people, believing that in the education of the people the true interests and safety of the Throne will be firmly

---

[6] The *Jewish Chronicle* also produced lists between June and September which showed that no other Jewish community had the foresight to make a similar public appeal. On 16th June there is a long list of London individual contributions amounting to £2,941.14s.3d. The 7th July list still has a preponderance of London individuals but also many provincial towns from subscribers with both Jewish and non-Jewish names together with a number of congregations giving over £300 in all as well as a few from the Commonwealth and Europe, notably a visit to Hanover by the Chief Rabbi that produced nearly £210. The 1st September list carried the following note: 'In consequence of pressure of time and being desirous to give the list of the Bristol collection correctly, we defer the continuation of the subscriptions till our next' – *Ed.Jew.Chron.* At least half of the 8th September list was occupied by Bristol's contribution amounting now to £823.19s.2d. The collectors were Moses Abraham, Abraham Mosely, John Braham, Jonas Rousseau, Isaac Ballin, Moses Blanckensee, the Misses Isaacs, Joseph Rothschild and the Misses E. and J. Rothschild, Charles Isaacs, D. Hyam, jun., S. Solomon and Isaac Solomon. The total collected was over £8,500.

based, to support which we shall always be found shoulder to shoulder with citizens, be their creed what it may, and believing in an infinite providence. These are the sentiments of the children of the house of Israel, located wherever they may be in the dominions of our glorious Queen, whom God in His infinite mercy protect, and that of her noble family, is the prayer of all of us, and of, sir,

yours truly,   I.B.[7]

A sadly unsurprising article, for the most part identical in both the *Bristol Times* and the *Bristol Mercury*, on 25th September, 1858, was the following:

> ELOPEMENT OF A JEWESS: Quite a commotion has been produced amongst the Jewish community in consequence of the elopement of Miss Gertrude Isaacs, daughter of Mrs. Isaacs of No. 24, Pritchard Street, Portland Square, who on Tuesday quitted the maternal roof for the purpose of executing some commission in the city for her mother, by whom her return was for several hours anxiously expected. Nothing transpired to show the real motive which had influenced her until two o'clock, when a note was received from her, stating that at nine o'clock she had been united in wedlock to Mr. Taylor, asking forgiveness, and assigning as a reason why she had acted in so clandestine a manner, her conviction that her parent and friends would never have given their consent to the match.

Whereas the *Bristol Mercury* alone continued:

> The elopement has – as we have before observed – produced a good deal of feeling amongst the followers of the ancient faith: for our own part we are inclined to regard it from a more cheering point of view, and to note in it another sign of the growing disposition of the age to overleap those religious and sectarian barriers which have too long divided the members of the common human family. We long since admitted the once despised and persecuted Jew to the rights of citizenship; but a few months have passed since the heaviest act of proscription – that which excluded him from his share in the great council of the nation – was swept away by the indignant voice of an outraged civilisation; and here we have a sort of double evidence, as it were, of our advancing civilisation. On the one hand, we see the maiden surmounting prejudices white with the hoar of ages, and breaking through a line of demarcation which has been deemed all but impregnable; while on the other is displayed a disposition

---

[7] *Bristol Times*, 14th and *Bristol Mercury*, 21st May, 1859.

to admit the daughters of Israel to the closest bonds of social union, to receive them as worthy to share the innermost emotions of our innermost hearts, to rule in the domestic temple, and to hold in our Christian families the honours of wifedom and maternity. May the young couple be prosperous, say we; and may the hearts of their kindred be gladdened by the happiness which they diffuse around them!

This was followed the next week by a letter to the *Bristol Mercury* from 'A Jew' (who could have been John Braham) in which he says that no commotion was caused, but her friends all regret Miss Isaac's decision. He went on to say that it is not another sign of the growing disposition of the age 'to overleap the religious and sectarian barriers which divide members of the common human family', but that Jews are quite content to join with others in political, charitable and other social action but in religious terms, having no desire to obtain converts, do not wish others to attempt to convert them. Finally he says:

> Here we have a maiden, apparently a Jewess at heart, observing the Day of Atonement according to the Jewish rites, on Saturday, and three days after kneeling before an altar in the Church of England, being married in the name of the Father, Son and Holy Ghost.[8]

Both the conversionist Societies (Society for the Promotion of Christianity among the Jews attached to Anglican Churches and Society for the Propagation of the Gospel amongst the Jews attached to Nonconformist Churches) continued their work and annual reports appear following meetings to encourage financial support for their work. The Hebrew School in Palestine Place, London, took in children of poor Jewish families and turned them into Christians but none appear to have come from Bristol, although there was a single, elderly man and just one family from Bath.[9] Many of these converts later became the Societies' missionaries both in England and abroad. In 1872, the *Western Daily Press* observed:

> They owed this most interesting people a debt of gratitude which could never be repaid. The prejudice of the Jewish people against conversion was very far from being extinct.[10]

---

[8] *Bristol Mercury*, 2nd October, 1858.
[9] Malcolm Brown and Judith Samuel, 'The Jews of Bath', JHSE, *Jewish Historical Studies*, XXIX, 1982–1986, pp. 144–147
[10] *Western Daily Press*, 19th March, 1872.

121

The *Jewish Chronicle* on 28th March, 1872, commented that these 'polite remarks . . . gave some idea of the amenities of those gentlemen'. According to the *Jewish Chronicle* there were only two replies to these articles. The first followed the report in the *Western Daily Press* of the annual meetings held on 31st May, 1886, of the Bristol and Clifton Auxiliary of the London Society for Promoting Christianity amongst the Jews held at the Victoria Rooms, Clifton. The morning meeting was presided over by the Rev. Talbot A.L. Greaves, supported by several clergymen and laymen. The evening meeting was not reported. The article opened with the financial report of the parent society and the help that the local auxiliary had provided. It continued:

> The report of 1886 is full of interesting, suggestive and encouraging information. It proves that in almost every possible way the middle wall of prejudice and distrust is being demolished and a knowledge of the truth spreading amongst the brethren of our Lord. Rabbinism is losing its hold on the Jewish mind in almost every part of the world.

They go on to admit that Jews who leave Synagogues do not necessarily turn to Christianity, the only raison d'être for the Society's existence. They feel strongly that this must be:

> the effect of the overthrow of faith in Talmudic teaching unaccompanied by the evidence and manifestation of Christianity and, while this state of things is to be deplored, it can only be mitigated or prevented by such operations as those carried on by this society.[11]

Two days later the *Western Daily Press* carried a reply from 'Yaled' (the Rev. Joseph Levy, minister to Bristol Hebrew Congregation) to the effect that that morning he had read with:

> curious interest the account in your columns of the so-called 'Jews' Society' meetings. This incorrect superscription attracted my attention and seems to me to be a key to the fallacies that follow. It is a lamentable and deplorable fact that objects 'chaste as ice and pure as snow' do not escape calumny; for the Jews are often made the aim of calumnious opinions, which a populace ready to believe any assertion made of a hitherto despised people are only too prone to accept as true and which they cherish with an earnestness becoming a nobler cause. The Jews may respect the motives that induce these opinions, but are not compelled to accept them.

---

[11] This report and subsequent correspondence appeared in the *Western Daily Press* on 1st, 3rd, and 10th June, 1886.

The writer of that report knows very little of the influence that Rabbinism has exerted and does still exert over us Jews. It has been our preserver in times past and today Rabbinism has a firm hold in the heart of the Jewish nation and its principles are rigorously adhered to; such, at least is my experience. In one year 100 baptisms have taken place. Who and what are these converts? Either unscrupulous individuals who are degraded from bad Jews to worse Christians, or poor, starving, deserted creatures to whom the alluring promises of home, food, help and money have been held out. . . . We have every esteem, regard and love for Christians, but little for Christianity and in our true and cordial esteem for our non-Jewish neighbours, we tell them (if I may be permitted to say so) 'Physicians heal yourselves'.

A week later another correspondent (who signed his letter Consistency) became involved. He wrote that he was:

. . . much struck with the courteous and manly rebuke administered to the members of the Society for Promoting Christianity amongst the Jews by your correspondent 'Yaled'. Reading that letter naturally led me to read the report of the meeting under the presidency of the Rev. Talbot A.L. Greaves. This took me back three years to a sermon preached and afterwards published by that rev. gentleman on the subject of the inspiration of the Bible and its providential preservation. . . . My object in now writing is to show what appears to me to be inconsistency in the Rev. Talbot Greaves presiding over the meeting for the conversion of the Jews.

The sermon in question mentioned the passing away of the generations since the time of Christ but:

What two things are left except the Bible and the Jew? The temple is gone, the Roman Empire has passed away, time, with relentless severity, has laid its hand on everything else, only two things have defied his touch, the Bible and the Jew. They have suffered more than all beside and they alone survive. Other books and other races have passed away, the two oldest – the Bible and the Jew – remain unchanged, two evergreens, as it were, of God's own right hand planting. They have stood side by side in the fiery furnace of man's persecution; like the burning bush of Israel's miraculous history they still bud and blossom and bear fruit. They have been contemporaneous from the beginning. They began the race together and they are destined to stand side by side all through the course of time till time itself shall be no more and if we would fight successfully the battle of the Bible, we must take our stand by the side of the Jewish people. This is the impregnable position of the Christian Church.

123

Yet the Rev. Talbot Greaves was supporting a society formed for the express purpose of sweeping away what he maintained was one of the 'evergreens' of God's own right-hand planting and which evergreens were 'destined to stand side by side till time itself shall be no more, for if the Jews are converted to Christianity or become infidels, they at once cease to observe their marriage laws and become absorbed in the Gentile population'.

The other reply was from Henry Simmons, President of the Bristol Hebrew Congregation. On 3rd March, 1893, the *Clifton and Redland Free Press* reported their interview with the Rev. H. Goldberg, a missioner to the Jews. The following Friday, 10th March, the paper carried Henry Simmons' reply:

> . . . Now let me ask you if it would not be better if these clergymen, ministers, &c., would attend to the spiritual welfare of their own unbelievers, and speak to them about the Saviour (Bristol has thousands who do not know, or wish to know, the name of God at all) rather than to interfere with a race who have at all times been God-fearing, and who have been chosen by God as His people. If he would use his energy and spend a little more time on behalf of his own adopted brethren, he might be of great service to Christianity. . . . He says that the Jews look upon the Founder of Christianity as one of the greatest impostors who ever lived and as one who taught his followers to serve idolatrous images and to persecute the Jews. If this is the case, whose fault is it, if not of those who have made the charge true by the worship of images and persecutions of innocent, unoffending, harmless folk? Let me tell Mr. Goldberg that we also believe in a blessed Messiah who is to come for the redemption of the people, but when that time comes the wolf shall lie down with the lamb and Judah shall not envy Ephraim, and Ephraim shall not envy Judah, for there will be peace over all the world. He also says you cannot get a Jew to enter a Church. I am a Jew and the President of the Hebrew Community here, and always attend Church when a public function requires it and I may venture to add with quite as much reverence as the Rev. Goldberg . . . .[12]

---

[12] Much of this chapter was originally a paper by the author, submitted at Ammerdown Study Centre, Radstock, Somerset, towards a Certificate in *Interfaith Dialogue and Jewish-Christian Understanding* in 1994. Now it has been somewhat updated.

Reform of National and Local Government: 1815–1868

Modern citizens of Great Britain might suppose that there has always been universal suffrage, at least for men. But this is not so. In 1815, representation in most, if not all, parts of the United Kingdom was controlled by the landed aristocracy. There had been little change in terms of wealth, interest or population since the seventeenth century. The most glaring example was Old Sarum, a notorious rotten borough, which was not even large enough to be called a village yet returned two members to Parliament. On the other hand, many of the new manufacturing towns of the Midlands and the North, where the industrial revolution took place, including Manchester, Birmingham, Leeds and Sheffield were not represented at all.

The first Reform Bill was drawn up by a cabinet committee and introduced to the House of Commons on 1st March, 1831. Towns with fewer than two thousand inhabitants would no longer be represented at Westminster. Seven large towns, including Manchester, Birmingham and Bristol, as well as four districts in London, were given two members each; twenty others would have one member each. The franchise in boroughs was to be uniform to include occupants of buildings of ten pounds rateable value. This bill failed in committee and there followed a general election. A new bill, similar to the first, was proposed but was defeated in the House of Lords and riots broke out. The worst riot occurred in Bristol three weeks after the first discussion of the bill when Sir Charles Wetherall, its Recorder, who had voted against both versions of the Reform Bill in the House of Commons, arrived for his normal duties. Soon after his arrival at the Mansion House in Queen Square, the mob attacked and returned the following morning to sack the house. The troops sent to safeguard Sir Charles lost their nerve; the mob broke into the prisons and burned the Bishop's palace and other buildings. Next day a cavalry charge restored order. The reformers dissociated themselves from the riots but the authorities feared similar disturbances elsewhere.

Ministers announced they would persevere with the bill and after further concessions and a threat from King William IV to create sufficient new peers to pass the bill, the House of Lords did as required and it became law in June, 1832.[1]

In 1867 the electorate for national government was increased by the addition of householders who paid rates and had been in residence over one year, in 1872 secret ballots were introduced, and in 1918 all men over the age of 21 and women over 30 if they were ratepayers or wives of ratepayers were entitled to vote. It was only in 1969 that everyone, both men and women, over the age of 18 years could vote.

Countrywide, municipal government was just as unrepresentative as national government. In Bristol it was the responsibility of several different bodies. The Bristol Incorporation of the Poor, formed in 1696, was the first local body to be elected by a city-wide popular election. By 1833 the Executive Officer, the Governor, his Deputy and twelve assistants, were coping with five hundred poor in the workhouse, St. Peter's Hospital, and up to ten times as many on outdoor relief. This was financed by a poor rate, agreed by the magistrates at Easter and shared among all the parishes.

The Select Vestry was the governing body in the parishes. It dealt with road mending, destitution relief and provided watchmen, as well as dealing with strictly church affairs. The church wardens also collected the rates. The aldermen were responsible for the City's twelve wards which consisted of single or combined parishes. (Synagogues were governed by a similar system.)

The Society of Merchant Venturers[2] dealt with the commercial interests of Bristol and levied many dues in the Port of Bristol, intended to maintain quays, wharves and cranes. They also licensed and controlled the pilots who navigated ships in coastal waters. That it could nominate one-third of the Dock Company directors gave it even more influence over port affairs. Membership of the Society was not easily won, election was by the society in private session and most were Tory members of the Corporation.

Central to Bristol was the Dock Company, founded in 1803 to promote the construction of the Floating Harbour and to control its operation. It was needed because of the excessively high tides in both the Severn and Avon rivers, leaving ships beached on the mud twice a day. The cost of the Floating Harbour was £600,000. Shipping immediately benefited but not the return to shareholders; a local difficulty for many years.

---

[1] Sir Llewelyn Woodward, *Age of Reform, 1815-1870* (second edition), The Oxford History of England, Volume 13, at the Clarendon Press, Oxford, 1962.
[2] Previously mentioned in Chapter 8.

So many bodies governing Bristol meant that improvements were often not carried out. The Corporation did not keep an efficient check on its finances which created a great problem for its successor. The dozen aldermen were elected during 'good behaviour', a euphemism for life tenure. Promotion to an alderman normally came after five to fifteen years' membership of the Corporation. Those who were rewarded had either drawn attention to themselves by their diligence or could thank their seniority.

The Government nationally realised that municipal government needed to become more efficient. A Committee looked into the matter and produced the Municipal Corporations Report. This emphasized that rationalized boundaries were a prerequisite of progress, and advocated inclusion of the entire parliamentary district within the new borough. This happened only gradually. The Municipal Corporations Act, which became law on 10th September, 1835, applied to all boroughs except those in London. New town councils would be elected by all householders who had been paying rates for three years or more but excluding lunatics and women and those freemen who were not ratepayers.

In Bristol twenty former members of the Corporation stood for election and six (five Conservatives and one non-party man) were defeated. However, the Council could not act until the aldermen had been selected and the Mayor chosen. Twelve Conservatives and three Liberals became aldermen. In Bristol as elsewhere, the chosen aldermen were mainly Conservative as was the Council, and those previously unsuccessful at the recent Council election were elected. Thus after the election there was but one new member on Bristol Town Council! Burgesses[3] in a city the size of Bristol had to enjoy an estate worth at least £1,000 or their property be rated at a minimum of £30 for valuation purposes, before they could aspire to a Council seat. Elected candidates who refused to take their seats could be fined £100 for a Mayor, £50 for alderman.[4]

But legally, Jews still had no place in municipal or national Government. They entered political controversy immediately following relief for Dissenters and Catholics who were able to vote and to be elected to national government from 1829. Since the repeal of the Test and Corporation Acts in 1828, the regular oath on taking a seat in Parliament included the words 'on the true faith of a Christian'. It

---

[3] Burgesses were persons holding privileges conferred by municipal corporations or representing the same in Parliament.
[4] Graham Bush, 'Bristol and its Municipal Government: 1820–1851', Bristol Record Society's Publications, Vol. XXIX, p.126.

is not certain whether this was framed with the intention of excluding Jews but it must have been passed in full knowledge that such would be its effect. Between 1830 and 1858 fourteen bills were introduced which attempted to remove Jewish parliamentary disabilities in the House of Commons and were rejected by the House of Lords. Lionel de Rothschild was elected by the City of London as their member in the House of Commons from 1847. He presented himself at the Table of the House in December, 1847 but his refusal to swear a Christian oath prevented him from taking his seat. Petitions supporting Jewish relief gathered over two hundred and fifty thousand signatures. Also in December, 1847, the Whig Prime Minister, Lord John Russell, proposed yet another bill which, had it passed into law, would have enabled Jews to sit in Parliament.

David Salomons stood for election in various towns from 1841. Finally he was elected as Member of Parliament for Greenwich in June, 1851, and similarly declined to take the oath. He took his place in the House and was asked to withdraw but remained in his seat. He was subsequently fined £500 for illegally voting in a debate. This story was reported in detail in the national press and copied in Bristol where the papers were sympathetic. The case drew the attention of the whole country to the question of Jewish disabilities.[5]

In December, 1857, Lord John Russell introduced yet another Oath's Bill, which was thrown out in April, 1858, by the House of Lords. Later that year, the resistance of the Upper House was finally overcome when Derby's Conservative government threatened that the Commons would alter its oaths independently and act in defiance of the Lords. In July that year, the House of Lords passed Lord Lucan's bill which allowed either House to modify the oaths it required members to take.

In the provinces progress came earlier. On 31st July, 1845, Lord Lyndhurst's Jewish Municipal Relief Act was passed enabling Jews to hold all municipal offices. Prior to this they had occasionally sat on Parish Councils in Portsmouth and Plymouth,[6] in spite of restrictions and probably because there were no others willing to take on the burden of attending meetings.

---

[5] Throughout his life, Sir David Salomons made strenuous efforts for the improvement of the status of his fellow Jews. He became the first Jew to hold the office of Sheriff, magistrate, alderman and was the second Jew to become a member of Parliament. His efforts were crowned by his election as Lord Mayor of London in 1855.

[6] The Act allowing Jews to sit on Municipal Councils is noted in Geoffrey Alderman, *Modern British Jewry*, Clarendon Press, Oxford, 1992. A copy of the Act was obtained from the Guildhall (City of London) Library.

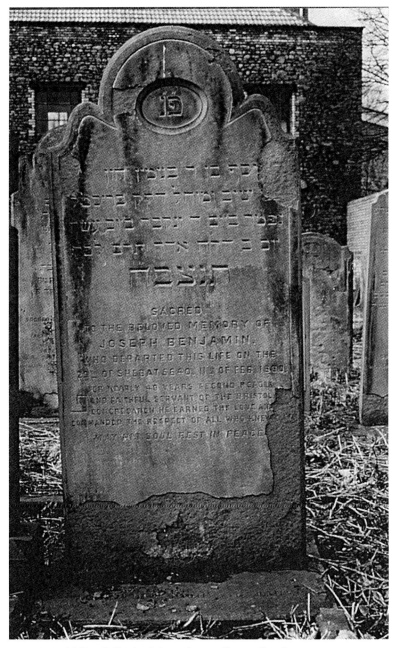

13 Joseph Benjamin's tombstone, Barton Road cemetery.
(photo: Simon Ferguson, 1992)

Bristol. On Monday, the Jewish Social and Debating Society gave a Purim treat to over 200 children who were provided with tea and an entertainment. Each child was presented with a toy and bag of sweets.—The Rev. H. Goodman, of Hanley, has been elected Minister of the Bristol Hebrew Congregation. Mr. Goodman was elected in July, 1905, Minister of the Hanley Congregation. He is a native of Portsmouth and was educated at the Grammar School in that city and at Aria College, and, after having matriculated, at Jews' College. He obtained the prize in logic at University College, and passed the intermediate examination in arts at London University. He acted for some time as assistant chaplain to Wormwood Scrubbs Prison.

Cardiff. On Sunday, under the auspices of the Dorshei Zion Association at the Oddfellows' Hall, Mr. J. Lewis presiding, Mr. Leo Joseph read a paper on "Character."

Rev. H. Goodman.

14 Rev. H Goodman. (*Jewish Chronicle* 15.3.1907)

15 Rev. Joseph Abelson. (*Jewish Chronicle* 2.11.1906)

16 Lazarus and Isaac Jacobs' noted Bristol blue glass.
(*Transactions* XXV, Plates XVI and XVII)

17 John Braham's shop at 17 St Augustine's Parade. (collection: Reece Winstone Archive)

18 Michael Jessel's shop on St Augustine's Parade. (collection: Reece Winstone Archive)

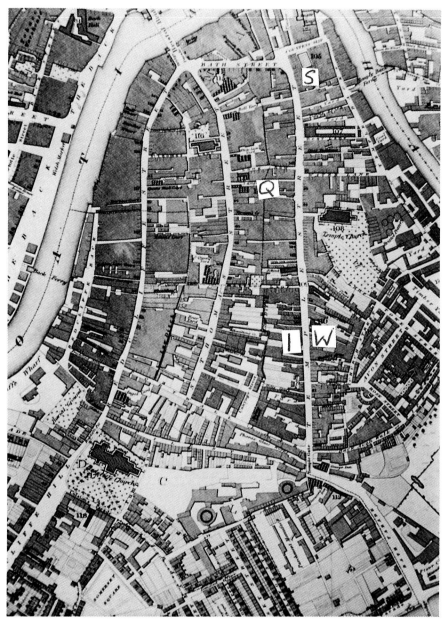

19 Temple Parish, from Ashmead's map. I = Stone Kitchen; W = Weavers' Hall;
Q = Quaker Meeting House; S = Synagogue south of Counterslip.

20 Henry Simmons. (*Jewish Chronicle* 29.1.1904)

21 Maurice Michael's shop on the corner of Bath Street and Thomas Street was demolished in 1869 to make way for Victoria Street from Bath Parade to Bristol Bridge. (drawing by Samuel Loxton, *Bristol as it was and as it is*, 1909).

22 Alexander gravestones at Barton Road cemetery. (photo: Simon Ferguson, 1992)

23 Victoria Street with the Platnauer Bros. shop.
(photo: Simon Ferguson, 1992)

Finally in 1866 the Parliamentary Oaths Act introduced a form of words for both Houses which required a conscientious speaker to believe in God but made no further demands. This Act signalled the virtual end of one phase in the politics of Jewish integration. Jewish and non-Jewish members of both Houses of Parliament henceforth swore the same oath on either the New or Old Testament. The Act's passage coincided with the revival of the issue of further parliamentary reform. The last major disability suffered by Jews was removed in 1871, when religious tests for entry to Oxford and Cambridge Universities were abolished.[7]

During the long-running saga to permit Jews to stand for local and national government, Bristol was in favour of reform. Unlike the Bath press whose leading articles were virulently against the change, the Bristol newspapers keenly supported the proposal. The city council voted on four occasions to send petitions to their Members of Parliament. On the first in 1836, the *Bristol Mercury's* leading article stated that:

> . . . to petition both Houses of Parliament for the removal of the disabilities of the Jews, is so honourable to the feelings of that body and contrasts so strongly with the selfish policy of the old corporation that, independent of the gratification it has afforded us as an act of justice to a much persecuted class of our fellow countrymen, we cannot fail to be pleased with it as manifesting to the world at large the predominance generally in our city of greater liberality than it has heretofore had credit for. . . .[8]

Joseph Frankel Alexander, the oldest of the three Alexander brothers, stood for election to Bristol City Council in 1835 but was not elected. He was possibly in failing health or was not approached in 1845 for he died on 23rd November, 1848 aged 60.[9]

With the passing of Lord Lyndhurst's Act in 1845, Abraham Alexander was elected the following November. It has been stated that '. . . some of the leading members of the Bristol Town Council wanted to have several prominent Jewish merchants as fellow councillors.'[10]

---

[7] Many details of the progress of Jewish emancipation from David Feldman, *Englishmen and Jews: Special Relations and Political Culture, 1840–1914*, Yale University Press, New Haven and London, 1994, pp.28–47.

[8] *Bristol Mercury*, 7th May, 1836. Newspapers of the period headed their reports: 'Bristol Town Council' – hence the apparent inconsistency in this book between 'city council' and 'town council'.

[9] Joseph Frankel and his brothers, Abraham and William Wolfe Alexander, who appear later in this chapter, also appear in chapter 4, page 62 and chapter 10, pages 140–143.

[10] Graham Bush, 'Bristol and its Municipal Government: 1820–1851', Bristol Record Society's Publications, Vol. XXIX, p.203.

A second petition was sent to the Houses of Parliament in 1841. A later petition was proposed by Abraham Alexander to the then mayor of Bristol and reported in *Felix Farley's Bristol Journal* of 8th January, 1848.[11] This was passed and sent to Bristol's members of Parliament.

Abraham Alexander represented the Docks interest from 1852 until his resignation from the Council. Bristol Town Council met on 19th November, 1845:

> mainly to discuss the possible arrangements with the Bristol Dock Company by which the Council may obtain possession of the Port and Harbour of Bristol. Mr. Alexander had taken some little trouble to prepare a statement as to the Dock dues and other charges on vessels entering the port. He read them out and then observed that 'These were enormous charges compared with Liverpool; if the Directors would go to Parliament and get a bill enabling them to reduce their dues . . . the port would be greatly improved. Captains would come here for they said it was the first port in Europe and they had no better accommodation in England only they paid too much for it. The report was adopted.'[12]

In February 1847 there was a proposal that Bristol should become a Free Port, which Abraham Alexander seconded. His other contributions that year concerned conditions for people working in the docks such as the pilots, the quay warden and so on. In October he seconded a motion for the purchase of the City Docks by the Council. Subsequently he is seldom reported in the press accounts of Council Meetings, beyond seconding various motions.

He kept his seat and was usually returned unopposed, as were most of Bristol councillors in those days; indeed, the local press grew quite perturbed at the lack of interest among the citizens.[13] His obvious popularity, though, can be judged from the newspaper remarks in 1866, when he decided at the age of 76 that he was too old to stand again.

In 1846, William Wolfe Alexander, Abraham's brother, was unsuccessful in the election in St. Augustine's Ward but in 1850 he was elected alderman by the councillors. He continued to be re-elected every three years until his death in 1874. The aldermen were all Conservative, which made life for the local Liberal party very difficult! He represented the Docks interest from 1866 in place of his brother

---

[11] Under the heading of Bristol Town Council.
[12] *Felix Farley's Bristol Journal*, 22nd November, 1845.
[13] 'The majority of councillors never experienced a setback on the hustings. . . . The typical Councillor represented only a single ward throughout his career as a Councillor which stretched out to a decade,' Graham Bush *Bristol and its Municipal Government: 1820–1851*, p.129.

and he appears to have spoken more than his brother in Council meetings, which are very fully reported in the local press. Bristol Town Council's fourth and final petition was sent to its members of Parliament in May, 1857. This time William Wolfe Alexander thanked his fellow councillors generously:

> Mr. W.W. ALEXANDER said he felt it incumbent on behalf of himself and his co-religionists to offer their sincere thanks to his esteemed friend, Mr. Shaw, for the generous and able manner in which he had brought forward the question, and also to thank his friend, Mr. Palmer, for the way it was seconded. He also begged to offer his thanks to the Mayor, who so ably and worthily filled the civic chair, for his vote, as well as to those gentlemen who gave it their support, and he trusted the legislature would this session mete out justice to a community who had ever proved themselves to be loyal and good citizens, and thus remove for ever the last link in the chain of religious exclusion.
>
> Extract from the
> REPORT OF BRISTOL TOWN COUNCIL
> in *Bristol Mercury*, 16th May, 1857

The Alexander brothers must both have worked hard behind the scenes or their presence would not have been as valued, as they must have been, judging by the tone of their obituary notices.

Once Jews were able to vote, to study at university, to own land, etc., they faced new challenges in theology and politics. The 'Judeophobia' of the late 1870s alarmed them. This arose when Benjamin Disraeli, no longer technically a Jew but generally seen as one,[14] was in trouble because of his actions in the Balkans. Communal leaders and Jewish writers denied that Jews could not be patriots and were indifferent to the universal claims of humanity. In 1871 the Anglo-Jewish Association was established in London to defend Jewish interests throughout the world.[15] In the first year of the Association's existence, only Liverpool, Manchester and Birmingham formed branches. The Bristol branch was founded in 1878 by John G. Levy, with Henry Simmons as President and Samuel Platnauer as Vice-President.

---

[14] Isaac Disraeli had left Bevis Marks Synagogue owing to a perceived injustice. As a result he had his children baptized. Nevertheless, his son, Benjamin Disraeli, felt himself to be a Jew and his books confirm this. However, had he still been a Jew, he could not have served as Prime Minister at this time.

[15] David Feldman, *Englishmen and Jews: Special Relations and Political Culture, 1840–1914*, Yale University Press, New Haven and London, 1994, p.122. The Anglo-Jewish Association is further discussed in chapter 13, pp. 162–164.

It is interesting to speculate why at this moment William Wolfe Alexander, who had died in 1870, was not replaced by another Jewish merchant on Bristol Council. It could be that Jewish merchants in Bristol were now less successful, but this political alarm may well have had an influence.[16]

The third member of the Jewish community on the Town Council at this period was Joseph Abraham who was elected in 1861. Michael Castle, J.P., and member of the Council, welcomed the new member. He drew attention to the distinguished traditions of the Jewish people and their ancient ancestry in a way that bears similarity to views expounded by such figures as Benjamin Disraeli and Aaron Levy Green on the matter of the disabilities suffered by Jews in public life at that time.[17]

From the start Joseph Abraham was much more vocal in meetings and more frequently reported in the local press. Examples include his remarks on the proposed improvements to Nicholas Street:

> Mr. Abraham directed the attention of the Council to the urgent necessity of carrying out these improvements which did not involve any difficulty, for which an Act of Parliament was not required and which ought at once to be dealt with. He had taken the pains to go through the matter with the surveyor and had arrived at the conclusion that they would not obtain such good terms with the owners and tenants as they might do now. He accordingly moved an amendment to the motion that this be done which was carried.[18]

On the new lease for the Black Rock Quarry:

> Concern was felt as to the safety of working the Quarry again, it being under the Downs. Mr. Abraham supported the adoption of the amendment to remove this lease from the report so long as there was the slightest danger to human life by the working of these quarries. He did not think the question of £250 a year ought to weigh for a moment with the Council. The amendment was carried.[19]

And on the health of the City:

> Mr. Abraham said they had much to congratulate themselves upon in this matter, but there was no doubt there was a great

---

[16] The Alexander and Abraham families also appear in chapter 4, p. 62 and chapter 10, pp. 140–143.

[17] Quoted in the 1986 exhibition '200 Years of Bristol Jewry'.

[18] *Bristol Mercury* and *Bristol Times*, 16th May, 1863.

[19] Earlier in this item, Black Rock Quarry was described as 'now disused'. *Bristol Times*, 1st October, 1864.

want of hospital accommodation. Fever still existed in the city and unless precautionary measures were taken it would become a matter of serious concern whether there might not be serious consequences. Seamen came to the city with contagious diseases and there was no place to receive them. . . . No decision was come to.[20]

From 1863 Joseph Abraham and William Wolfe Alexander were repeatedly asked to become Mayor. This was not a very popular honour at the time since it was expensive, both in time and money. For a man with a business to run which required his personal attention, this was time that could ill be spared.[21] However, in November, 1865, Joseph Abraham agreed.[22] An interesting note among so many others in the local press after his election reads:

THE MAYOR'S CHAPEL: The appointment of a gentleman of the Jewish persuasion to the office of Chief Magistrate will, we need hardly say, have no effect on the service at St. Mark's. It is the Mayor's Chapel; but it is as well the civic chapel for the members of the Town Council, who will attend as usual, the chaplain being their chaplain. We understand the Mr. Abraham will do as Mayor what he has hitherto done as Town Councillor – namely attend the chapel on those occasions when it is usual for the Corporation to go in state.[23]

From a perusal of the Council Minutes it was possible to determine which Jewish councillors were present and when. Joseph Abraham was present at the meeting when he was formally voted into the Mayoralty on 9th November, 1865. At the next meeting on 1st January, 1866, Mr. Phippen, acting Chairman:

regretted, and he knew he should be expressing the feelings of the council at large, that he was obliged to take the chair in consequence of the illness of Mr. Abraham (hear, hear). He was sorry they had not got him there that morning to guide them in

---

20 *Western Daily Press*, 2nd August, 1865.
21 'There were several disagreeable features of the office. Three or four business hours were required daily and Fripp (an earlier Mayor) for one, attended almost every Committee. Also at risk was their personal wealth,' Graham Bush, 'Bristol and its Municipal Government, 1815–1851', Bristol Record Society's Publications, Vol. XXIX, p.127.
22 The *Jewish Chronicle*, 18th October, 1889, in the obituary of Sir B.S. Phillips observed that: '1865 was particularly distinguished in Anglo-Jewish history. There were no less than three Jewish Mayors elected in addition to Alderman Phillips in London, there were Joseph Abraham in Bristol and Mr. S.M. Emanuel in Southampton.'
23 *Saturday Bristol Times and Mirror*, 11th November, 1865.

their deliberations, with that ability and discretion he had always shown (hear, hear); and he could only say that he trusted they would soon have him amongst them (hear, hear). Mr. Phippen expressed the hope that the city would continue to increase and prosper for many years to come and in conclusion he wished all present a happy new year.[24]

Joseph Abraham attended only two more meetings in April and May. The local press relates that he took to his bed, occasionally recovering to take 'carriage exercise'. He went to Weston-super-Mare, hoping a change of air would improve his health, which it appeared to have done for a short while. Letters he wrote on Council business to Alderman Phippen, his Deputy, are printed in the local press. He sent regrets for his absence and suggested what he wanted the Council to do. His reappearance in the spring was greeted with great pleasure. He was well enough to attend his daughter's wedding at this time. Unfortunately he had a relapse and took to his bed again. He died on Wednesday, 30th January, 1867, of heart disease. The *Bristol Times* of 2nd February, 1867, reported:

DEATH OF THE EX-MAYOR, MR. JOSEPH ABRAHAM. – It is with sincere regret we announce that this melancholy event took place on Wednesday, Mr. Abraham having expired at his residence, Tyndall's-park. The deceased gentleman, who suffered from a severe heart disease, had been for the past eighteen months in failing health, and although he appeared occasionally to rally, and thus afforded his friends some slender hopes that his life might yet be prolonged, it was nevertheless felt that he might at any time be called hence, and his death, although we believe it occurred somewhat suddenly, has consequently not taken his immediate friends by surprise. We hear that Mr. Abraham was engaged in conversation with his medical man, when he suddenly ceased talking, and almost immediately expired. The deceased gentleman, was affable, pleasant, and genial in his disposition, and was greatly esteemed by a numerous circle of friends and fellow-citizens. When in the Town Council, and enabled to take an active part in the city business, he evinced most painstaking industry, good judgement, and intelligence, which he brought especially to bear in connection with the Local Board of Health. By the death of Mr. Abraham, a vacancy occurs in the Central Ward, for which he had sat as representative in the Town Council for many years.

---

[24] Bristol Town Council Minutes reported in the *Daily Bristol Times and Mirror*, 2nd January, 1866.

The funeral was conducted by Joseph Benjamin at Joseph Abraham's home, Stafford House, Tyndall's Park, Clifton, and at Rose Street Cemetery in Great Gardens.[25] The new Council elected as a result of the Municipal Corporations Act, 1835, proposed much new work. The street improvements in the City exercised the Council for many years. An Improvement Committee was formed in July, 1840, and in May, 1842, a memorial was read from 'certain inhabitants of Temple Street and the neighbourhood in respect to the formation of a new street to lead to the Terminus of the Great Western Railway.'[26] As can be seen from the map in ill. 19, Temple Street was not wide or direct enough for passengers in a hurry to catch a train from Brunel's new railway. Reports in *Felix Farley's Bristol Journal* and the *Bristol Mercury* described the recent Council Meeting at which the Improvement Committee stated:

> the present thoroughfare is narrow, inconvenient and dangerous and means should be adopted to afford the facility of approach from the centre of the city to the railway demanded by the increased traffic. The Committee also pointed to the lamentable state not only of the health but of the morals of many of the inhabitants through which the proposed street would pass. They also referred to the wretched state of the drainage in that part of the city. The improvement would sweep away a mass of houses of the lowest description and would produce a current of pure air which would necessarily be beneficial to the neighbourhood.[27]

What it would also do was to destroy all three buildings used at various times for Jewish worship, those previously known as the Stone Kitchen, the Weavers' Hall and the Quaker Meeting House. By 1844 plans had been produced and continued to be discussed by the Committee and Town Council for many years. In September, 1846, a bill was submitted to Parliament which included the proposed new street as well as numerous other works. In the 1850s there was no

---

[25] This burial ground was purchased by Moses Abraham, father of Joseph Abraham, in 1830 after Isaac Jacobs' bankruptcy. Other burials in this cemetery, besides Joseph Abraham, were those of his mother and father, his brother, John, and, according to the *Western Daily Press* in its report on 4th February, 1867, members of the Alexander family, who were related to the Abrahams' family.

[26] Minutes of the Improvement Committee of Bristol Town Council dated 31st May, 1842.

[27] *Felix Farley's Bristol Journal* and the *Bristol Mercury*, 16th August, 1845.

D O N ' T   F O R G E T   T H I S !
GUNS, PISTOLS, WATCHES, CLOCKS & MUSICAL
INSTRUMENTS are SELLING at
M. MICHAEL'S, PAWNBROKING ESTABLISHMENT,
2 *BATH-STREET.*
Fifty per cent. Cheaper than any other House in the City.

	£	s.	d.
New and Second-hand Watches, by eminent makers,			
in silver cases (each), from	2	2	0
Patent Lever Watches	3	10	0
Jerome's American Clock, goes 30 hours, best make ..	0	18	6
Handsome 8-day Clocks, mahogany cases	4	10	0
8-Keyed Flutes, German silver, double action, metallic			
tube and slide	1	3	6
6-Keyed ditto	0	19	6
4-Keyed ditto	0	14	6

Also a large assortment of Second-Hand FLUTES made by *Wood & Ivey*,
at very Reduced Prices.
    Second-hand, first-rate SHIP CHRONOMETER for Sale,
Price 25 Guineas.
        INSTRUMENTS of every description always on Sale.
    A large assortment of First-rate ACCORDIONS, cheap.
            THE TRADE SUPPLIED.
        Observe! – 2, BATH-STREET, BRISTOL.

Maurice Michael's advertisement in the *Bristol Mercury and Western
Counties Advertiser*, 15st January, 1848.

progress owing, it is said, to diversity of opinion both among members
of the Committee and the public.[28]

In October, 1865, a New Streets Committee (part of the Local Board
of Health) was formed and work began on the new street, to be called
Victoria Street. Several members of the Jewish community found
themselves with property to be compulsorily purchased. They were
required to name their price, which the Council's surveyors discussed
and reduced whenever possible. The arguments are recorded in the
New Streets Committee minute books and the local press and make
fascinating reading. There was only one person who was not easily
satisfied. This was Maurice Michael, pawnbroker, jeweller and silversmith, whose shop was on the corner of Bath and St. Thomas Streets.[29]
(See ill. 21.) One of his advertisements appears above. His annual
profits were stated to be from £1,500 to £1,600. In the opinion of the

---

[28] 'In 1852 a final, despairing effort to get the Victoria Street scheme under way
failed because of the animosity of ratepayers,' Graham Bush, 'Bristol and its
Municipal Government 1820–1851', Bristol Record Society's Publications, Vol.
XXIX, p.165.

[29] Maurice Michael has already appeared in Chapter 4, page 51.

TREMENDOUS REDUCTION
OF PRICES
AT JOSEPH MICHAEL'S,
PAWNBROKER AND GENERAL SALESMAN
61, *CASTLE-STREET.*

The Cheapest House in the city for Guns, Pistols, Gold and Silver Watches, Gold and Silver Watch-Guards, Flutes, Musical and Mathematical Instruments &c.

	£ s. d.
Superior Double Bass and Bow	8 0 0
Ophicleides	4 0 0
Cornopeans (Herr König's improved)	2 8 0
G Trombone, £1 10s., C. Trombone	1 5 0
Violoncellos	from 1 10 0
Violins in great variety	from 0 2 3
Patent Lever Silver Watches	from 3 10 0
Youths' Silver Watches	from 2 2 0
Gold Guards	from 1 10 0

Fentun's London-made Flutes, metallic tube and slides,

8 Keys	1 3 6
6 Keys	0 19 0
4 Keys	0 14 0

A Second-hand CHAMBER ORGAN and Four DRUMS.

Liberal allowance to the trade. – Country Orders punctually attended to upon receipt of a Money-order.

Observe! – 61, CASTLE-STREET.

N.B. – MONEY LENT ON VALUABLES, &C.

Joseph Michael's advertisement (who is believed to have been a brother of Maurice Michael) in the *Bristol Mercury and Western Counties Advertiser*, 1st January, 1848.

arbitrator the property itself was worth from £200 to £220 per annum; taken at 20 years' purchase that would give a capital value £4,500. As compensation for the business, which would be entirely destroyed, Mr. Michael considered that not less than three years of his net profits ought to be allowed him, and these, counsel went on to point out, amounted to £1,500 a year. The final decision was adjourned to a later date, the case to be held in London but was not recorded either in the minutes or the newspapers. However the conveyance, dated 23rd December, 1868, shows that the local Board of Health bought the property for £7,940, a not unreasonable outcome in the circumstances.[30]

---

[30] The sale of Maurice Michael's premises was discussed in Bristol City Council's New Streets Committee minutes (among the minutes of the Local Board of Health) from 9th June, 1868, to 10th May, 1870.

The arrangements between Samuel Platnauer, President of Bristol Hebrew Congregation, and Bristol City Council for the sale of the Synagogue in Temple Street and purchase of the land previously occupied by the Little Sisters of the Poor in Park Row, have been described in Chapter 5, pp. 71–73.

Notable Jewish Families
c. 1750–1883

J oseph Alexander settled in Portsmouth in the early 1700s and came
to Bristol about 1740 or 1750. It is said that he originally established
himself by copper-bottoming ships, necessary in Bristol before the
construction of the Floating Harbour.[1] Here he created a dynasty. His
sons became well-known as merchants and ship-owners in the town.

His eldest son, also Joseph Alexander, had married Dinah and they
joined his father in Bristol in the 1750s. They ran a general trading
business which thrived and prospered from an address 'on the Quay'.
Their business was ships' brokerage. When a vessel entered the Port of
Bristol, a broker would undertake to divide up the cargo and sell it on
behalf of the ship's owner.[2] From the Registry of Ships help by Bristol
Record Office it appears that they also lent money towards purchase
of ships by other mariners.

Joseph and Dinah Alexander had six children, two girls and four
boys. The oldest son, Michael, died at sea in 1816 aged 35.[3] The
political life on Bristol Town Council of Abraham Alexander and
William Wolfe Alexander (their third and fourth sons) has already
been discussed.[4]

Abraham Alexander's marriage to Matilda, daughter of Isaac Jacobs,
in 1817 joined ship brokers with the great glassmakers of the past whose
business became increasingly unprofitable. Their marriage contract is
preserved in the Bristol Record Office. Their four eldest children,
Adeline, Dinah, Henry and Rachel Rosetta were born in Queen
Square, but some time before the birth of Phillip Douglas in November,
1830, they had moved to Park Street. After that they had four more
children, George, Frankel Isaac, Edward and Charles David.

The Synagogue's ceremonial spice box (a Georgian pepperette,
hallmarked 1724) was given by Abraham Alexander, president, in

---

[1] Quoted in the 1986 exhibition '200 Years of Bristol Jewry'.
[2] Quoted in the 1986 exhibition '200 Years of Bristol Jewry'.
[3] The entry in the family Chumash does not relate whether he was a passenger or a
seaman but, judging by the family's business interests, it seems more likely that he
was a seaman.
[4] See Chapter 4, page 62 and Chapter 9, pages 129–132.

1845. The Alexander brothers served as consuls for a variety of European states. Joseph Frankel Alexander (the second son of Joseph and Dinah Alexander) represented Hanover, Saxony, Bremen, Frankfurt and Russia; on his death in 1848, Abraham took over the Russian consulate, and when he died, his son Philip Douglas Alexander became Russian Consul in his place. William Wolfe Alexander was for a time consul for Greece and for somewhat longer for the Kingdom of the Two Sicilies.[5]

Abraham Alexander died on 22nd July, 1870, and there were obituaries in several local papers:

> We regret to record the death of Mr. Abraham Alexander, of Lansdown Place, Victoria Square, which sad event occurred on Friday evening. On the previous Sunday he was seized with a paralytic fit, and had been since then attended by Dr. Lyon. His condition was from the first considered extremely critical, and for the last day or two no hopes whatever were entertained of his recovery. Mr. Alexander, who had attained the ripe old age of 81 years, was, during the greater part of his life, engaged in the commerce of Bristol. He was a member of the Hebrew body, and it speaks well for the tolerant spirit of the age, and was no less honourable to our citizens than to himself, that in 1844 he was elected one of the representatives of the Bristol Ward in the Municipal Council, and held that position until his voluntary retirement from it, after twenty-two years service in November, 1866. The deceased gentleman was one of the few surviving members of the old Bristol Volunteers, and he was not more respected for his probity in commercial life than he was esteemed in the circles in which he was best known for the frankness and geniality of his disposition.[6]
>
> . . . He belonged to a family which, for two generations, have been leading members of the Jewish community ·in Bristol. He was closely and largely associated with the trade of the port, and always bore a high character for honour, and uprightness. . . .[7]

William Wolfe Alexander married Angelina Brandon on 21st May, 1829, and at first they lived in Great George Street and from 1841 in Berkeley Square, both just off Park Street. They had three sons and three daughters.

---

[5] Paragraph from R.R. Emanuel 'The History of Bristol Jewry' in the Newsletter, No. 4/88 of Temple Local History Group, Bristol.
[6] The *Clifton Chronicle and Directory*, Wednesday, July 27, 1870.
[7] The *Daily Bristol Times*, Monday, 25th July, 1870.

Some of their correspondence has been preserved and was given to the Bristol Jewish History Group. Two letters are particularly entertaining. They were sent to Angelina from her mother in the course of a three-month tour of the north of England and Scotland. A complete transcription appears in Appendix III.[8]

The letters to William Wolfe Alexander from 1829 to 1838 cover many subjects. Some deal with his appointment as Consul to the King of the Two Sicilies. Others refer to his trade with a French wine merchant, with his brothers-in-law, Henry H. Cohen of London and Charles Mozley of Liverpool.[9] These often include family matters as well and gifts being sent by mail coach of, for example, a turtle (from Henry Cohen), turbot and lobsters (from Gabriel Brandon, his brother-in-law). Another from Henry Cohen dated London, 11th September, 1833, after he had returned there in haste on business, is worth quoting in part:

> . . . the brig, Elizabeth . . . will be put in train of settlement. They could not get the wreck off. She is advertised to be sold on Monday next at public sale. . . . I have sent you by tonight's Company Coach from Basing Hall Street to deliver to you in the morning and carriage paid: a basket of prime smoked Salmon, a basket of prime Yarmouth herrings, 20 Keg of prime Dutch Herrings and 20 Keg of prime Dutch Pickled Cucumbers which you will oblige me by accepting. I hope they will arrive in good time for Rosh Hashanah. . . . I leave by mail tomorrow night for Cheltenham. I hope to remain there 4 or 5 weeks.[10]

Three days later, Angelina Alexander came to Cheltenham, where her parents, Joseph Israel and Rachael Brandon were staying. She wrote to her husband, describing a ball they attended and other social events. Finally she requested that 'William does not eat too many of the Dutch cucumbers that Henry sent, please to save one or two for her!' She wished him a very happy New Year.

Other letters from Israel Brandon deal with his sons' quarterly allowance. It is William Wolfe Alexander who sends David and

---

[8] Family details of the Alexander family (copied by Mr. Tony Reese) come from a family Chumash found with the letters and other documents owned by Mr. Abbot and donated to the Bristol Jewish History Group. They are now kept in the Bristol City Archives.

[9] Mozley was Mayor of Liverpool in 1863 and President of the Hebrew Schools from 1854 to 1866. He owned a bank; thus there was money in the family. He, too, was not known for his adherence to Judaism.

[10] The gifts quoted suggest a degree of assimilation by this family, yet their acknowledgement of Rosh Hashanah shows that it was only partial.

Edward Brandon cheques to put in the bank. These run from 1833 to 1837. A vivid description of him and his life style appears in *At the Port of Bristol*:

> He lived with his wife, three daughters and three sons in Berkeley Square. He was generally popular and esteemed for his sound common sense and courtesy to all who came in contact with him. In appearance he was of good height, well set up, invariably dressed in black, of slight build, grave looking but very genial and pleasant in conversation, and an active man who carried his years well. His yellow barouche was a well-known object in Clifton in the fifties and sixties. His daughters were among the foremost leaders of fashion in the district, much admired, and very popular everywhere.[11]

His death on 1st August, 1874, was recorded in both the local and Jewish press:

> Mr. Alexander was a man of the highest honour and integrity, and was justly held in great esteem by his fellow-citizens, he and his family having been associated for two generations with the commerce of Bristol. He was a man of great courtesy and kindness of heart, of a very cultivated mind and tastes, with a singularly delicate consideration for the feelings and convictions of others, however his own feelings and convictions might have differed from theirs. He and his brother, the late Mr. Abraham Alexander, were amongst the first of the Jewish persuasion elected to municipal office in England. On three or four occasions he was solicited by the Conservative party (of which he was a consistent and intelligent member) to allow himself to be nominated for the mayoralty – to which, we have no doubt, he would have been unanimously chosen; but his quiet habits induced him to decline the honour. . . . His fellow citizens of various creeds respected him highly. Alderman Alexander was connected with the Bristol Jewish community for upwards of fifty years. He was a very regular attender at divine Worship and showed his interest in communal affairs by constant attendance at the general meetings of members. He was beloved by all – Jew and gentile alike. He was a staunch supporter of Bristol Jewish and non-Jewish charities and many metropolitan institutions. He greatly elevated the political and social status of his brethren.[12]

Tombstones of the Alexander family appear in ill. 22.

---

[11] W.G. Neale, *At the Port of Bristol, Volume 1, Members and Problems, 1849–1899*, Port of Bristol Authority, 1968. It includes details of Abraham Alexander, William Wolfe Alexander and Arthur Albert Levy-Langfield.

[12] *Bristol Times*, 22nd and *Jewish Chronicle*, 28th August, 1874.

Two of William Wolfe Alexander's sons, Edward (who died young in Bath) and Alfred, were associated with him in business for a time. Alfred left to become Secretary of the Bristol Water Works Company. The family letters show that, as an infant, Brandon, their older brother, had been seriously ill. His very survival was in doubt. But he recovered and in due course trained for and was called to the Bar in January, 1858. Some of his correspondence with his younger brother, Alfred, from July, 1867, has been preserved.[13] He was writing from Cava dei Turnum near Naples. It must be assumed that he had gone to live in a warmer climate for the sake of his health. His life there was enlivened when he found some kindred spirits with whom he could make music, and his violin was sent out, which helped although his relations with possible accompanists were sometimes stormy. His letters to Alfred are mournful about his state of health but entertaining about the people with whom he came into contact. Sadly the letters cease suddenly in June, 1878, and it has been impossible to discover when or where he died.[14]

The third member of the Jewish community whose career on the Council has already been mentioned was Joseph Abraham. His father, Moses Abraham, was born in London about 1772 but he lived for some time in Frome[15] where all his children were born. Three of his daughters married Sephardim from London and their marriage details[16] show that he was an optician.

Moses Abraham had two sons. The elder, John, married Caroline and they had a daughter named Hester. In April 1867 she married Samuel Nuñes Carvalho of London. The brothers, John and Joseph, were in partnership together in the wine trade. They leased the Coopers' Hall in King Street from 1850 where they carried on their trade until John died in 1856 aged only 51 years. Joseph Abraham continued without him. After Joseph's death in 1867, the property passed to Mr. Carvalho, son-in-law of John Abraham. It was finally sold by Mrs. H.F.N. Carvalho in 1919.

The King David Tavern existed from at least 1752 on the corner of Upper Maudlin Street and St. Michael's Hill. From 1860, Joseph

---

[13] The letters were given to the Bristol Jewish History Group – see note 8, page 141 above.

[14] The Alexander family and the Abraham brothers are recorded in chapter 4, page 62, and chapter 9, pages 129–135.

[15] The town has a long Jewish connection in that Butler and Tanner have for years published the High Festival prayer-book which is standard in this country.

[16] From the Marriage Registers of the Spanish and Portuguese Synagogue, Lauderdale Road, London. Miss Miriam Rodrigues-Pereira's assistance in this matter was invaluable.

Abraham owned the building, by then renamed the King David Inn, until his untimely death in 1866. He leased the building to Mrs. Ann Willey, landlord of the Inn.[17]

Joseph Platnauer was born in Wreschen, near Posen, in Poland, three miles from the Russian border.[18] He came to England, lived in Newport and Pontypool before settling in Bristol in 1834[19]. The naturalization papers dated 1858 and 1859 of Joseph Platnauer's sons, Michael Joseph, Samuel, George, and Louis, show that they were born respectively in 1820, 1822, 1826, and 1835.[20] They had been living in England for a little over twenty years, suggesting that they arrived in 1838 or thereabouts. Michael Joseph Platnauer does not seem to have been in business with his father and brothers, although it is not clear what he did for a living, since none of them advertised in the local press. A photograph of Victoria Street with the Platnauer Bros. shop appears in ill. 23.

Samuel Platnauer, second son of Joseph, sometime President of Bristol Hebrew Congregation, has been mentioned in connection with the move from Temple Street to Park Row.[21] He was also instrumental in obtaining the Abraham Solomon Palmer legacy for the Bristol Hebrew Congregation. It seemed reasonable to surmise that Abraham Palmer of Exeter and Samuel Platnauer of Bristol were related but this has been impossible to prove. Certainly Samuel Platnauer was one of the executors of Abraham Palmer's will in which donations to the Shochet and to the Jewish poor of both Bristol and Exeter were made as well as endowments to two relatives and for a scholarship to Jews' College.[22]

Moses Blanckensee came to England from Hohne, Prussia, in 1837 and took out British citizenship in 1858.[23] He appears in the *Jewish Chronicle* as President of the Bristol Hebrew Congregation in 1867. He

---

[17] The King David Inn in the eighteenth century appears in *Bristol Inns and Alehouses in the mid-18th Century* by Patrick McGrath and Mary E. Williams, published by the City of Bristol. Nowadays the building is called the King David Hotel.

[18] Formerly, Wreschen had one of the largest Jewish communities in South Prussia, but was badly treated in the seventeenth century.

[19] Mr. Tony Reese's study of the Platnauer family provided this information.

[20] The Public Record Office, Kew, hold naturalisation certificates C54/15281 p. 29, C54/15281 p. 30, C54/15281 p. 31 and C54/15344 p. 56.

[21] He also appears in chapter 4, page 50 and chapter 5, page 72.

[22] Mr. Arnold Greenwood, treasurer of Bristol Hebrew Congregation, provided information about Abraham Solomon Palmer. Neither his will nor naturalization papers threw any further light on the subject.

[23] Naturalization certificate at Public Record Office, Kew, no. C54/15272 p.38.

married a London girl and they had nine children. His obituary states: 'He was held in esteem by people of all denominations.'[24]

Despite its attractions, Bristol has too often been a temporary home for Jews. It is interesting that children of both the Platnauer and Blanckensee families married nine Londoners, two people from Birmingham and two from South Africa, of whom one came from Kimberley, a migrant from England, and the other from Cape Town, who may also have been born in this country. Finally there was one each from Swansea, Middlesborough and Philadelphia, U.S.A. For daughters this meant that they left Bristol, never to return. Three of the Platnauer sons remained in Bristol for one further generation but no longer. Memorials to Samuel Platnauer and Moses Blanckensee can be seen in ills 28 and 29.

The fact that girls marry and leave Bristol suggests that settlement patterns here are similar to those found in Bath. In each generation the Jewish Congregation loses members to other cities either at the time of marriage or later, when a growing family seeks a larger Jewish community in which their children can grow up. The difference in Bristol is that newcomers regularly arrived to take their place, especially the twentieth century academics. It also means that it is not possible to follow families through more than two, or at most three, generations as the community grows and develops. In almost every period it is a new generation who enjoys the old places and organizations. This has not changed and in the 1990s Bristol continues to have a mobile Jewish population.[25]

---

[24] *Jewish Chronicle*, 16th November, 1883.
[25] This is not uncommon in provincial communities. However, in larger centres, Zionism has exerted a pull on its supporters to make Aliyah (to emigrate Israel). Increasing academic opportunities since the late-nineteenth century has meant that children leave home to go to universities and do not return. Luckily, Bristol University has been a strong attraction that brings in new blood.

The Social and Artistic Life of the Congregation: 1881–1968

W hat can be gleaned about the social and artistic life of the
Congregation? Prior to the 1880s very little, but after that
date correspondents to the Jewish press become much more
voluble and many more and varied reports appear. In addition to
being Secretary of the Bristol Branch of the Anglo-Jewish Association,
founded in 1878, Mr. John G. Levy was a founder member of the
local Parliamentary Debating Society, which was said to have a good
attendance of Jewish members. He was also Vice-President of the
Bristol Hebrew Literary and Debating Society, already holding its
third session, as reported in the *Jewish Chronicle* of 18th February,
1881. It is not reported again in this newspaper and must have died
an early death. Twelve years later, in 1893, an opening concert by the
Bristol Jewish Literary and Debating Society was held:

> . . . The room was very prettily decorated for the occasion, with
> flags, fairy-lamps, flowers, &c., and the whole presenting a very
> cheerful appearance. The following ladies and gentlemen kindly
> rendered their services. Mrs. Jessel, Misses Hyman, Frances
> Jacobs, Alice Jessel and Annie Salanson; Messrs. J. Jacobs, F. and
> S. Goldman, H. Levy and L. Norden. Each item of the pro-
> gramme was well carried out. The large audience, consisting of
> members and friends, showed their appreciation by their hearty
> applause. During the interval twenty ladies and gentlemen
> wishing to become members gave in their names. The concert
> opened with the singing of the hymn, Maoz Tsur, which was
> particularly suitable for the occasion and was capitally rendered.
> Very much praise is due to the President, Mr. A. Salanson, and
> the Committee, Messrs. S. Jacobs, F. Goldman, J. Jacobs, H.
> Israel, S. Festenstein and A. Jacobs, for the able manner in which
> the whole entertainment was carried out.[1]

They held fortnightly debates, lectures and concerts, the occasional
dance and play-reading, as well as conversaziones. Some subjects for

---

[1] *Jewish World*, 8th December, 1893. The concert took place on Sunday, 3rd
December, the first night of Chanukah, for which Maoz Tsur is a traditional hymn.
The festival ended on the evening of Sunday, 10th December.

debates or lectures in 1894 included 'Jews and Politics', 'Cremation', 'Women's Franchise', 'the History of Metals', and 'Don Israel Abrabanel'. They provided a regular Purim treat for the Religion School children, the first of which, in 1894, was reported as follows:

> The Jewish Social and Debating Society gave a Purim treat to over one hundred children in the schoolroom on Sunday. The children were provided with tea, oranges and sweets, and entertained with a magic lantern exhibition and other amusements.[2]

The following year 'the Committee having provided rather generously, the surplus refreshments were sent to the Children's Hospital.'[3] The numbers attending varied over the years from over a hundred to about 250 children in 1908. In March, 1898 'a plentiful tea was provided and a ventriloquist was greatly enjoyed. A threepenny piece was given to each child.'[4]

A novel entertainment was reported in the same newspaper on 23rd March, 1900:

> After a substantial meal, the children were entertained with a series of magic lantern views, exhibited by Mr. H. Salanson, after which some interesting feats of jugglery were performed by Mr. Leon Schneidermann, which created much amusement.

On 20th March, 1903, the *Jewish World* reported that:

> the Jewish Social and Debating Society gave its annual Purim treat last Sunday, when 175 children attended. Mr. Levy sang and Mr. H. Salanson, Vice-President, gave a magic lantern entertainment.

Other Purim events were arranged that weekend by the newly formed Jewish Girls' Club and the Jewish Social Club. In March, 1905, two Purim parties were held, one at the Canynge Rooms, Montpelier, organized by the Jewish Social and Debating Society, and another by the Jewish Girls' Club at 20 Portland Square. In March, 1911, the Society entertained two hundred children at the St. James Parish Hall who:

> were provided with tea, after which games, etc., were indulged in, followed by a concert in which several of the children took part. During the evening, the distribution of prizes gained by pupils of the Hebrew school, in the recent examination by Dayan

---

[2] *Jewish Chronicle*, 6th April, 1894. Purim that year was on 21st/22nd March.
[3] *Jewish Chronicle*, 15th March, 1895.
[4] *Jewish Chronicle*, 18th March, 1898.

Hyamson took place. The Rev. H. Goodman presided and the prizes were handed (out) by Mrs. H. Goodman. On leaving each child was presented with a bag of sweets and an orange.[5]

In February, 1913:

In memory of her husband, and in remembrance of the keen interest he always showed in the religious education of the young, Mrs. Henry Simmons of Kingsland House, Clifton, generously treated the pupils of the Congregational Hebrew School with a visit to the pantomime 'Dick Whittington' at the Prince's Theatre on the 5th instant. Mrs. Simmons also presented each child with buns, oranges and a box of chocolates. A most enjoyable evening was spent by all and the children heartily voiced their appreciation of Mrs. Simmons' kindness.[6]

This was the first of many visits to the pantomime organized by Mrs. Simmons until 1920, the year of her death.

The Annual General Meeting of the Society, held on Sunday 23rd September, 1894, elected the following: President – Mr. Alfred Salanson; Vice-President – Rev. L. Mendelssohn; Hon. Treasurer and Secretary – Mr. F. Goldman; Committee – Messrs. S. Bertish, H. Felsenstein, A. Israel and A.J. Jacobs.

On 1st April, 1896, the Society held a special meeting:

. . . to accept with sincere and profound regret the resignation of its able and worthy President, Mr. Gerald Platnauer, who is leaving Bristol. A motion to create Mr. Platnauer a life-member of the Society was agreed. Mr. Henry Salanson was elected President of the Society and the vacancy thereby caused in the office of Hon. Secretary and Treasurer was filled by Mr. Sam Festenstein. A hearty vote of thanks was accorded to Mr. Henry Salanson for his past services as Hon. Secretary and Treasurer. Mr. S.H. Jacobs was elected a member of the Committee in place of Mr. Festenstein and the following ladies, the Misses Gertrude Platnauer, Annie Oppenheim, and Golda Israel were elected additional members of the Committee.[7]

At the Annual Meeting of the Society held on 16th October, 1898:

The following were re-elected: President – Mr. Henry Salanson, Vice-President – Mr. F. Goldman, Hon. Secretary and Treasurer – Miss R. Jacobs, Committee – Messrs. A.J. Jacobs, Ely Epstein

---

[5] *Jewish World*, 31st March, 1911.
[6] *Jewish World*, 14th February, 1913.
[7] *Jewish Chronicle*, 10th April, 1896.

and Solly Bertish, Misses G. Platnauer, A. Oppenheim and M. Salanson.[8]

By 1900, the Committee had changed:

Mr. F. Goldman was unanimously elected President, Mr. H. Salanson was unanimously appointed Vice-President, the new Hon. Secretary was Mrs. Walter Michael. The Committee were all re-elected with the addition of Mr. S.H. Jacobs.[9]

The Annual Meeting of 1905 was fully reported and the following elections recorded:

Mr. H. Salanson – President, Mr. M. Bertish – Vice- President, Mr. S. Epstein – Hon. Secretary and Treasurer, Committee – Rev. J. Abelson, B.A., Messrs. A.J. Jacobs, L. Goldberg, J. Belcher, F. Goodman, Mrs. A.J. Jacobs, Misses Salanson, G. Platnauer, R. Jacobs, E. Oppenheim and E. Goldsmid. Thanks were offered to the retiring President, Mr. A.J. Jacobs and Secretary, Mrs. E. Oppenheim.

Annie Oppenheim was a regular contributor to the Society. She first appeared on 12th April, 1895, reported in both the *Jewish World* and *Jewish Chronicle*, as a contributor to an invitation concert at the Hamilton Rooms when she sang and gave a piano solo. On 17th January, 1896, both papers reported:

On Sunday evening last an interesting paper was read . . . by Miss Annie Oppenheim, Cert. R.A.M., entitled 'A Few Musical Composers with Selections from their Works'. The paper was thoroughly enjoyed by a large audience and provided one of the most interesting events of the season. Her fine execution when rendering each of the selections drew hearty and well-earned applause from the audience and, in two cases, encores were demanded. Many thanks were given to Miss Oppenheim for her kindness in giving the paper, she being the first lady who has favoured the society in this manner.

Thereafter, she gave regular lectures and assisted at all subsequent musical entertainments. As already noted, Henry Salanson was frequently elected as President of the Bristol Hebrew Literary and

[8] *Jewish Chronicle*, 21st October, 1898.
[9] *Jewish Chronicle*, 16th November, 1900. Since the Annual Meeting had not been reported since 1898, one can only guess at the names of the Committee in between those dates.

Debating Society. He was a photographer and until very recently (1995) there was a camera shop in Bristol bearing his name.[10] He worked the limelight or lantern at illustrated lectures. In 1900, the members of the Society presented Annie Oppenheim and Henry Salanson with a 'handsome, massive flower-stand on the occasion of their marriage, in recognition of the services which they have both rendered to the Society for many years past.'[11]

They are recorded on its Committee at the Annual Meeting held on 10th April, 1910, and maybe thereafter, but this is the last report of the Bristol Hebrew Literary and Debating Society. Annie and Henry Salanson had no children and on his retirement, he sold the business to his staff, whose successors continued to run it. They were members of the Congregation until they moved to London in 1946.

Another regular lecturer was the Rev. Joseph Polack, B.A., whose subjects included 'the Story of a Converted Jew' in January, 1894, 'Jews and Crusaders' a year later, a paper on 'The Problem of Nationality' in November that year. 'The Revolt of Bar Cochba' in November, 1898, which he repeated in 1901, 'The Life and Works of Moses Mendelssohn' in November, 1899, and 'Nathan the Wise' in February, 1904. He spoke on 'Socialism in Judaism; Ancient and Modern' in November, 1911 (when he had just been elected as President of the Union of Jewish Literary Societies, whose annual conference was held in Bristol in June, 1912).[12] See ills 25 and 26 for portrait and memorial plaque.

A famous author started his education in Bristol. Moses Zangwill was a Russian refugee who had come to England when a boy in 1848 to escape the severe decree of Jewish child-conscription instituted by Tsar Nicholas I. He married Hannah Marks and their son, Israel, was born in London on 14th February, 1864. The family moved to Plymouth where other children were born and later to Bristol where Israel attended Redcross Street School. Here he showed such promise that the family returned to London, where he was sent to the Jews'

---

[10] The Bristol Jewish History Group in the 1980s was told that, at one time, Henry Salanson's camera shop was the only one of its kind in Bristol. They sold compasses and camera parts and imported German cameras, which caused a fuss in 1938 because he was dealing with Germany.

[11] *Jewish Chronicle*, 4th May, 1900. The marriage took place on Monday, 30th April, 1900.

[12] *Jewish Chronicle* and *Jewish World*, 26th January, 1894; *Jewish Chronicle*, 25th January and 15th November, 1895; *Jewish Chronicle*, 18th November, 1898 and 29th May, 1901; *Jewish Chronicle*, 24th November, 1899; *Jewish Chronicle* and *Jewish World*, 26th February, 1904; *Jewish World*, 17th November, 1911. The conference was reported in the *Jewish Chronicle*, 28th June, 1912.

Free School at Spitalfields. There he distinguished himself by winning scholarships and in due course, being articled as a teacher.[13]

Another son of Bristol who did not survive the war was Isaac Rosenberg. His father, Barnett Rosenberg, was born in Lithuania, and left Russia to escape conscription in 1887. His wife and baby daughter joined him when he had settled in Bristol in 1888. Isaac Rosenberg was born on 25th November, 1890, at 5, Adelaide Place, near St. Mary Redcliffe. Two sisters and another brother were born in this city. Barnett Rosenberg had many different jobs, finally as a pedlar. His wife took in washing and needlework. Certainly the family received help from the Jewish community and its charitable organizations. Poverty and the hope of a better life took them to the East End of London in 1897. Unfortunately, their prospects did not improve in the metropolis. Isaac Rosenberg was seven years old when they arrived in London to live in a slum, povery-stricken and ill-educated. Later he wrote that: 'Nobody every told me what to read, or even put poetry in my way.'

At school in the East End, he was lucky to encounter a teacher who encouraged him to draw and to write poetry, at both of which he excelled. But he left school to work as an engraver (which he disliked) to help the family finances. In 1907, he attended art classes in the evenings. In 1911, he found patrons to send him to the Slade School of Art, where he did well, but sadly few of his works have survived. His friendship with the son of the Minister at Bristol, brought him back for frequent visits from 1897 to 1914.[14] In the winter of 1914, apparently suffering from T.B., he went to visit his elder sister, who was married and living in South Africa. This journey was financed by the Jewish Educational Aid Society. By Autumn, 1915, he had enlisted to provide his mother with an income which he did by having his salary sent to her. (It was normal practice for servicemen to send part or all of their salary home to wives or parents.) He joined the 'Bantam' Battalion of the Suffolks at Bury St. Edmunds, because he was so small. In June, 1916, he went to France with his regiment and was killed on 1st April, 1918. His poetry writing started in 1905, when he was only just 15. Only part of one of his poems has anything to do with war. In his biography of Isaac Rosenberg, Ian Parsons quotes the words of Siegfried Sassoon in an earlier biography of the poet:

---

[13] Israel Zangwill attended London University graduating with triple honours. Later he became a journalist and discovered his talent for writing. Memories of his early life appear in his novels, particularly *Children of the Ghetto*. He was also a fervent supporter of Theodor Herzl and Zionism for much of his later life. He died in 1926. From 'An Exhibition on Israel Zangwill' at the Van Dyke Gallery, Bristol, in September, 1985, and the *Dictionary of National Biography*.
[14] This could have been a son of either the Rev. Eisenthal or Rev. Ritblatt.

I have recognised in Rosenberg a fruitful fusion between English
and Hebrew culture. Behind all his poetry there is a racial
quality – biblical and prophetic. Scriptural and sculptural are the
epithets I would apply to him.[15]

CLIFTON COLLEGE

Legends abound as to how the Jewish House at Clifton was founded
but two facts exist to support them: first, the future Bishop of
Hereford, John Percival, Clifton's first Headmaster, had thought of
such an institution for some time. 'He was gravely dissatisfied with the
method that scattered Jewish boys through the other houses, cut off
from any facilities for their own observances' wrote William Temple
in *The Life of Bishop Percival.*

Second, the School's own constitution stated that no boy should be
refused admission because of his religious beliefs. In some ways
Percival's intention went beyond the constitution, but it turned out to
be acceptable and has been supported strongly to the present day by
most members of the School Council.

It was not altogether a new idea: three other schools had Jewish
houses too; but their Housemasters were not integrated into the staff
of the School, thus making them outsiders and causing their failure in
due course. The Housemaster of Polack's has always been a member
of the teaching staff. This encouraged him to play a part in school life
often far in excess of his duty.

Its success lies as much in this fact, as in the quality of the founders
themselves and of the boys who set the tone for providing the future
leaders of Anglo-Jewry, as well as the unqualified support of what is
essentially an Anglican school.

What of the legend? Well, it is certainly true and has been related
in several places, notably the *Centenary Essays on Clifton College,* the
Jewish part of which was written by Albert Polack himself.[16] Cyril
Hershon told the story as Albert Polack told him with the great relish
that he brought to all his tales:

---

[15] Ian Parsons, ed., *The Collected Works of Isaac Rosenberg,* Chatto & Windus, London,
1979, reprinted 1984, and C.P. Hershon, *Centenary of a Great Bristol Poet,* West
Quest Magazine, No. 5, Spring, 1990. See also: Charles Tomlinson, *Isaac Rosenberg
of Bristol,* Bristol Historical Association.

[16] Son of the Rev. Joseph Polack, second Housemaster of the house that came to
bear his name. Albert's wife was Betty Polack, who appears later in this story.

In the nineteenth century Hot Wells in Clifton was a growing spa where people came to take the waters. Lionel L. Cohen was a regular visitor. He was an early Jewish Member of Parliament, a devout Tory. On a certain visit to Hot Wells, he found himself sitting next to a clerical gentleman also taking the waters, the Rev. John Percival, one of the foremost proponents of Radicalism in the country. But both sides came together for their mutual benefit. After introductions, the conversation might have gone like this:

'Mr. Cohen, you are a prominent M.P., are you not? I would dearly love to seek your help for the School over which I preside at Clifton. We do not have a charter as yet, and I would welcome your assistance in piloting one for us through the House . . .'.

'That sounds perfectly reasonable . . . and it might do a service to the Anglo-Jewish Community if Jewish boys were properly admitted to your School.'[17]

That is probably how their conversation went. Clifton received its charter and Jewry saw the opening of a small Jewish House for ten boys in 1878. If this romantic beginning had been the only cause of the House's opening, it might never have happened. Percival was also realising his pet scheme. On 16th November, 1877, the *Jewish World* reports that a concession had been granted for Mr. Bernard Heymann to establish a house for Jewish boarders. The article states that:

> . . . no longer would Jewish boys have to attend religion classes. Hebrew instruction was to be personally conducted by Mr. Heymann.

Thus Hamburg House, No. | 1, Percival Road, with Bernard Heymann at its head, came into being. Who was this nebulous gentleman whose faded portrait hangs on the walls of the house today and who looks quite at home in the sepia group photographs of the staff of the time, since everyone wore beards? There is a small portrait of him in writing made on the occasion of the endowment of a £20 prize for Modern Languages '. . . founded by members of the Jewish Faith in recognition of the establishment of a Boarding-House for Jewish boys.'

---

[17] Lionel Louis Cohen was elected as an M.P. for North Paddington, London, in the General Elections of 1885 and 1886. The meeting between Lionel Louis Cohen and the Rev. John Percival is likely to have taken place in 1876 or 1877. Mr. Cohen, as a descendant of Levi Barent Cohen and therefore related to many other notable Anglo-Jewish families involved in Parliamentary affairs, could, without being a Member, obtain a affirmative answer to the Rev. Percival's request from a Jewish Member of Parliament. L.L. Cohen died on 14th January, 1890.

His father was Zadok Heymann of Hamburg and he was born in 1835. His education was typical of a German Jew of humble circumstances: he studied at the Talmud Torah School under the Chief Rabbi of the city, Dr. Isaac Bernays. He came to England as a young man, and between 1854 and 1878 earned a living giving private lessons in London. Perhaps surprisingly, he was invited by Percival to look after the new house, which he called Hamburg House, after his native city. He must have made some reputation for himself in London, because he was recommended by Mr. Mundella and Mr. Montefiore, well-known leaders of contemporary Anglo-Jewry.

Candidly, as a foreigner and cheder-teacher, his success was a miracle. Neither he nor the boys knew anything of British public schools, their traditions and way of life. But he was determined to make Hamburg House a success and the boys must have been very loyal to him. He gained a reputation for taking snuff and disliking ventilation. If a man's greatest asset is his wife, then Mrs. Heymann won love and esteem for both of them by her tact and charm. He taught German in the School in general and Hebrew to his boys. He stayed at Clifton until 1890 and left a healthy House to the Rev. Joseph Polack, Chief Minister of the Prince's Road Synagogue, Liverpool, to found a dynasty at Clifton. During his tenure, it was decided to stabilise the names of Clifton Houses by giving them the title of the current Housemaster for all time. Thus it is Polack's and not Heymann's or Hamburg House. Subsequently his son Albert Polack served as Housemaster from 1922 to 1948, followed by his cousin Philip from 1948 to 1964 and finally Ernest (Joseph's grandson) from 1964 to 1979.

A valuable correspondence about Jewish boys in English Public Schools which gives further background to the situation at the time appeared in the early part of 1878 and was summarized in the *Jewish Chronicle* of 26th July in that year:

> It is well known that Jewish lads are pupils at Rugby, although no provision is made for training them in the religion of their fathers, nay, even though they are not exempted from joining in the religious services of their Protestant comrades. It is sad to reflect upon the consequences which must inevitably ensue from such a course of action. . . . A few Jewish lads, likewise, go to Harrow, and we are glad to know that in their case attendance at Chapel is not made compulsory. The lads also return to their parents' homes over the Sabbath and kosher meat is supplied to them in the house of the Master with whom they reside. . . . But even these arrangements are far from being satisfactory. . . . Thanks to the zealous efforts of a few energetic members of our

154

community, a School house has been established by Mr. Bernhard Heymann, in connection with Clifton College – a large public school with nearly six hundred pupils, situated on Clifton Downs, a few miles from Bristol. Mr. Heymann is in all respects competent for this task, having been long and favourably known in London as a successful instructor of youth. He has been appointed German and Hebrew Master at the College, and enjoys the entire confidence of the Head Master, the Rev. Dr. Percival. . . . The pupils of Mr. Heymann's House have, of course, been exempted from taking part in any of the religious exercises in connection with the College and the School. They are permitted to be absent ón Saturdays and on our Festivals. Special arrangements have been made for the Jewish pupils to prepare the lessons missed and they obtain their marks accordingly. . . . It now rests with Jewish parents to contribute to the success of an undertaking which has been entered upon not as a commercial speculation, but solely for the benefit of the community. Mr. Heymann's house forms one of what are technically called 'small houses' which are limited to ten or twelve boys. It is earnestly to be hoped that this house will always have its full complement of boys and that the Jewish students of Clifton College will distinguish themselves by their *morale*, their diligence, and their religious consistency.

The only other schools now remembered as having Jewish houses for boys are Harrow, Cheltenham and The Perse School, Cambridge.

Few local boys attended the College over the years and the House had very little to do with the Bristol Hebrew Congregation either then or later. However, the Rev. Joseph Polack (the second Housemaster) alone became a notable figure in Bristol Jewish circles. He was founder and President of the Bristol Jewish Board of Guardians soon after his arrival in Bristol in 1890. He was vastly experienced, having been Hon. Secretary of the Liverpool Board of Guardians since 1883. Its first mention in the *Jewish Chronicle* is in December, 1894, when the Bristol Jewish Social and Debating Society held a concert in aid of the funds of the Board and it was reported that a substantial sum had been realised. He retained the post of President until 1930 when he became Honorary President until his death in 1932. His memorial plaque stands at the side of the Ark in the Synagogue at Park Row. These charitable concerts continued to be a regular feature of local Jewish life until in 1904 the Prince's Theatre was first hired for the performance of a play, a practice that continued until comparatively recently. Today the Welfare Society of Bristol Hebrew Congregation carries on the work both of the Board of Guardians and the Bristol Hebrew Ladies' Benevolent Society.

Polack's House produced a number of pupils who subsequently became Members of Parliament, cabinet ministers and members of the House of Lords, among them Leslie Hoare-Belisha and Edwin Montague.[18] They have produced many leaders of Anglo-Jewry, writers and painters and there is a long tradition of going into the theatre and the media.

During the Second World War, Polack's had a very narrow escape when at ten to six on 2nd December, 1940, a large bomb dropped immediately at the back of the house. The impact was such that they were all thrown to the floor. Had it been twenty yards the other way there would have been no-one left alive in the house. Fortunately about ten minutes earlier, Betty Polack[19] had just said to Albert, her husband: 'This is getting rather unpleasant, do bring in the staff'. There was a reinforced shelter in the basement which had been used until the outside shelters were built. Everybody was very shaken. Then one of the boys said to Albert Polack: 'Sir, I think this is getting past a joke', whereupon they all laughed and felt better. So much damage was done that King George VI came down the next day. He stood in the crater and Betty Polack was very upset that she was not told that he was there. Afterwards, nobody was allowed into the house even to pick up their hats and coats; they all had to travel home that morning without any possessions. The school was evacuated to Bude in Cornwall from February, 1941, and was entirely cut off from Bristol. They returned in 1945 to find the house in a very poor state. What the enemy had not done their friends had. The American and British armies had been in Bude and the College swapped places with them. The Americans did some repairs to part of Polack's so the house could be used. Most of the roof was off; one could stand indoors and see the stars, and it was some time before the house was properly repaired.

On leaving Polack's House in 1948, Albert Polack became Education Officer of the Council of Christians and Jews in London until he retired from that work in 1968 and with his wife returned to Bristol.

---

[18] Noted in the 1986 exhibition '200 Years of Bristol Jewry'.
[19] Betty Polack (who told this story) was a grand-daughter of Lionel Louis Cohen, mentioned above.

Expansion: 1893–1897

I n the 1880s there were portents suggesting the Bristol community was not flourishing. The Rev. David Fay and the Rev. Moses Hyamson both remained in Bristol for only four years each, and others stayed for even shorter periods.

Early in 1893 Mr. Henry Simmons wrote to the Bristol School Board requesting that a Jewish teacher be attached to one of the Board Schools where all the Jewish children could attend. The Board recommended that they do their best to accommodate the wishes of Mr. Simmons and in June that year the Board School minutes note that Mr. Joseph Jacobs had been appointed as Hebrew Assistant Master. In February, 1894, the minutes note that owing to the failure of the arrangements, no successor to Mr. Jacobs would be appointed.

Subsequently, in November that year, the *Jewish Chronicle* announced that:

> at the monthly meeting of the Bristol School Board on Monday last, the Management Schools Committee reported that a letter was read from the head mistress of the Hotwells school, pointing out that Rebecca Wolfson, being a Jewess, could not do any written work at the Centre classes on Saturdays nor take the Government examinations, which were always held on that day, and notifying further that she had been absent for several days on account of religious festivals. Letters were read from Miss Wolfson's father and from the Rev. L. Mendelssohn, Minister of the Hebrew Congregation, asking that the girl might not be dismissed.

The outcome was that she was allowed to remain as a candidate but it was noted by a member of the committee that 'the School Board never entered into any agreement to engage girls at the end of their training.'[1]

In August, 1893, the Bristol Hebrew Congregation advertised for a replacement for the Rev. A.H. Eisenberg who had transferred to Bridge Street.

---

[1] *Jewish Chronicle*, 2nd November, 1894. Helen Vegoda kindly provided these extracts from the School Board minutes.

On 18th August, 1893, Jack S. Platnauer, Secretary of the Bristol Hebrew Congregation, wrote to the *Jewish Chronicle*:

> That it had been brought to the knowledge of Henry Simmons, President, that some Jewish residents of Bristol were applying in the name of the congregation to their co-religionists in London and elsewhere for assistance towards the purchase of a burial ground. These applicants have no authority from the Bristol Hebrew Congregation to make this appeal which has been set on foot by a few malcontents who have seceded from the congregation and are, by setting up a rival place of worship in this city doing much mischief to the vital interests of the existing community.[2]

In reply, Mr. Goldberg, Hon. Secretary of the Bridge Street Congregation, wrote to the *Jewish Chronicle* stating that Mr. Platnauer:

> . . . says 'that it has been set on foot by a few malcontents.' The answer to this is that there are but a few 'contents,' for I know, for a fact, that the President of the Bristol Hebrew Congregation with his most intimate friends, including those who make their appearance for about two hours a year in the synagogue, would hardly be a sufficient number to make up a Minyan, and all the others that are still under his guidance are not entirely content.

His letter is followed by a copy of the circular which they had sent out that gave rise to Jack S. Platnauer's letter in the first place:

> Bristol, 1st August, 1893.

> For many years past many residents and members of the Bristol Hebrew Congregation have noticed the gradual decline of the congregation in consequence of the removal – by degrees – of the ancient Land Marks from the Jewish Rites and Customs and the deplorable neglect of the Hebrew Education of the children is indescribable.
>
> This being the case and believing that there is no likelihood of a change for the better under the existing state of affairs, we, the undersigned, together with a goodly number of our co-religionists, have decided to form a congregation and thank God we have succeeded in obtaining the requirements for Synagogual Services and have purchased ground for a Beth Olem (cemetery) and as we find that we are deficient in means to complete the purchase, we are obliged to solicit the assistance of our co-religionists and therefore beg of you, that you will aid us in our

---

[2] *Jewish Chronicle*, 18th August, 1893.

endeavour with any amount you may feel inclined to Subscribe or obtain through your influence. Trusting that you will give this your earnest consideration. –

We are, dear Sir, Yours faithfully,

H. GOLDBERG, 21 St. Paul Street, Bristol

N. JOSEPH, 35 Windsor Terrace, Totterdown, Bristol

P. MILLET, 9 Newfoundland Street, Bristol.[3]

On Thursday, 17th August, 1893:

The Bridge Street hall was consecrated in regular orthodox style as a synagogue. The service was ably and impressively conducted by Mr. H. Feather, an accomplished Chazan from Russia, with a choir trained by himself. The Wardens (Messrs. H. Goldberg and N. Joseph) discharged their duties creditably. The hall was filled with members and visitors, and the gallery with ladies.[4]

The Rev. Emanuel Ritblatt came to serve the Bridge Street Congregation later in 1893. They announced that:

at Bridge Street on Rosh Hashanah and Yom Kippur, the attendance was fairly large and every available seat was occupied. . . . Mr. H. Feather, the Russian Chazan, read Musaph, Kol Nidre and Neilah, proving conclusively that a good Chazzan not only can draw a large congregation but can keep his congregationists in rapt attention owing to the impressiveness of his reading. The Rev. E. Ritblatt before Neilah delivered an extempore sermon. Taking his text from Joel, II, 11–14, and in enlarging upon it, he showed the great principles which should govern repentance and concluded with a touching peroration. . . .[5]

By October, 1894, the Rev. A.H. Eisenberg had made his mark on the Bridge Street Congregation:

. . . The services during the Festivals were ably rendered by the Rev. A.H. Eisenberg, assisted by the Rev. E. Ritblatt, the synagogue being well attended.

On Sunday last the general meeting of the Bridge Street Congregation was held . . . Mr. H. Goldberg, retiring President,

---

[3] In reports of services and other events at their premises in Bridge Street much is made of the excellent Jewish education provided for young members. This was similar to the dissatisfaction with the level of religious practice and education that gave rise to the Machzike Hadath in London in the 1890s and against Reform in 1842.

[4] *Jewish Chronicle*, 25th August, 1893.

[5] *Jewish World*, 20th September, 1893. 'Congregationists' is the word used in the newspaper; nowadays we would say 'congregants'.

thanked Mr. L. Lowenthal for his kindness in acting as teacher, also the Rev. A.H. Eisenberg. . . .[6]

Bridge Street as it was in 1921 and later in 1992 can be seen in ills 24 and 27.

Rev. A. Levinson is first reported in Bristol in October, 1894. During his time in Bristol the following note appeared in the *Jewish Chronicle* of 17th April, 1896:

> It is gratifying to be able to report that immediately before the recent festival (of Passover) an amalgamation was effected between the two congregations in this city. The schism took place about two years ago when a number of the members of this congregation, suffering under some grievance, either fancied or real, established a separate congregation, acquired a piece of ground for a cemetery and secured a house in Bridge Street for worship. It has long been evident that there was no room for two congregations and the evil effects of the rivalry have told upon the prosperity of both bodies. In these circumstances a number of the dissentients approached the President of the Old Congregation, Mr. I.M. Jacobs, who at once entered upon negotiations for bringing about a reunion and it is greatly owing to his tact and zeal that the amalgamation has been effected upon terms satisfactory to all parties. One of the first beneficial results of the cordial relations which have now been established is that a determined effort is being made to reconstruct the Hebrew and Religion classes in connection with the Synagogue. Owing to the split in the congregation and the other causes, the classes have fallen into a state of disorganisation. It has now been arranged that the Rev. A. Levinson should be relieved of a portion of the duties he has hitherto performed, in order that he may devote more time and attention to the religious education of the children. Mr. Henry Simmons, who for many years has conducted a class gratuitously on Saturdays and Sundays, has kindly consented to contribute his valuable cooperation and Mr. Levinson will in addition to those days give instruction on weekdays. It is to be hoped these new arrangements will succeed in placing the classes upon a better footing and raising the standard of knowledge among the children of the congregation.

Now that peace was restored in Bristol, Rev. Eisenberg returned to, and the Rev. Ritblatt joined, the Bristol Congregation and both men served it well. Rev. Eisenberg stayed in Bristol until his retirement in 1902.

In June, 1897, the Rev. Joseph Polack, Housemaster of the Jewish House at Clifton College, examined the children and:

---

[6] *Jewish Chronicle*, 26th October and 2nd November, 1894.

expressed himself quite gratified with the zeal and energy with which the children were taught. He found a distinct advance from the previous occasion. The boys and girls had been instructed carefully in reading, translation and religion. He congratulated Rev. A. Levinson, the Headmaster, on the good discipline and smartness of the pupils and on the manner in which he had instructed them during the short time he had the children under his control. . . .[7]

In August, 1899, the Rev. Levinson was unanimously elected Second Reader and Hebrew Teacher to Brighton Congregation.

---

[7] *Jewish Chronicle*, 4th June, 1897.

Consolidation: 1878–1938

I n addition to David Nyman, the other migrant from Bath to Bristol was Alfred J. Goldsmid, younger brother of Michael J. Goldsmid of Birmingham, who died in Manchester in May, 1892. Alfred had lived in Bath since 1874 where he had a boot and shoe warehouse in Union Street. Like Nyman, Alfred was made bankrupt in 1895 owing to family worries. He, also, found life in Bristol more beneficial. He had been treasurer to Bath Hebrew Congregation for a number of years. Two of his sons, Arthur and Ernest, have appeared in reports of Bristol Grammar School successes. His daughter, Ethel, was noted in several reports of the Bristol Jewish Social and Debating Society. Once settled in this city, he took his part in the local congregation's affairs, acting as treasurer of both the Board of Guardians and the Synagogue, for which he was also secretary for a number of years between 1909 and 1915.[1]

International events were having an effect on local affairs in England generally, and some time later in Bristol as well. On Sunday, 12th May, 1878 a short-lived Bristol Branch of the Anglo-Jewish Association was founded by John G. Levy, with Henry Simmons as President and Samuel Platnauer as Vice-President and a good attendance of members and friends of the congregation. The Rev. A. Löwy and Mr. A. Hoffnung were present as a deputation from the parent body. This excerpt from the Rev. Löwy's speech gives a good idea of what the Association stood for:

> The aim of the Anglo-Jewish Association was truly Jewish. It was that there should be unity amongst the free Jews throughout the world. They were not, as had been asserted by those who reviled Judaism, without honestly studying it, a people merely caring for themselves, nor had they occasion to send missionaries to bring men of different creeds to Judaism. . . . The aim of the Association in promoting unity was to remove intolerance . . . by means of education . . . and to encourage Jewish journals in the East (of Europe) and thus to diffuse knowledge in such a way as would tend to instruct those who had hitherto received teachers from persons devoid of affection for the Jewish religion, persons who asserted

[1] Malcolm Brown and Judith Samuel, 'Jews of Bath', JHSE, *Jewish Historical Studies*, XXIX, 1982–1986.

they were out to catch the souls of Jews and who sought to introduce a religion which was not Jewish. . . .[2]

Sadly, there are no further reports of the branch. But then, on 15th April, 1881, three days of anti-Jewish violence broke out at Elizavetgrad. It spread to other towns in south-western Russia such as Kiev, Kishineff, Yalta and Odessa in the Ukraine. Elsewhere in Lithuania and White Russia in particular the authorities took measures to protect Jews.[3] At a subsequent meeting in Bristol held in June, 1881[4] much concern was expressed for 'the unfortunate Jewish subjects of the Tsar'.

That became a deputation to the Mayor of Bristol and public meetings were held the following year. This caused the Society of Merchant Venturers to donate twenty guineas to help persecuted Jews in Russia.[5] No doubt many others gave generously as they had in 1854 but, not for the last time, local reports at this exciting stage in proceedings fail to appear.

Also at this meeting Dr. A. Macgowan was elected to the Committee:

> There was doubt expressed as to non-Jews being members and a lively debate ensued. It was decided that non-Jews should be encouraged.

A week later the *Jewish Chronicle* announced that the Council of the Association was not in favour of non-Jewish members, so presumably Dr. Macgowan had to leave. Once again reports cease, in this case for eighteen years.

On 3rd November, 1899, another branch of the Anglo-Jewish Association was formed. The President was H.M. Kisch, late Postmaster General of Bengal,[6] and the Hon. Secretary, the Rev. Joseph

---

[2] *Jewish Chronicle*, 17th May, 1878. The *Jewish World* of the same date also reported the meeting.

[3] *Englishmen and Jews*, David Feldman, Yale University Press, New Haven and London. 1994, pp. 97–122.

[4] *Jewish Chronicle*, 3rd June, 1881.

[5] *The Merchant Venturers of Bristol*, Patrick McGrath, published by the Society of Merchant Venturers, Bristol, 1975, p.390. Ms. Madge Dresser of the University of the West of England kindly provided this information.

[6] Herman Michael Kisch, C.S.I., born 1st December, 1850, was educated at City of London School and Trinity College, Cambridge. From 1873, he served in various capacities in Bengal. He retired and lived in Bristol for a while, sending his two sons, Cecil Herman and Frederick Herman to Polack's House, where they gained numerous prizes. They both excelled in national affairs: Cecil in politics, for which he received a knighthood, and Frederick in the army. F.H. Kisch served in Europe and Mesopotamia, earned many awards, both French and English, reaching the rank of Brigadier. H.M. Kisch died 7th November, 1942; Temp. Brig. F.H. Kisch died 7th April, 1943 and Sir C.H. Kisch died 20th October, 1961. *Who Was Who*, 1941–1950 and 1961–1970.

Abelson. Mr. C.G. Montefiore and the Rev. Dr. Löwy addressed a well attended meeting in Hamilton's Rooms, Park Street, Bristol.

By 1903 Kisch had moved to London and the Rev. Joseph Polack became President with Abelson continuing as Secretary. The only other reports of the Association appear in 1910 and 1911 when H.M. Kisch, once again President, returned from London to attend meetings.

The Rev. Abelson was Headmaster of the Hebrew Schools and led several special Chanukah services for the children. He served as President of the Bristol Jewish Social and Debating Society from 1899 to 1906 and sat on its committee thereafter. He lectured to the Society in Bristol and took part in their debates as well as lecturing to similar societies in Cardiff, Swansea, Newport and Merthyr. His association with the Zionist Association appears:

> On Sunday last the first annual meeting of the BRISTOL ZIONIST SOCIETY was held, Mr. A. Harrisberg, the Treasurer, presided. The usual routine of business was gone through. The Auditors, the Rev. J. Abelson and Mr. L. Goldberg, gave their report and congratulated the Society on having a balance on the right side. The election of officers resulted as follows:– President – Mr. L. Goldberg, Vice-President – Mr. L. Schneidermann, Treasurer – Mr. P. Cirelstein, Hon. Secretary – Mr. L. Lowenthal, Committee – Messrs. H. Cohen, S. Fox, D. Liberman, S. Kirsch, M. Shindler, D. Strimer, M. Goldman, H. Berkovitch and M. Bertish and A. Harrisberg as past officers.[7]

Just to show that it is not only congregations that have difficulties:

> The quarterly meeting of the original Bristol Zionist Association was held on Sunday at the Synagogue Chambers. Notwithstanding the rupture that recently occurred there was a fair attendance. The Rev. J. Abelson presided. It was unanimously resolved not to elect a President till the end of the financial year, so as to avoid intensifying differences. The most important matter on the agenda was the formation of a Zionist Social Club. A committee of six was nominated to propose a scheme and to report thereon as soon as possible.[8]

A week later:

> At a meeting of the Bristol Zionist Society, held at the Synagogue Chambers, Park Row, on Sunday, Mr. L. Goldberg was unanimously elected delegate to the conference of the English Zionist

[7] *Jewish Chronicle*, 8th and *Jewish World*, 15th February, 1901.
[8] *Jewish Chronicle* and *Jewish World*, 18th October, 1901.

Federation to be held at Manchester on Sunday next, the 27th inst.[9]

After the Congress Mr. Goldberg chaired the meeting:

> On Sunday last, a public Zionist Meeting was held at Synagogue Chambers. The Rev. J. Abelson moved the resolution of the day and dilated on the hold the Zionist movement had taken through the wide world. Mr. L. Schneidermann seconded and Mr. Harrisberg supported the resolution. Mr. I. Belcher followed with a Drosha. Mr. D. Soilovichi gave Yiddish recitations and songs. A vote of thanks proposed by the Chairman, seconded by Mr. G. Jackson and supported by Mr. M. Schwartz, to the Rev. J. Abelson was carried unanimously. Votes of thanks were also passed to Mr. I. Belcher and Mr. D. Soilovichi.[10]

The rupture mentioned in February, 1901, seemed to have been cured when the Zionist Association held a meeting on 9th February, 1902. Mr. Louis Goldberg was elected President, Mr. L. Schneiderman Vice-President and the Rev. Abelson Secretary.[11]

The Association then met regularly until August, 1909. While he was in Bristol, Joseph Abelson frequently lectured to the local Zionist Association and, as for the Jewish Social and Debating Society, to similar groups in South Wales. He was about to open a session in Plymouth. He also lectured to Bible groups in Bristol, Cardiff and Bath.

The Boer War was mentioned in a sermon at the special thanksgiving services on the 1st Day of Pentecost. The sermon was preached by the Rev. J. Abelson, B.A., from the text 'May the Lord give strength unto His people, may the Lord bless His people with peace.' The sermon appeared *in extenso* in the *Western Daily Press*. . . .[12]

Emanuel Harris came to Bristol from Sheffield in the early 1900s. He built the Triangle and Whiteladies picture houses which introduced new standards of luxury in the emergent cinema industry. The Triangle cinema was destroyed by enemy action in the Second World War, but the Whiteladies cinema still survives as a multi-screen theatre. In December, 1908, Emanuel Harris married Mary Jane Wilson at the Park Row Synagogue and is entered in the synagogue register of the period. The popular singer, Anita Harris, is their granddaughter.[13]

---

[9] *Jewish Chronicle* and *Jewish World*, 25th October, 1901.
[10] *Jewish Chronicle* and *Jewish World*, 20th December, 1901.
[11] *Jewish Chronicle* and *Jewish World*, 14th February, 1902.
[12] *Jewish Chronicle* and *Jewish World*, 20th June, 1902.
[13] Recorded in the 1986 exhibition '200 Years of Bristol Jewry'.

Two personalities who figured permanently and prominently in the life of the St. Philips area were remembered by Benjamin Price:[14]

Amos Raselle had a pawnbroker's shop in Old Market opposite the Almshouses and Jacob Street. Amos always wore a black astrakhan coat and a small round astrakhan hat. He was about five feet tall with a little goatee beard and looked very much like King Edward VII and was known as a friend to the poor. As his business was founded amongst the poor and needy in St. Philips and places like that, he was well-known. For instance in the School Emanuel, (a Church of England School which I attended) every year at the annual prize giving a considerable amount of prizes, which were usually books, were purchased with a donation from Amos. He often visited our school, everyone knew him. We kids thought he was marvellous because he always tried in our hearing to get the Headmaster to let us off early that day. Though Mr. Raselle had ceased trading there for some time, the shop that bore his name still existed in the 1980s.

Post World War One, things were really rough. A young cousin of mine was really hard up. They had a large family and his father had not worked since the war. Now, Amos presented the school with a gold watch for the best boy in the school, academically the best boy. My cousin won it. A gold watch in a family with about seven kids and an unemployed father would not have a long life but this one did. It went into Amos' pawnbroker's shop and out again every week until 1935 when conditions began to improve.

In 1938 Moseley's Black Shirts rented a shop as a local headquarters in West Street, diagonally across the road from Raselle's shop. In spite of his shop being what they regarded as a soft target, they left him severely alone. It was too risky not to.

Another poor man's banker was Mr. Rose of Lamb Street who was a scrap metal, rag and bone merchant. His business provided many hard-up families with some cash enabling them, at least, to survive. He was a dapper little man, who wore spats, he was extremely neat and tidy with a large gold watch and chain with a gold Albert and had little gold-rimmed glasses. When going into his establishment, the first thing that hit you was the smell because he dealt with rags and bones and some of those bones had meat on them which could have walked on its own. Nevertheless he was always there, he paid out in cash himself. He went into his office. He called every regular by their first name and he earned the affection and respect of all his clientele. I remember him specifically because every time I went there with my father, I received a

---

[14] Benjamin Price also contributed valuable information about the Jews' Cemetery in Barton Road, Bristol, see chapter 5, pages 75–77.

penny and that was a small fortune. A visit to Rose's Rag and Bone Merchant was an experience. Impossible to forget and impossible for an outsider to comprehend. But those who knew Mr. Rose will never forget him. He was, as the saying goes, really the salt of the earth.

The minutes of Bristol Hebrew Congregation show that it ran its own butcher shop. This business had been a useful source of funds for the Synagogue in addition to subscription income. However, when a new porger was needed in 1906 and Mr. B. Paletz was engaged, the cost was more than its income could cover. As a result a tax was instituted (probably of one penny per pound weight or so) on the cost of meat and poultry.

Some time in the 1920s, a rival butcher shop was opened by Mr. Aaron Campbell. In September, 1926, the minutes state that it was agreed the Communal Meat Supply should be the sole purveyor of meat. At the same time, £200 was paid to the trustees of the late Aaron Campbell's estate, being a voluntary contribution to his successors on their retiring from the meat trade by 1st November that year if not earlier. A committee was formed to run the communal butcher shop which was to be called 'The Shechita Board'.

In the 1930s the Congregation must have been losing members[15] because it could no longer afford to provide meat independently. So W.J. Harris, Ltd., of Dighton Street added a separate department to their butcher shop for kosher meat with Miss H. Campbell (Aaron Campbell's daughter) as manager. In 1939 Harris's complained they were making a loss and asked that the tax to the Congregation be reduced. This was agreed. During the war years, 1939–1945, payments to the Congregation ceased altogether. In 1946, W.J. Harris closed their branch in Dighton Street and the kosher department moved to Clarence Street, where they had another shop.[16]

In 1909, Dr. Selig Brodetsky[17] came to Bristol to lecture on 'The Talmud: Legendary and Scientific' to the Bristol Jewish Social and Debating Society. In 1914 he was appointed as a lecturer in applied mathematics at Bristol University and remained in the city well into the inter-war period. He was a fervent supporter of the local Zionist Society and when money was required for needy Jews in Eastern

---

[15] The Bristol Jewish History Group in the 1980s was told that 'there was very little Yiddishkeit in the town. The only Kosher shop was Harrisbergs, run by a nice kosher Yiddish family'. See pp.170–171 for more about Aaron Harrisberg.

[16] The story of the Kosher butcher is completed in chapter 14, pages 185–186.

[17] Brodetsky had been educated at the Jewish Free School, London, and at Trinity College, Cambridge, where he had a brilliant career, after which he spent some time at Leipzig University.

RULES
OF THE
BRISTOL HEBREW LADIES'
Benevolent and Religous Education
Society
FOR THE RELIEF OF POOR FAMILIES,
(Residents in Bristol,)
PECUNIARY OR OTHERWISE,
during confinement, sickness, mourning,
general distress and at festivals.

⤜⤛

BRISTOL:
PRINTED BY W. FISHER AND CO.

1902

Europe, his name was always there in the list and generally as a collector. He also joined the Council of the Bristol Hebrew Congregation in 1918 and served as its President in 1920. From 1949 to 1951 he was on the Board of Governors of the Hebrew University in Jerusalem. He continued to work for Zionist causes and for the State of Israel. He died on 18th May, 1954.[18]

After the Synagogue itself, the Hebrew Ladies' Benevolent Society must have been the longest lasting Jewish society in Bristol. A rather dilapidated booklet (the front page of which is copied above) given to the author containing the rules of the Society and the remaining minute books prove this to be correct. A later undated, rule book, found in the minutes, which must be from the 1940s, no longer includes 'Religious Education' in its title.

The efforts of the Society towards children's education was discussed in Chapter 5 under Sabbath Schools. The twentieth-century minutes of the Society give some idea of its later affairs. Charity was given to a more or less regular list of clients. Sometimes this was done in conjunction with the Bristol Jewish Board of Guardians, when the Board gave two-thirds and the Benevolent Society one-third. Special

---

[18] *Jewish Year Book, Who Was Who* and History Group observations, *Jewish Chronicle*, 2nd April, 1909, 30th January, 1914, 19th March, 1915, 15th February, and 28th June, 1918. *Jewish World*, 9th April, 1909, 17th March, 21st April, 1915, 7th March, and 5th December, 1917, 20th February, and 3rd July, 1918.

payments were made at Passover together with clothing for children at Passover and the High Festivals. Miss Gertrude Platnauer was President of the Benevolent Society from 1910 to 1920 when she left Bristol to live in London. She was succeeded by Mrs. Albert Michael who resigned in 1924, also on leaving Bristol. The next president of the Society was Mrs. Salanson (née Oppenheim) who remained in office until 1946.[19]

When the Bristol Jewish History Group interviewed members of the Congregation in the 1980s the Benevolent Society was well remembered. It was felt to have been organized by the more comfortable members of the community. People had to appear before the Society and state their case and were questioned exhaustively to obtain perhaps a shilling a week. One of the good things that the Society did was to pay for poor girls to learn shorthand and typewriting.

Achei Brith (Brothers of the Covenant) was a Jewish Friendly Society which, before the advent of National Insurance and the National Health Service, helped its members over sickness and death. To raise money, they arranged functions including an annual dance at either the Grand or Royal Hotel to welcome new members and no doubt to encourage others to join the Society. (See ills 30 and 31, listing the Presidents of the male and female societies.)

The First World War found the Jewish community as ready to serve King and Country as their neighbours. The loss of the choir, commemorated on a plaque in the Synagogue has already been mentioned (see ill. 32). Another very sad loss occurred to the Housemaster of the Jewish House at Clifton College. The Rev. Joseph Polack and his wife had three sons, two of whom joined up and both were killed in the summer of 1916. To avoid the family being wiped out, the middle son, Albert Polack, was not allowed to go to war. In due course he took over from his father as head of Polack's House, creating a tradition.[20]

The story of Isaac Rosenberg who did not survive the war, dying in its final year, has already been mentioned in Chapter 10.

In August, 1934, Polack's Branch of the Royal British Legion was founded in Bristol and is commemorated on a plaque in the Synagogue in Park Row. (See ill. 33.)

---

[19] Minutes of the Hebrew Ladies Benevolent Society from 1910–1952.

[20] *Jewish World*, 26th April, and *Jewish Chronicle*, 5th May, 1916, announced the death of 2nd-Lieut. B.J. Polack of the Worcestershire Regiment, eldest son of the Rev. J. Polack. *Jewish World*, 2nd, and *Jewish Chronicle*, 4th August, 1916, announced the death of Lieut. E.E. Polack of the Gloucester Regiment, youngest son of the Rev. J. Polack. It was Betty Polack, Albert's widow, who told the writer why he had not followed his brothers into the Army. The memorial plaque to the brothers and other Polackians who died in the Great War stands in the House Synagogue.

The Bristol Jewish History Group's discussions with members of the Congregation old enough to remember the inter-war years, found that in the 1920s the Congregation numbered about 100–120 families and those families had more children than today. Of this number about 90 families were enthusiastic members of the synagogue, taking part in services and social events regularly. There were loud arguments as to who should hold office on Council. This may have been because it was not a popular honour, as had been the case with the choice of the Mayor earlier in our story.

It is clear from the minutes that there were problems. On four occasions, between 1902 and 1966, nobody was willing to stand as President and the Congregation resorted to governing themselves with a committee. But this did not work for more than a month or two since every congregation requires a President to direct Shabbat services as well as to lead it and be responsible for the day-to-day running of affairs. But from 1919 to 1932, in order to solve this problem in the administrative part of the President's duties, the Rev. Joseph Polack was elected as Chairman of the Synagogue Council. When he died on 14th September 1932 the *Jewish Chronicle* printed its own obituary, followed by contributions from many who had known him and bene-fitted from the experience. The Rev. Arthur Barnett wrote:

> . . . In spite of his many and arduous duties at Clifton, he found time to fill the office of Chairman of the local Community for many years. And this was a task that demanded much patience, diplomacy and zeal. For the congregation (the only one in Bristol) is naturally composed of many heterogeneous elements, representative of varying religious outlooks, and it was due in no little measure to the profound influence that he exerted as its Chairman that the Congregation remained a solid unit. At times, when there were threats of secessionist movements, Joseph Polack was able, by his commanding respect, to maintain peace and unification. His innate dignity, his just administration, his sym-pathetic attention to all points of view and his patent desire for the Community's welfare, enabled him to succeed where many might have failed. . . .[21]

In the 1840s and 1850s when some members of the community in Temple Parish had bettered themselves and moved to the parishes of St. Pauls, St. James, St. Augustine and finally to Clifton, it was clearly divided between those living in the poorer and the richer areas. In the twentieth century, matters were no different. Jewish residents of St.

---

[21] *Jewish Chronicle*, 23rd September, 1932. Other obituaries appeared in the same newspaper on 30th September, and 11th November, 1932.

Pauls in Bristol were descended from immigrants of the 1880s (who created the short-lived Congregation in Bridge Street). In the 1920s, they still had workshops in their own houses and generally did outside tailoring or cabinet-making. Some of those interviewed by the Bristol Jewish History Group said that people living in St. Pauls on the wrong side of the railway were not recognised by those living in Redland and Clifton. Others could see no difference between residents in the two areas.

A well-remembered resident of St. Pauls was Aaron Harrisberg, who came from Vilna in Russia (now Lithuania). He had been living in Bristol from at least 1886 when the Congregation's birth register records the birth of a daughter named Rose at Chesterton Square, Michael born in Totterdown in 1887, Sarah born in a different address in Chesterton Square in 1888 and David born in Adelaide Place in 1892, where they were neighbours of the Rosenbergs. He was elected to the Committee of the Bridge Street Congregation in 1894.[22] Once the amalgamation between the two communities had taken place in 1896, he served on the Jewish Loan Society founded in October that year, the Chevra Kadisha and Bikur Cholim Society in November.[23]

> On Sunday, the scholars of the Talmud Torah Class, Thomas Street, were examined by their president, Mr. M. Moore. The knowledge displayed by the pupils throughout was of an excellent character and reflected great credit on their teachers, Messrs. I. Belcher and A. Harrisberg; especially as the class has only been in existence about three months and some of the children had to be taught the elements of Hebrew.[24]

He remained on the Chevra Kadisha until 1898 and continued teaching the Synagogue's children for many years. He taught Joseph Orman, aged 12, from Blaenavon, Monmouthshire, a pupil 'who received First Prize of four handsome volumes for an essay at Colston's School.'[25]

The *Jewish Chronicle* states that Aaron Harrisberg and I. Belcher assisted with High Festival overflow services in 1899 and 1905, but they may well have done so more often than was reported.[26] He was a moving spirit in the Bristol Zionist Association founded in January,

---

[22] *Jewish Chronicle* and *Jewish World*, 2nd November, 1894.
[23] *Jewish Chronicle* & *Jewish World*, 9th October and 27th November, 1896.
[24] *Jewish Chronicle* and *Jewish World*, 16th April, 1897.
[25] *Jewish Chronicle*, 6th January, 1899, under 'Prizes and Certificates'. Unfortunately the newspaper did not tell us the subject of the essay.
[26] *Jewish Chronicle*, 22nd September, 1899, *Jewish Chronicle* and *Jewish World*, 6th October, 1905.

1900, being elected Vice-President and Treasurer. He took part in lectures until 1905 when the Association ceases to be reported. However, it was reconstituted in June, 1909, when he seconded the vote of thanks to the speaker. This was a single report and there are no subsequent meetings.[27] He served on the Council of Bristol Hebrew Congregation from 1908 to 1919 and was Vice-President of the community from 1919 to 1925.[28]

The Harrisbergs lived at 25, Newfoundland Street from 1900 to 1932. At the front of the house they ran a grocery shop, which many congregants from both sides of the divide recollected with great pleasure. At the back was the living room with a small yard to one side and garden behind. At the back of the yard was the kitchen and bakery where his wife, Rachel, baked bread not only for Jewish customers but also for Harvest Festivals in local churches. Behind that was another kitchen, only used for cooking at Pesach. She also made cream cheese for the grocery shop and their salt herring and pickled cucumbers were often recalled in discussions about the 1930s. Aaron Harrisberg gave Hebrew lessons to ten to twenty children in the yard beside the kitchen. This must have been in addition to the Synagogue's Hebrew School, or alternatively the Talmud Torah School quoted earlier.

Aaron's death was announced on 19th November, 1926, in the *Jewish Chronicle*. Both Rabbi Swift and the Rev. Ritblatt wrote to the paper:

> The Bristol Hebrew Congregation has sustained a very grievous loss by the death of Mr. Harrisberg. The deceased was for many years Vice-President of the congregation and devoted himself heart and soul to its welfare. . . . He was a member of the Council up to the time of his death. He was also one of the founders of the local Lodge Order Achai Brit and acted as its President. The sorrow of his widow and children is sincerely shared by all the community.

Mr. Emanuel Ritblatt had arrived in Bristol in 1893 to serve the Bridge Street Congregation. Once the two communities were reunited, he joined the Bristol Hebrew Congregation and lived in Synagogue House. He was remembered as the shochet who killed chickens for the community on the premises.[29] He was a member of the various Zionist

---

[27] *Jewish Chronicle* and *Jewish World*, from 26th January, 1900, almost monthly meetings to 13th May 1904 and *Jewish World*, 11th June 1909.

[28] *Jewish Chronicle* and *Jewish World*, from 25th December 1908 and Bristol Hebrew Congregation Minutes.

[29] This raises a question as to whether it had ever occurred before, for example in the Temple Street premises or by previous Ministers. The lack of written information of any kind until the twentieth century means such enquiries cannot be answered.

societies that were formed in Bristol, as well as the Bristol Jewish Social and Debating Society. Both he and his wife were members of the Achai Brit. He died in Bristol in 1927 and his obituary says that he was much loved as '. . . a good scholar, a man of great piety and inflexible loyalty to traditional and orthodox Judaism. . . . He was a person who thought only of others, never of himself.'[30]

After the death of her husband, Mrs. Ritblatt was allowed to live in Synagogue House for a further two months from 1st May, 1927. She would receive a grant of £250 after leaving the building she had shared with her husband and family since 1896. She was also paid £2 a week for six months and £1 a week for a further six months. Synagogue House continued to be occupied by the minister of the time until 1959, although from 1942 complaints were frequently made about the state of the building.

The Council minutes relate that in 1902 it was agreed to form a private school which would use the Synagogue's committee room and an independent teacher would be engaged. Income was insufficient; in 1904 the President made a donation to cover the deficit and in 1906 the Congregation filled the gap. Thereafter it must have closed, for it is not referred to again. In 1912 a Talmud Torah was planned, but may not have come to fruition. In 1919 a new School Committee was formed and this time the school was more successful, at least until 1922.

The Bristol Jewish History Group was told that:

> Cheder in the 1920s was attended by about forty children taught by two Rabbis and two assistants. Classes were held on Tuesday and Thursday evenings, before or after the service on Saturday and on Sunday mornings. The lesson before the Saturday service was a Shiur on the week's portion given in Yiddish and lightened with songs.

In 1925 the chairman resigned from the Committee, which was not reinstated until 1927. Later minutes are silent about the School Committee, which suggests either that it closed down or that all was running smoothly. In 1936 the school required a third teacher. During the war years, 1939–1945, the school closed and children of that generation had particular difficulties as there were very few of them remaining in Bristol, with no-one capable of teaching them. However, in November, 1945, classes appear to have restarted, although attendance was frequently a problem. In 1953, a Talmud Torah was created which ran

---

[30] *Jewish Chronicle*, 15th April, 1927.

better in spite of financial troubles and difficulties with teachers and the Rabbi of the time.[31]

When Henry Simmons ceased acting as choirmaster in 1903, he was succeeded by Frank Goldman until 1907 and Montague Belcher who remained in charge to 1917. In 1921 the Synagogue Council agreed that a new choir be formed with Frank Goldman again as its organizer. In 1932 he suggested a mixed choir, but since this met with objections, he continued as before. In 1934 he resigned owing to ill health. Replies to enquiries by the Bristol Jewish History Group confirm that while there was a choir, those attending were paid 3d. a week and 6d. on festivals. The choir is said to have ceased to exist on this occasion because women wished to join in.

It is worth noting the attempts made by members of the Bristol Hebrew Congregation towards women's suffrage in their communal affairs (which may be have been similar at this time to other Anglo-Jewish communities). At a general meeting of the Congregation in October, 1926, various proposals were put forward to enable women to become full members of Council. It was agreed that Council should consider the matter and bring a proposal to the General Meeting three months later. The following May it was proposed:

> That female seat holders shall qualify for free membership and shall be eligible for membership of the Council and for honorary offices, except that of President and Vice-President, provided that not more than two ladies shall be members of Council at the same time and that on no occasion shall a husband and wife be elected on the Council at the same time and further that such ladies elected to Council shall not exceed more than half of the male members.

In November, 1928, Mrs. Gazina Sacof was elected as Hon. Secretary of the Congregation, a post she held for only twelve months. The reason for this was not mentioned in the general meeting held on 10th November, 1929, but it was minuted that Mrs. Sacof proposed the new secretary, Mr. Maxwell Levy. Mr. Nat Sacof, her husband, was elected a new member of the Council at that meeting. In the absence of Council minutes at this time one can only imagine the heated arguments that must have gone on behind the scenes. However, nothing more is heard of the idea for many years.

Under 'Provincial News Items' the following report appeared in the *Jewish Chronicle* on 2nd December, 1932:

---

[31] Minutes of Bristol Hebrew Congregation, 1902–1953.

174

A lecture on 'The Legal Difficulties of Jewish Women' was delivered to the Jewish Literary Society last week, by Miss L. Hands. Rabbi Swift presided. Messrs. A. Polack and W.S. Morris proposed and seconded respectively a vote of thanks to the lecturer.

Council minutes from 1938 make the story much more comprehensible. In November, 1943, the newly formed Women's Jewish Council, chaired by Gazina Sacof, requested representation on the Congregation's Board of Management, which was not permitted. At a Council meeting in May, 1944, a member suggested that women be eligible for membership. This appears not to have been discussed but in July, 1944, he proposed that:

> wives of members be automatically regarded as full members of the Congregation with the right to attend and vote at General Meetings and to be eligible for election to Council. Widows and single women to have the same rights on payment of a membership fee.

Discussion was adjourned until April, 1945, when the meeting did not pass a resolution and the matter appears to have been shelved. On 27th May, 1946, the local Council of Jewish Women requested representation on the Synagogue Council. Later that year, the Council proposed that the Congregation's rules be altered allowing ladies to be admitted as members on payment of the minimum subscription of one shilling a week. A subsequent general meeting quashed the proposal and, though it reappears in 1951, 1953 and 1960, nothing more is heard about the idea until December, 1965. At this time, in answer to an enquiry from the Congregation, the United Synagogue wrote that it was in order for women to attend meetings and vote but not to be voted for. Therefore after amendments to the constitution, Council proposed that lady members paying subscriptions in their own right be allowed to attend General Meetings with full voting rights and that a total of two lady members be elected to Council though not to hold office. This was carried and from March, 1966 to 21st June, 1971, and no doubt thereafter, there were always two women on Council.[32]

The Jewish Social and Debating Society changed its name in 1915 to the Jewish Literary Society. It continued to invite guest speakers. One respondent to the Bristol Jewish History Group remembered the Rev. Joseph Polack, who, as has already been noted, spoke to the Society on many occasions. Before 1939, there was a separate Drama Group of which Muriel Epstein was an outstanding member. She

---

[32] Minutes of Bristol Hebrew Congregation, 1926–1971.

married Ernie Morris, who was also active in the group. The plays chosen were similar to those generally selected for amateur productions by non-Jewish groups. They put on benefit shows, when the theatre was booked for one wonderful night. Everyone wore evening dress, it was a glittering occasion and well supported by Jews and Gentiles alike. The Society not only supported the Hebrew Ladies' Benevolent Society and the local Jewish Board of Guardians with a regular play at the Prince's Theatre but also put on fund-raising functions for refugees from Nazi Germany, for victims of pogroms, towards the war effort, and so on.

A hall for social functions was built behind the Synagogue in 1926 and used frequently. During the Second World War it was a haven for many groups. Unfortunately, after 1945 its upkeep was neglected to the extent that from the 1970s it gradually became too dangerous to use.

On 6th March, 1921, Samuel Lazarus, son of the late Barnett and Maria Lazarus, died at his home in Cotham Grove. He had served on the Council of Bristol Hebrew Congregation and been President from 1895 to 1902.[33] At a Council meeting of Bristol Hebrew Congregation in October, 1935, it was agreed that gates six feet high and eight feet wide be erected at the entrance to the Synagogue. This was done and paid for in part or entirely by the Lazarus family in his memory.

[33] Barnett Lazarus appears in Chapter 4, page 50. Samuel Lazarus' service on Council reported in the *Jewish Chronicle* and *Jewish World*, 25th January, 1895, as Vice-President, *Jewish Chronicle*, 22nd January, 1897. He resigned as President having held the post for five years, *Jewish Chronicle*, 14th March, 1902. From the Congregation's minutes he was on Council from 1st February, 1903 to 30th December, 1906, when he was elected Vice-President. He served on Council from 22nd December, 1097 to 3rd December, 1911, when, once again, he was Vice-President. He was President from 7th December, 1913 to 9th February, 1919, after which he does not appear in the Minutes.

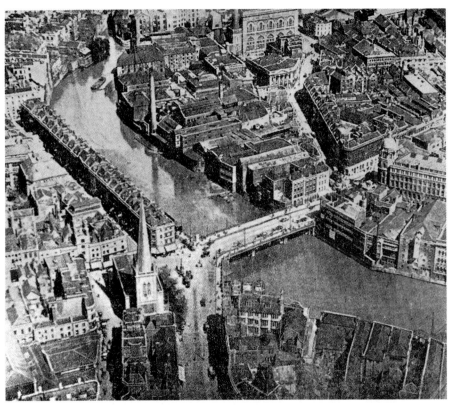

24 Bridge Street from the air, before the Second World War blitz, running along the waterfront towards the top left hand corner of the photograph. (*Western Daily Press* 10.3.21)

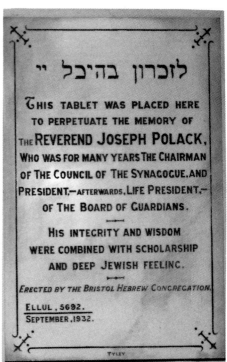

לזכרון בהיכל יי

ᵀᴴⁱˢ TABLET WAS PLACED HERE
TO PERPETUATE THE MEMORY OF
ᵀʰᵉREVEREND JOSEPH POLACK,
WHO WAS FOR MANY YEARS THE CHAIRMAN
OF THE COUNCIL OF THE SYNAGOGUE, AND
PRESIDENT,–ᴬᶠᵀᴱᴿᵂᴬᴿᴰˢ,LIFE PRESIDENT,–
OF THE BOARD OF GUARDIANS.

HIS INTEGRITY AND WISDOM
WERE COMBINED WITH SCHOLARSHIP
AND DEEP JEWISH FEELING.

ERECTED BY THE BRISTOL HEBREW CONGREGATION.
ELLUL , 5692.
SEPTEMBER ,1932.

TYLEY

25 and 26 Rev Joseph Polack (*Jewish Chronicle* 28.6.1912) and plaque in Park Row Synagogue (photo: Michael Wagen, 1997).

27 Bridge Street today. (photo: Simon Ferguson, 1992)

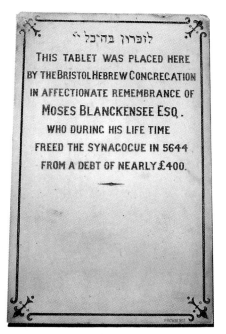

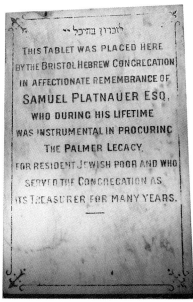

לזכרון בהיכל

THIS TABLET WAS PLACED HERE
BY THE BRISTOL HEBREW CONGREGATION
IN AFFECTIONATE REMEMBRANCE OF

MOSES BLANCKENSEE ESQ.

WHO DURING HIS LIFE TIME
FREED THE SYNAGOGUE IN 5644
FROM A DEBT OF NEARLY £400.

לזכרון בהיכל

THIS TABLET WAS PLACED HERE
BY THE BRISTOL HEBREW CONGREGATION
IN AFFECTIONATE REMEMBRANCE OF

SAMUEL PLATNAUER ESQ,

WHO DURING HIS LIFETIME
WAS INSTRUMENTAL IN PROCURING
THE PALMER LEGACY.
FOR RESIDENT JEWISH POOR AND WHO
SERVED THE CONGREGATION AS
ITS TREASURER FOR MANY YEARS.

28 and 29 Memorial tablets to Moses
Blanckensee and Samuel Platnauer.
(photo: Michael Wagen, 1997)

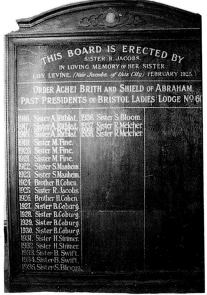

THIS BOARD is PRESENTED by
BROs H.FOX & S.FOX.
In Loving Memory of Their FATHERS
TO THE SIR JULIAN GOLDSMID LODGE No 26 Bristol.
ORDER. ACHEI. BRITH. & SHIELD of ABRAHAM.
26 SHEBAT. 5689. 6TH FEB, 1929.
PAST PRESIDENTS.

1904. I.J.Bloom.	1924. A.Coburg.
1905. L.J.Bloom.	1925. H.Fox.
1906. M.Schwartz.	1926. H.Fox.
1907. M.Schwartz.	1927. I.Freeland.
1908. H.L.Goodman.	1928. W.Reed.
1909. A.Harrisberg.	1929. W.Reed.
1910. H.Salanson.	1930. H.Cohen.
1911. M.Schwartz.	1931. H.Garcia.
1912. M.Schwartz.	1932. H.Garcia.
1913. I.J.Bloom.	1933. Rabbi H.Swift.
1914. A.Harrisberg.	1934. Rabbi H.Swift.
1915. A.Harrisberg.	1936. H.Cloot.
1916. A.Harrisberg.	
1917. B.Ronigsberg.	
1918. B.Ronigsberg.	
1919. Revd.B.Paletz.	
1920. A.Coburg.	
1921. A.Coburg.	
1922. H.Cohen.	
1923. H.Cohen.	

THIS BOARD IS ERECTED BY
SISTER R.JACOBS.
IN LOVING MEMORY of HER SISTER
LILY LEVINE. (Née Jacobs. of this City) FEBRUARY 1925.
ORDER ACHEI BRITH AND SHIELD of ABRAHAM
PAST PRESIDENTS of BRISTOL LADIES LODGE No 6

1916. Sister A.Ribblat.	1936. Sister S.Bloom.
1917. Sister A.Ribblat.	1937. Sister R.Melcher.
1918. Sister A.Ribblat.	1938. Sister R.Melcher.
1919. Sister M.Fine.	
1920. Sister M.Fine.	
1921. Sister M.Fine.	
1922. Sister S.Manheim.	
1923. Sister S.Manheim.	
1924. Brother H.Cohen.	
1925. Sister R.Jacobs.	
1926. Brother H.Cohen.	
1927. Sister B.Coburg.	
1928. Sister B.Coburg.	
1929. Sister B.Coburg.	
1930. Sister B.Coburg.	
1931. Sister H.Strimer.	
1932. Sister H.Strimer.	
1933. Sister B.Swift.	
1934. Sister B.Swift.	
1936. Sister S.Bloom.	

30 and 31 Achei Brith. (photo: John Adler, c.1990)

32 1914–1919 & 1939–1945
memorial plaque to 'the fallen'.
(photo: Michael Wagen, 1997)

33 British Legion memorial plaque. (photo: Michael Wagen, 1997)

PRESENTED TO THE
BRISTOL HEBREW
CONGREGATION
BY THE
JEWISH PERSONNEL
OF THE
UNITED STATES ARMY
IN DEEP APPRECIATION
OF THEIR
FRIENDSHIP AND HOSPITALITY

PURIM FEBRUARY 1945

כל ישראל חברים

34 US Army plaque. (photo: Michael Wagen, 1997)

THREE SISTERS canvassing in the by-election at St. George East, Bristol, talk to Mr J. Williams. The sisters are (left to right): Mrs Jeanette Britton, Mrs Helen Bloom (Labour candidate) and Mrs B. Sacof.

35 Newspaper cutting: Mrs Helen Bloom electioneering, supported by her sisters. She went on to become Lord Mayor in 1971. (*Western Daily Press* 8.5.64)

BRISTOL HEBREW CONGREGATION
1871 SEPTEMBER 1971
THIS PLAQUE WAS UNVEILED
TO COMMEMORATE THE
CENTENARY OF THIS SYNAGOGUE
BY
THE RT. HON. THE LORD MAYOR OF BRISTOL.
ALDERMAN MRS. HELEN BLOOM.
THE FIRST JEWISH LORD MAYOR OF BRISTOL.
26TH SEPTEMBER 1971.
7TH TISHRI 5732.

36 Centenary plaque. (photo: John Adler c. 1990)

37 Scroll and cover depicting the Tree of Life at the Bristol and West Progressive Jewish Congregation's Synagogue, Bannerman Road, Bristol. The scroll is on permanent loan from Westminster Synagogue, London. (photo: Michael Wagen, 1996)

38 Jo Shapiro taking the scroll out of the ark. The ark was once at Polack's House, Clifton College, now at Bristol & West Progressive Synagogue, Bannerman Road, Bristol. (photo: Michael Wagen, 1971)

War and Peace: 1939–1971

U nexpectedly, at this late stage in the story, we have some detailed personal stories of newcomers to the Bristol Hebrew Congregation. It is worth noting the ease with which these people were accepted in the community, probably because of the constant need for new members to replace families and individuals who had departed to other centres of Anglo Jewry throughout its existence.

The Bristol Jewish History Group spoke to members of Bristol Hebrew Congregation who had left Nazi Germany in the late-1930s and come to Bristol. One explained the hardships of leaving home. Some people had never left their homes before, for others it was a treat to go to a new home. The children did not realise it meant losing the loving care of their parents and being in unfamiliar places. Also there was the difficulty of learning a new language. It often took quite a while for them to become used to the new social climate in which they found themselves. However it cannot have been easy for the foster-parents either, having to cope with war-time shortages and rationing as well as a foreign guest.[1]

Another woman pointed out that her family (in common with many Jews in Germany) felt they were so well known in their little town that they would come to no harm. After Krystalnacht (9th November, 1938) when Nazis attacked all Jewish communal buildings and many private houses, they realized their mistake. It became increasingly difficult to live a normal life in Germany or to get a visa to leave the country. To be accepted in a British or American home they required a sponsor who would guarantee their financial viability and that they would not be a burden on the state. So there were many who were unable to escape.[2]

In 1939 Jewish children were being rescued from Germany and Austria, mainly by the Quakers, and sent to England and safety. Today the subjects of this rescue are known as 'kinder-transport children' and many have recorded their experiences. The journey was fraught with

---

[1] From an essay written by Greta Meyer. She came to England in 1939 as a young woman and went into domestic service. With her husband and small son, she came to live in Bristol in 1947 or 1948, where the family remained.

[2] Kate Lever mentioned this in memories of her childhood.

danger but most arrived safely. Once in Holland, they boarded ship for England and were put up at Dovercourt, a holiday camp in Gravesend, closed for the winter. There was no heating and the weather was bitterly cold. So for children from comfortable, middle-class homes, it was a very painful experience to be put up in such Spartan surroundings. In addition, not knowing when or if they would see their parents again must have made it very distressing indeed. In due course, the children were given homes with Jewish and non-Jewish families. In some cases this meant they were expected to attend church on Sundays, an experience which must have been another shock for them. In Bristol, Gazina Sacof was the moving spirit in finding temporary homes for refugees who were welcomed and looked after for the length of their stay. Many had to travel, yet again, to a more permanent life in America or elsewhere.[3]

Another woman very nearly did not make the journey. It was September, 1939, and it took a long time to organize the necessary papers. She boarded the last train out of Cologne for Holland. They were not held up, although some Nazis boarded the train and asked if any of the travellers were Jewish. It is not surprising they received no affirmative replies. The refugees were met at the Dutch border by a Rabbi who told them that war had been declared at eleven o'clock that morning! They were found lodgings in Rotterdam, while they waited for the final leg of their journey to England. Some time earlier, the woman's husband had been allowed to leave Dachau Concentration Camp on condition he left Germany, which he did. He came to England and joined the Pioneer Corps. Thus he was able to help his wife to leave Rotterdam by ship and come to Gravesend and safety. A job as a domestic servant with a Jewish family had been arranged for her. She said they treated her very well.[4]

One gentleman who spoke to the History Group had a very eventful time. He was born in Czechoslovakia and, in 1933, had a confrontation with two Nazis who were not supposed to be wearing Nazi insignia in Prague. He came off best but thereafter was known as a trouble maker. He went to Palestine for his own safety. While he was there his passport expired. When he went to the embassy to renew it, they pointed out he was due for military service and would have to return. So in 1938 aged 24, he went home. He was in Prague when the Germans invaded and he left for Poland. Here he continued

---

[3] A few papers from the Refugee Committee given to the author by Mrs. Sacof's daughter tell this story.
[4] Told to the author by Kate and Ernest Lever who came to Bristol soon after the end of the war.

the work he had been doing with refugees until, one day, he was called to the British Embassy in Katowice where he was living. He was told he had to leave as war was imminent, and he arrived in England with four days to spare. He joined the Pioneer Corps and trained at Sandwich in Kent. He married just before embarkation for France, after Dunkirk, he was stationed in Avonmouth. His wife joined him there, and this was why, since the war, they have lived in Bristol, where they became members of the Bristol Hebrew Congregation.[5]

Another Bristol resident was sent to a forced labour camp in Crakow in Poland, aged only 15 years. He survived a variety of other camps where he suffered much hardship so that by 1945 he weighed only 4½ stone. It took him a long time to recover. He tried to go to Palestine but was unable to do so. So he came to England and waited at a camp in Cirencester. While there, he visited his cousin in Southend, where he received an introduction to a family in Bristol. Thus he came to visit them, although his English was insufficient to explain his needs. However, the family took him in and in due course he married their daughter.[6]

Towards the end of 1940, there were a series of bombing raids, later known as Baedecker raids, as places of historic rather than military importance were attacked. The central shopping area (what is today known as Castle Park) was largely destroyed.

One member of the Bristol and West Progressive Jewish Congregation told the Group of her experiences on the night of the big air raid on Bristol in August, 1940. In those days (long before the Progressive Congregation was founded) she and her family were members of the Bristol Hebrew Congregation. Her father, I. Freeland, was on the Council and served as Secretary of the Congregation for many years. She lived with her family at the top of a house over their furrier's shop in Bond Street (opposite where John Lewis's department store now stands). That night she had gone to stay with some friends. Central Bristol was burnt down, the Upper Arcade was gutted and the shops next door to where she lived were destroyed. Her brother was not yet in the Army and he put a hose to the house and saved the shop, but they could not live there any more. Her parents and aunt were trapped in the cellar for some time. They feared they might never escape, but they were rescued. When she arrived home the following morning, one of the firemen told her she could not go into the house, but she replied 'I live here', and had a good look round. Her parents were gone and

---

[5] Part of the story told to a member of the Bristol Jewish History Group by Bill and Ray Schlesinger, which is continued later in this chapter.
[6] Told to a member of the Bristol Jewish History Group by Sam and Ann Nirenberg.

she did not know where they were. Finally she found them staying with another aunt in her big house in Redland.[7]

The whole of the Synagogue building was damaged and the roof of the big hall was weakened and in need of repair. From the outbreak of war in 1939 to at least 1941 arrangements were made to hold High Festival services at such a time that they would finish before black-out was needed.[8] However services continued to be held. But membership was decreasing because people were joining the services or moving away.

Not long before the outbreak of war in 1939, Bristol Hebrew Congregation received a letter requesting the use of a room in the Synagogue for Jewish refugees living in and around Bristol. This was granted and a sub-committee was formed to make the necessary arrangements. Later that year a class for physical instruction of refugees and other ladies was held in the Hall weekly on Thursday evenings. In March, 1940, the Bath Refugee Committee wrote asking if religious services could be provided for refugees and evacuees in their city. After discussions, Jewish instruction classes started in Bath in May. At the same time in Bristol classes for the religious instruction of evacuee and refugee boys were held regularly. In both cases it is not clear how long the classes continued.[9]

In 1941, the Jewish Forces Club was founded by Hilda and Queenie Schrieber, Rose Perchersky and Anne Freeland. It was for single Jewish men and women – no married couples. Music, refreshments and organised events were held in the little room at the top of the first flight of stairs on the shul premises or occasionally in the big hall. At first there were not many servicemen and women and events had to close at nightfall since they had no black-out curtains. The Bristol hosts took one or two servicemen home to have a meal and a chat. These were refugees who had joined the Pioneer Corps. Later there were people who came to work at the Bristol Aeroplane Company (later British Aerospace). At the end of 1942 the numbers rose when three thousand American men and women arrived in Bristol. (See memorial plaque in ill. 34.)

In July, 1941, Gazina Sacof, on behalf of the Women's Advisory Council of the W.V.S.,[10] asked to use the hall behind the Synagogue to store clothes and for distribution to victims of bombing. This was

---

[7] Told to a member of the Bristol Jewish History Group by the late Ann Chalmers who died in 1994 leaving her husband (Myer) to remember her.

[8] Black-out was required so that no lights would show in the event of an air-raid. Even traffic lights were dimmed.

[9] Bristol Hebrew Congregation minute books.

[10] Women's Voluntary Service, now W.R.V.S., Women's Royal Voluntary Service.

agreed, but distribution should not take place while services were in progress.

Shortly after the end of the Second World War a corner of the Downs became Speakers' Corner and was used by Fascists, Communists, Seventh Day Adventists, Spiritualists, men selling tracts, and so on. (The minutes of the time confirm this: in August, 1946, Council was asked that action be taken regarding speeches made by a certain person on Durdham Down on Sunday evenings. It was agreed that a letter be written to the congregation's representative on the Board of Deputies requesting him to inform the Board's Defence Department.)

An agitator by the name of John Alban Webster held meetings on behalf of the British Workers' Party of National Unity on the Downs. He recruited young men who caused trouble, lighting a fire outside the Synagogue entrance and even threw a blazing branch into the building. (A Defence Committee was formed and R. Landau, L. Jacobson, D. Malin, J. Burke, V. Schlesinger, H. Cohen and the wardens were elected.) They organized parties to go to the Downs to break up the meetings.

This is confirmed by an item in the *Jewish Chronicle* of 1st August, 1947:

> Police had to intervene to prevent a stormy scene developing into a general fight at a meeting on Durdham Down, Bristol, organized by the Bristol Workers' Party for National Unity.
> Heckling began as soon as the meeting opened and the speaker complained that 'Communists and Jews' were deliberately attempting to cause a disturbance.
> After the Police intervention, the meeting continued without further incident. No arrests were made.
> The Bristol Workers' Party is one of the four regional parties advertised in UNITY, the organ of the pro-Mosleyite Union for British Freedom, headed by Victor Burgess.

A Mr. Cohen brought a group from the Association of Jewish Ex-Servicemen (AJEX) in London to hold counter meetings. On one side there were the Fascists and on the other side the group defending the Jews. Homeless, unemployed boys were housed in a flat belonging to John Webster. The boys were said to be burglars who sold stolen property and dealt in Fascist tracts. The group provided alternative accommodation for some of them and organized an attack against the Fascists. Eventually this information was passed to Mr. Payne of the CID, a personal friend of Mr. Schlesinger,[11] and with his help, the

---

[11] Part of his story has already been related earlier in this chapter.

members of Webster's group were all arrested and convicted. Thus the Fascist organization in Bristol was defeated. Could it have been Mr. Schlesinger's influence that persuaded John Webster to write the following letter to the *Jewish Chronicle*, printed on 20th January, 1948?:

JEW HATER RECANTS:

To the Editor of the Jewish Chronicle

Sir, Through the medium of your paper (which I know is perused religiously by many Jew-haters), I should like to make public a confession of error, which, having been made publicly, in justice must be so repudiated.

For many years I have, through the columns of the Press and on the platform, asserted my conviction of the existence of a 'Jewish World Plot' to control and dominate all other races and peoples.

My political life, dominated by this illusion, has inevitably meant discrimination against the whole of the Jewish community, seeking to persuade my fellow countrymen to the same action.

I now see the folly and resultant misery of such action, and repudiate the notion which engendered it, and hope by this public statement to undo some of the harm possibly caused to many people, both Jew and Gentile.

Let it be understood that this statement is an apology to those my past anti-Jewish activities might have led into error or conflict, and must not be regarded as a political statement of right- or left-wing sympathies.

Lastly, I make this statement of my own free will, please or offend whom it will.

JOHN ALBAN WEBSTER,
Leader of the British Workers' Party,
Bristol, England.

Mr. Webster subsequently announced that he was dissolving the British Workers' Party.

The Defence Committee continued in being with help from AJEX.[12] The threat from the National Front and similar organizations is something modern Jews are perpetually aware of and need to guard against. So little has changed.

---

[12] Information from Bill Schlesinger and Julius Burke during interviews with the Bristol Jewish History Group in the 1980s. Corroborating items in brackets from Bristol Hebrew Congregation's minutes. *Jewish Chronicle* items in support. There were, of course, similar events in many other towns such as Manchester, Liverpool and Glasgow, as well as London, Cardiff, Birmingham and Brighton, *Jewish Chronicle*, 8th August 1947.

Repairs to the Synagogue building from war damage in 1940 took some time to be effected. After 1945, the War Commission awarded the Congregation over £3,000, a substantial sum of money at that time. The architects and builders employed to do the work were said to have merely plastered over the walls by the stairs to the Ladies' gallery.

Since the minister was no longer living in the synagogue house, Council agreed to engage a caretaker in 1945. This may have been necessary, owing to the extreme housing shortage at the time. In June, 1946, Ray Schlesinger was told they needed some Jewish people to take over. So Bill and Ray Schlesinger moved into the house. Before the war, only minimal sums had been spent on upkeep of the Synagogue buildings, and now, owing to further neglect throughout the war years and bomb damage, it clearly needed regular cleaning and repair. Bill cleaned it up, and found the eighteenth-century brass Menorah, broken and with parts missing. It was repaired and re-assembled. The big iron gates (a gift in memory of S. Lazarus, President of the Congregation in 1914–1919) were repaired.[13] The Schlesingers stayed in the house for four years, after which non-Jewish caretakers were engaged.

In January, 1944, a circular had been received from the Child Exchange Movement about Jewish children having non-Jewish Guardians with no opportunity for Jewish education. In addition many of these children were taken to church and in due course baptized. The minutes are sadly silent about any outcome of this problem. However an interview with Miss Patience Mostyn filled in some of the gap. She explained that the Central British Fund (C.B.F.) in Bloomsbury House was closely involved in the work of re-educating the children and employed her and others in the work.[14] The Bristol Refugee Committee, of which Mrs. Gazina Sacof was Chairman, was closely connected with the C.B.F. Miss Mostyn said that Mrs. Sacof was delightful to work with and organized an expense account for her. In October, 1945, the Council of Bristol Hebrew Congregation was asked if Miss Mostyn could hold a Chanukah service for the refugee children. It was agreed the Synagogue Schoolroom could be used for their tuition during the week of Chanukah.

Miss Mostyn had been asked to look after the children in the West Country, which she agreed to do. It was not easy and many of the

---

[13] From the interview with Bill Schlesinger by members of the Bristol Jewish History Group in the 1980s and the Synagogue minute books of the time.

[14] The emergency Refugee Committee in Britain educated thousands of Jewish children up and down the country.

children had considerable difficulty in learning about Judaism but she was clearly a gifted teacher who cared greatly for her charges. Her area covered Bristol, the Cotswolds, Gloucestershire, Wiltshire, Somerset, Devon and Cornwall. Throughout the period that she was teaching she never slept in the same bed for two nights running.

In addition Mrs. Sacof had been asked to provide a teacher for several English Jewish pupils studying at Badminton School in Bristol. Miss Mostyn taught them every Sunday morning. On Sunday afternoon she went to Cheltenham where there were four refugee children requiring her help. That night she would return to Bristol. On Monday mornings she taught in Bristol and on Tuesdays and Thursdays was either in the Cotswolds, Wiltshire, Gloucestershire or Devon. These last four were monthly visits. She walked miles up and down country lanes.

Each Wednesday, she travelled by train to Exeter, St. Davids. She was taken from the station by car, and ferried to and from each lesson. The orthodox community made her work a priority as all the children were in danger of being baptized. She only had time to teach her pupils about Judaism and sufficient Hebrew to read the prayer book. After such a busy day, it was sometimes a race to get back to the station for the last train but, with the help of her taxi-driver, she never missed one!

Once a week she went to the Gloucestershire office to meet the C.B.F. Welfare Officers there. In Cornwall, refugee children were visited about twice a term, otherwise their tuition was mainly by correspondence.

Only one of her children was reunited with his mother. This was difficult at first, as she spoke only Polish and, of course, he knew only English. However, he learned his mother tongue and was able to communicate with her. He celebrated his Bar Mitzvah in Golders Green. After that Patience Mostyn lost touch with him.

By 1948 most of her charges had grown up. The Bristol Committee, being responsible for fewer children, ceased to exist. She continued to work from London reporting to the Jewish Refugee Committee at Woburn House and to the C.B.F. offices at Bloomsbury House. Miss Moos (a much-loved teacher at the Liberal Jewish Synagogue in St. John's Wood) had written correspondence courses for all ages of Jewish children. She used these to cover for the weeks she could not visit and teach her pupils. With the course and to keep in touch, she would write a personal letter to each child. In 1948, Miss Olga Lazarus (a teacher and member of West Central Liberal Jewish Synagogue), who had also been teaching Jewish refugee children in the Greater London area and Southern England, took over the education of the remaining refugees in the South West. Patience Mostyn went on to do welfare work for the Stepney Jewish Primary School in East London and later with the Association of Jewish Youth.

Since 1939 membership numbers in the Bristol Hebrew Congregation had been falling, with people leaving to go into the forces or to be closer to other family members. This had a serious effect on the Congregation's income. Synagogue House, where the minister lived, and the Synagogue itself had been severely damaged (as noted earlier). It was a historic building and they would have liked to sell it and build a new one. Indeed between 1956 and 1969 Bristol University appeared interested in buying it. The Council of the Congregation understood they would have paid a large sum for it, but in the event the sale never took place,[15] as the University authorities changed their mind.

A report by the Jewish Memorial Council on Small Communities dated 9th April, 1962,[16] stated that:

> the present Synagogue . . . contains pleasant airy Classrooms, a large hall and fair sized kitchen. The community has its own kosher butcher.
>
> The Jewish population . . . is at the moment composed of fifty families or about 120 individuals, whilst thirty children attend the Hebrew Classes.
>
> With the financial assistance of Hillel House of London and under the kind supervision of Mrs. Yoffey, the wife of Professor J.M. Yoffey, President of the Congregation, twenty-one Jewish students are being served daily with kosher luncheons. The community has for some time been without a Minister in spite of repeated advertisements in the *Jewish Chronicle*, offering a fair salary and free accommodation. . . .

Regarding the provision of meat for the Congregation, Miss H. Campbell[17] who had been working in the kosher department of the butcher's shop since the 1930s, requested an increase in her salary from the Congregation in March, 1955. Accordingly, her allowance was raised to £10 per half year. In November, 1960, the Treasurer had contacted Mr. Wise who agreed to give Miss Campbell a pension of £1 a week. He further agreed to discuss with Mr. Wise the

---

[15] Bristol Hebrew Congregation minutes and History Group interviews in the 1980s.
[16] This report with many of the papers from the Office of the Chief Rabbi are now available for study with permission from that Office, at the Greater London Record Office. It was previously noted in chapter 4, p. 48.
[17] Miss H. Campbell was a daughter of Mr. Aaron Campbell who ran the Butcher Shop in the early 1900s, see previous chapter, page 167.

necessity of engaging Miss Campbell on a part-time basis, as Shomer at Messrs. Wise's new premises at 5, Byron Place, which was done.

In 1960, Martin Meyer joined the firm, now known as Wise and Harris, to train as a kosher butcher under Miss Campbell. In January, 1961, it was reported that the butcher shop was running smoothly and a letter of thanks was sent to Miss Campbell for remaining while Mr. Meyer was training. The Council proposed that a pension of £1 a week be given to Miss Campbell in addition to that paid by Messrs. Wise. They also agreed that a gift of a canteen of cutlery be made to her in view of her long years of service. This was done on Shabbat 22nd and delivered to her on the Sunday, 23rd July, 1961.

In that month the kosher butcher department left Wise and Harris and moved into part of the Co-operative Society's shop in Whiteladies Road, with Martin Meyer continuing as manager. Sadly, the shop never made a profit. Early in 1963 the congregation purchased premises at 23, Redland Road. Unfortunately he had no greater success here. After a year's trading the shop had made a loss of £103, which did not take into account the cost of buying the premises! In June, 1963, Meyer resigned owing to lack of support. The shop continued to make a loss and finally closed in November, 1964. For some time kosher meat was purchased from Cardiff but for many years it was left to individuals to make their own arrangements until in May, 1988, the Kosherina opened on the Synagogue premises. It opens fortnightly on a Sunday morning and sells frozen kosher meat and groceries to all who require it.

Since the 1970s, Bristol has had a new brand of members – no longer tradesmen and artisans or middle-class members who had risen from similar roots, but doctors and surgeons serving the Bristol Royal Infirmary and other hospitals or lecturers at Bristol University and the Polytechnic, now the University of the West of England. To anyone coming to Bristol in the 1980s, the congregation was flourishing.

From 1939, when there was no minister, the need to visit local Jewish prisoners was recognised and the name and address of the President was given to the Governors of Horfield and Gloucester gaols. From about 1960, Mr. Schlesinger started visiting Leyhill Prison, the open prison near Bristol. He recorded that:

> if an orthodox Jew got a prison sentence he would automatically be sent to Leyhill because of the Synagogue in the Prison. Its inauguration was a very special event. A Rabbi or Dayan, I don't remember his name, came to open it. We made a big dinner in Leyhill with the Governor and after that they had regular services there. We provided them with everything for Pesach and they had a Seder which lasted until two o'clock in the morning and the Governor participated. Before that, at an earlier Pesach,

186

they came by bus and I laid on a breakfast in Shul for them with Matzah and so forth. Up to a dozen Jewish prisoners came to Shul for the service and afterwards I arranged a cooked dinner in the Shul. Then they returned to Leyhill. It fell to pieces when I gave up. Since when there have not been many Jewish prisoners in shul.[18]

The Bristol Hebrew Ladies' Benevolent Society ceased functioning in 1941 and recommenced in 1946. At their first meeting after the war they contributed to the donation by the local Jewish Board of Guardians to the Cardiff and West of England Home and Hospital for the Jewish Aged. From time to time contributions continued to be made and the Home sought two members of Bristol Hebrew Congregation as representatives to attend their meetings.

Later in 1946, a meeting was held to reform the Society which had been dormant for nearly four years of war. However, the chairman, Mrs. Salanson, was no longer living in Bristol and wished to resign. Therefore she was elected President and Mrs. Polack[19] was elected Vice President. It was further suggested that the wife of the President of the Congregation should be Chairman during her husband's term of office. They intended to charge subscriptions from the following June and to revive all their payments to various Societies as in the past. The death of Annie Salanson, née Oppenheim, in 1948, was recorded at a Council Meeting on 14th April that year when all present stood in silence as a mark of condolence with Mr. Salanson. Henry Salanson was similarly remembered when he died in February 1956.

However, the next minute of the Society is dated 27th September, 1947, when a joint meeting with the Board of Guardians was held. It was agreed that the two societies should merge under the title of the Jewish Welfare Society.[20] But again the Congregation needed time to consider, for the next recorded event is a general meeting of the Congregation on 17th February, 1952, when:

the proposed amalgamation of the Board of Guardians and the Ladies' Benevolent Society was hotly debated. . . . It was proposed and agreed that this be adjourned for a fuller meeting.[21]

That meeting was held on 23rd November, 1952, to create the new Bristol Jewish Welfare Society. Its objects would be to dispense funds

---

[18] Related by Bill Schlesinger.
[19] Betty Polack, wife of Albert Polack, then housemaster of Polack's House, Clifton College. They both appeared in chapter 11, in the section on the College.
[20] Minutes of the Bristol Hebrew Ladies' Benevolent Society.
[21] Minutes of Bristol Hebrew Congregation.

to needy cases of the Jewish faith. Membership of the Society would be by subscription as before.[22] From the brevity of the minute, the strong feelings suggested in the February meeting must have been dealt with as the Welfare Board continues to function to this day.

Helen, Berta and Jeannette Strimer were founder members of the Fabian Society in Bristol during the war and followed its teaching in their political work. They realized that injustice could be changed only by political action and legislation. They joined the Labour Party and the first sister to be elected to the City Council was Helen Strimer in 1945 when she represented Avon Ward. In the 1947 election she won 3,530 votes, Mr. I.R. Westlake (Citizens' Party) had 3,134 votes and John A. Webster (British Workers' Party), having returned to Bristol, received only 485 votes.

Helen married Sidney Bloom on 2nd January, 1950, at the Synagogue in Park Row. It appears she did not stand for re-election in 1951, but in the elections in 1956, she was elected for St. George East and Berta Sacof (her sister) for Somerset Ward. Berta told the Bristol Jewish History Group that when she stood for election in 1956 she did better than any other Labour candidate in Clifton, because so many of the voters knew her mother. She was also a magistrate for fifteen years. In 1964, they were joined on the Council by their sister, Jeannette Britton, and newspaper headings celebrated 'Three Sisters sitting on Bristol Council together'. (See ill. 35.) In that same year Helen Bloom was honoured by being chosen as an alderman. This caused a by-election in St. George East. No longer were aldermen outsiders brought in at the whim of the City Council! Berta Sacof left the Council in 1968 and Jeannette Britton in 1983.

The first Civic Service held in the Synagogue took place on Sunday, 1st April, 1962, when the then Lord Mayor, Alderman Charles H. Smith, J.P., requested an invitation. The second was at the request of Lord Mayor Alderman Cyril Hepplethwaite and was held on Sunday, 6th November, 1966.

Helen Bloom was elected Lord Mayor in 1971.[23] She was the third woman Lord Mayor and the second Jew to hold such high office. Her term of office was more propitious than her Jewish predecessor. It so happened that 1971 was the centenary of the consecration of the Synagogue in Park Row. (See ill. 36.) So the Bristol Hebrew Congregation's

---

[22] Minutes of the Bristol Hebrew Ladies' Benevolent Society.

[23] Readers will have observed that Joseph Abraham was a Mayor. Helen Bloom was a Lord Mayor by virtue of a visit to Bristol on 21st June, 1899 when Queen Victoria gave the City a charter by which its Chief Magistrate became a Lord Mayor.

Council agreed that there should be a Civic Service with the Lord Mayor, Alderman Mrs. Helen Bloom, and her husband, Sidney Bloom (Vice-President of the Congregation), together with other members of the City Council in attendance. This was held on 26th September and was followed by tea at the Mansion House.

Helen Bloom remained on the Council until 1979 when she became an honorary alderman. She died on 7th December, 1987. Her obituary states that:

> . . . She played a central role in the development of health services in Bristol from the post-war period until her death. Her concern for the rights and well-being of others had been evinced previously in her work for the Achei Brith, the Jewish mutual help health insurance society that existed prior to the establishment of the National Health Service. She was subesequently vice-chairman of the Bristol United Hospitals and served on the committees of several other local hospitals.
>
> She also took a keen interest in education. She was a governor of many schools in the region and was a member of the university court. . . .[24]

Councillor Mrs. Berta Sacof died on 23rd June, 1989. Mrs. Jeannette Britton was Councillor from 1964–1983, when she, in her turn, became an hon. alderman. She died on 10th May, 1991.

---

[24] *Jewish Chronicle*, Friday, 11th December, 1987.

Bristol & West Progressive Jewish Congregation: 1961–1971

L en Hart came to Bristol from York in 1959 with his wife and their five children. He had been brought up in an orthodox Jewish home but became interested in Liberal Judaism. He had tried to found a Liberal community in York but failed on account of the small number of Jews in that city.

When he arrived in Bristol he joined the Bristol Hebrew Congregation and his children attended Cheder. In conversation with other parents waiting to fetch their children, he discovered sympathizers for a Liberal Congregation in Bristol, a city with a thriving Jewish community which seemed a better proving ground than York for such an undertaking.

He put the idea to the Union of Liberal and Progressive Synagogues, who were not optimistic. However, Len Hart was not defeated by their pessimism. During the following year he delved into the local telephone and street directories and other sources. He contacted all those with possibly Jewish names by letter or by telephone. One was an amazed West Indian called Abrahams. Thus he created a small group of like-minded people. Finally he placed an advertisement in the *Bristol Evening Post*, which brought in others and the new organisation was named the Bristol Liberal Jewish Group.

The lay-minister of the Union at that time, Mr. Joseph Ascher, attended a meeting early in 1961, when some twenty people were present. The principles of Liberal Judaism were explained and plans made for regular services, for adult study and children's religion classes. A committee was formed with Len Hart as Chairman and Hon. Secretary, Henry Springer as Treasurer and Bulletin Editor and Leah Papworth, David Burnard and Jo Schapiro.

David Burnard was a stalwart member of the Group for many years. He was the middle son of a successful Birmingham business man. He had been brought up as an Anglican but found it unsatisfactory. As a result he became interested in Liberal Judaism. At last he thought he had found a creed which, as a rational person, was worthy of respect. He completed his studies and was converted. Once he and his wife were living in Bristol, he took a full part in running the new-born congregation.

Friday evening services were held at members' homes. At this stage they did not have a Sefer Torah, indeed the children did not see a Scroll for many years. They used copies of the Union Prayer Book on foolscap sheets. They gained in numbers; a few came from the Bristol Hebrew Congregation, others through Len Hart's efforts and gradually the group grew too large for house meetings. Then they hired a room at the Friends' Meeting House in Hampton Road for Friday evening and Festival services. Members felt that they were part of a family and enjoyed this community feeling. The first baby blessing in 1960, for Sarah, eldest daughter of Peter and Mavis Hyams, took place at the home of Michael and Isobel Wagen.

Religion classes were held at the home of David Burnard, their first teacher. Various attempts were made at adult education; discussion groups, Hebrew classes and so on, but none lasted for very long. Reading the Bulletin and talking to founder members, one is aware of new projects but seldom of their closure, merely a slow demise, which is no different from other Jewish congregations.

However, interviews show that there were certain personality differences between the members of the committee. Len Hart was very single-minded and found it hard to accept alternatives. But peace was maintained. The first Annual General Meeting was held at the Friends' Meeting House in Redland on Sunday, 4th March, 1962, when the Hon. Lily H. Montagu, C.B.E, J.P., was elected Hon. President and Joseph Ascher, B.A., Officier de l'Académie, Hon. Vice-President. Jo Schapiro was elected as Chairman, David Burnard as Vice-Chairman, Len Hart as Hon. Secretary and Henry Springer as Treasurer.

One family joined the new Congregation from Bristol Hebrew Congregation. Their knowledge of Hebrew was poor and they found traditional services hard to follow, but for many years they worked very hard for the Community. Their eldest son was the first to have his Bar Mitzvah with the Bristol Liberal Group. However, in the end the call of traditional Judaism was too strong and they returned to their roots some time in the late-sixties.

Affiliation to the Union of Liberal and Progressive Synagogues was accomplished by June, 1962. This acceptance meant that help was available from the Union both financially and by the provision of visiting and Student Rabbis. During subsequent years the Group consolidated its routine, holding fortnightly Friday evening services at the Friends' Meeting House. These services were taken by members, quite often with a sermon or talk delivered by another member of

Council. In January, 1963, the Hon. Lily Montagu died and the Group mourned the loss of its very recently appointed Hon. President. It appears she was not replaced.

In 1965, the Czech Scrolls had been gathered together at the Westminster Synagogue[1] and were on permanent loan to congregations, of which the Bristol Liberal Jewish Group was one, and Polack's House another. It has been a source of spiritual comfort ever since. At this time it was used for Friday evening services, as the Group still did not hold Saturday services. It came from the Synagogue in Kutna Hora in Czechoslovakia, five kilometers from Prague. That building is now (1997) used as a church. (See ill. 37.)

Len Hart last appears in the list of Council members in March, 1963. According to the Bulletin, the last service he led was on 11th February, 1966 and he later he emigrated to Israel. He was held in high regard by many members and, without his influence, Jo Schapiro (and no doubt many others) would not have returned to Judaism. He was a most active member of the Group. He sang beautifully though his speech was marred by a stutter when he became excited.

In 1966, the Group lacked Rabbinic support for the Yom Kippur service. The Bulletin tells us that a panel of readers made an effort worthy of the day and many were impressed by the sincerity of this communal effort.

In 1969, it was proposed the Group change its name to the Bristol and West Progressive Jewish Congregation and this was carried a month later.

At some time in the early 1970s, Mr. Albert Polack, Housemaster of Polack's House, Clifton College, taught the congregation's children and in 1971 he and his wife became members of the Group. In the same issue there was a momentous decision, that Friday evening services should be held weekly, as has been the case ever since. The first Saturday morning service was held on 4th July, 1970, and thus began the tradition of a Sabbath service on the first weekend of every month.

At the A.G.M. in February that year, Mrs. Rosita Rosenberg announced the new scheme of Foster Rabbis for small communities. In April, members were told that Rabbi Dr David Goldstein had been appointed to Bristol and would visit in May. This was a popular choice. He made frequent visits while he held the post.

---

[1] These scrolls and other artifacts were collected in a Prague synagogue. They were intended to be part of an 'exhibition of the Jews, an extinct race', to be put on by the Nazis after the success of their Final Solution. Some time after their defeat in 1945, the building and its treasures were found and brought to the Westminster Synagogue in London.

Mr. David Burnard had been a tower of strength to the community from its beginnings in 1961. He had served as Chairman, Treasurer and Secretary as well as leading the Religion School. He and his wife are remembered today as superb hosts at many congregational functions. After some months of illness he died on 3rd June, 1970. His obituary in the Bulletin recorded that:

> He taught us how to be good Jews and as a person he taught us
> how to be good people. He taught us not by exhortation but by
> example, not by theory but by practice. He taught us and our
> children how to live and in the end, he taught us how to die. He
> was a good man and a kind man – we shall miss him.

When he died, the embryonic Chevra Kadisha of Peter Hyams and Martin Bogod and others were wonderful at arranging his funeral and shiva.[2]

His widow, Josie, remained in Bristol for some time and continued to take a full part in the life of the Congregation until she left for London. She now lives in Hereford and is a member of the small Jewish community in that town.

In August, 1973, the Bulletin stated:

> We have long been conscious that our Scroll is not very worthily
> housed and the Council are now making arrangements for a
> better Ark to be made. This will be a permanent asset, which we
> can keep at Hampton Road and use at all services.

It was made at Colston's School and was plainly functional.

The Bristol and West Progressive Jewish Congregation had been using the Friends' Meeting House in Hampton Road, Bristol, since 1961. The community was growing and started to feel the need for a permanent Synagogue. In 1971 it was proposed to purchase 61, Princess Victoria Street at a total cost of £3,705 for the building and £1,405 for renovations. An Extraordinary General Meeting agreed that subscriptions would rise to £10 per annum for a single person and £16 for family members from 1st November and that the building should be purchased. Unfortunately another buyer was successful.

In November, 1972, Mrs. Hilary Kay was going about her professional business in Easton and saw 43, Bannerman Road for sale. She approached the estate agents and a long-drawn out series of negotiations took place between them and the Building Committee consisting of Hilary Kay, Jo Schapiro and Henry Harris, reaching

---

[2] Recollections of Josie Waldron, late Burnard, whose memories were very helpful in much of this chapter.

completion only in 1974. Members of the Congregation did all the necessary interior work, including laying a concrete floor, installing a new electric light system, painting and decorating. Mr. Albert Polack donated the Ark and the Ner Tamid as they were constructing a new synagogue for Polack's House. This took the place of the first Ark, which continued in use upstairs for the Religion School. A photograph of Jo Shapiro taking the scroll out of the ark appears in ill. 38.

Rabbi Dr. David Goldstein helped with the Consecration Service which was held on 8th February, 1975.[3]

---

[3] Thanks to Peter & Mavis Hyams, David Wolfe and Mr. & Mrs. Henry Singer for information. Also to Jo Schapiro whose old copies of the Bulletin were invaluable. The minute books since 1966 and sundry papers dealing with the purchase of No. 43 Bannerman Road, Easton, Bristol provided further information.

Conclusion

B ristol has never had large numbers to boost its Jewish community, but it has survived well. There were Jews in Bristol before 1290 who had some success until the kings became too greedy. Once again, they flourished from the 1750s. Though numbers ebbed and flowed, new members continually came to revive the community and to keep the congregation strong. Their troubles in 1825/35 and 1893/1896 were undoubtedly due to newcomers with different standards but on both occasions unity was re-established without too much difficulty.

Relations with non-Jewish Bristolians were generally good in spite of the country-wide trouble at the time of the Aliens Act in 1753 which also affected Bristol. The letter from Candidus reporting the consecration of the Synagogue in the Weavers' Hall shows how someone's feelings could change in favour of the Jews from a pleasant experience with another person. In business the association between Lazarus Jacobs and Michael Edkins was trouble-free, assuming that Edkins was not a Jew. Much later, Henry Simmons worked as hard for the Jewish community, of which he was President for many years, as he did for St. James' Parish, where he had his business. Ministers who gave lessons to non-Jews to augment their income included Aaron Levy Green who taught Hebrew language, grammar and literature and the Rev. Meyer Mendelssohn who offered German to residents of Bristol. The Rev. Joseph Levy appears to have been the first Minister to speak to a non-Jewish Group about Judaism, confirmed by the attendance of Jews and many non-Jews at his marriage. In the twentieth century, the Rev. Joseph Abelson lectured to Bible groups in Bristol, Cardiff and Bath and the Rev. Hyman Goodman did likewise at least once in Bristol. Finally and more practically, there was Rachel Harrisberg who not only baked bread for her Jewish customers but also for Harvest Festivals.

The conversionist societies had little success in Bristol in spite of their strong statements. It is, perhaps, surprising that they were only twice answered by the Jewish community in the local papers. The brief confrontation with the National Front immediately after the Second World War was dealt with efficiently by members of Bristol

Hebrew Congregation with help from the Board of Deputies Defence Department in London.

It is clear from the language used in *Jewish Chronicle* and *Jewish World* notices that most Bristol Jews were very assimilated. Hebrew names for Festivals do not occur until the period after the Second World War. This is borne out by the tombstones at the Barton Road Cemetery which at first are mostly in Hebrew; by the mid-1800s there is more English and in particular the date of death is more often according to the English calendar, although some do include the Hebrew year. Further proof is given by the presents sent to members of the Alexander family in spite of their strong commitment to the Synagogue management and High Festival services.

Members of Bristol Hebrew Congregation were either tradesmen or manufacturers served by ministers of high quality, who commenced their careers in Bristol, leaving for the Metropolis and high honours. Whereas in Bath the local press during the conflict to allow Jews to become Members of Parliament was virulently against the move and the City Council petitioned their Member not to vote for the bill, in Bristol the feeling was very different. Four separate petitions in favour of the change were encouraged both by the Town Council and local press. Abraham Alexander was one of the first Jews in the provinces to become a Town Councillor after the passing of the Municipal Reform Act. Thus the name and reputation of Bristol was repeatedly in the public eye through the Jewish press. It is curious, however, that the triumvirate, Abraham Alexander, William Wolfe Alexander and Joseph Abraham were not followed by other members of the Jewish Community on the City Council. It is unlikely that Arthur Albert Levy-Langfield was, in fact, a practising Jew when he joined Bristol Council and thus he has not been included. He was a councillor from 1896 to 1913, when he became an alderman. He died on 18th August 1927 age 65.

Nowadays members are more likely to be lecturers at Bristol University or the University of the West of England or doctors and surgeons at the local hospitals or in general practice. Bristol was always a good place for Jews to live in and one must hope that this will always be so.

In the period covered by this book, there have been three Civic Services: in 1962, 1966 and 1971. No doubt there have been others since that time. The Lord Mayor would attend, accompanied by most, if not all, of the aldermen and councillors. This must be a measure of the improved attitude between the City Council and its Jewish population.

The Rev. Arthur Barnett, in his obituary of the Rev. Joseph Polack, described the Bristol community as being:

... naturally composed of many heterogeneous elements, representative of varying religious outlooks and it was due in no little measure to the profound influence that he exerted as its Chairman that the Congregation remained a solid unit. . . .[1]

It is likely that this is no different nowadays with two separate Congregations. However, they do make attempts at co-operation, through the Liaison Committee founded in 1981, which meets two or three times a year and has members from both communities. Then there is the Western Jewish Social Club which started in the early 1990s as a meeting place for non-working Jewish people of both Congregations. The Club meets at the Progressive Synagogue in Bannerman Road since there is easier access from street level. Davar, the Jewish Institute in Bristol, can be an influence for growth in both communities. It would help if some of the Jews who live in the area but are not committed to either synagogue decide that it is worth joining one or other of them. This should be a great force for the future of Bristol Jewry.

Once the Bristol Hebrew Congregation employed a Minister/Reader and Chazzan, who would double as Shochet and Mohel as required. Only in the 1940s were they reduced to one full-time Minister and since the retirement of Rev. Moddel, they have had to exist with a part-time Rabbi who is also Chaplain to University Jewish students. One hopes that they will be able to employ a full-time Rabbi in future and that, once again, the name of Bristol's Jewish Community will be recorded as a centre of excellence as when the *Jewish Chronicle* said it was:

... the nursery of many of our most distinguished preachers and readers.[2]

---

[1] *Jewish Chronicle*, 23rd September 1932.
[2] Rev. Abraham Barnett's obituary, *Jewish Chronicle*, 29th October 1886.

APPENDIX I

Ministers and Officers of the Bristol Hebrew Congregation

The following list is clearly far from complete. From 1765 to 1803 information comes from rate books and street directories. The Birth Register 1829–1830 & 1849–1893 gives some further useful facts. From 1833 to 1906 the *Jewish Chronicle* is a valuable source and the Congregation's minute books are thereafter.

DATES	MINISTERS
1765–1785:	Isaac Collish or Zevi Hirsch Kalisch
1798–1803:	Moses Levy
1829–1830:	Solomon Levy
1829–1838:	Rev. Abraham Barnett
1833–1835:	Prof. D.M. Isaacs
1838–1851:	Aaron Levy Green
1844–1880:	Rev. Joseph Benjamin
1851–1855:	Rev. Jacob Lindiner
1855–1858:	Rev. Samuel Landeshut
1859–1864:	Rev. Isaac Samuel
1867–1878:	Rev. Meyer Mendelssohn
1871–1878:	Rev. Barnett (Berman) Berliner
1872–1879:	Rev. Abraham Muller
1880–1884:	Rev. David Fay
1880–1893:	Rev. A.H. Eisenberg
1893–1896:	Rev. A.H. Eisenberg at Bridge Street
1893–1896:	Rev. E. Ritblatt at Bridge Street
1885–1889:	Rev. Joseph Leonard Levy, B.A.
1890–1892:	Rev. Moses Hyamson
1894–1895:	Rev. Lewis Mendelssohn, B.A.
1897–1902:	Rev. A.H. Eisenberg
1897–1927:	Rev. Emanuel Ritblatt
1894–1899:	Rev. A. Levinson
1899–1906:	Rev. Joseph Abelson
1907–1916:	Rev. Hyman Goodman
1907–1919:	Rev. Bernard Paletz
1920–1924:	Rev. Arthur Barnett
1925–1934:	Rabbi Harry Swift

198

1934–1944:	Rev. Simon L. Sussman
1935–1947:	Rev. Louis Sanker
1944–1959:	Rev. Freedman
1949–1955:	Rev. H. Lerner
1956–1957:	Rev. Wolfson
1959–1961:	Rabbi Dr. A. Ehrman
1962–1992:	Rev. Max Moddel

The list below is equally incomplete as that for ministers. Except for Barnet Lyon Joseph, whose story comes from Dr. Anthony P. Joseph, all other information is derived from the *Jewish Chronicle* (and occasionally the *Jewish World*) and from February 1903, the Congregation's minute books. Where available, names of Gabbai, Secretary, etc. are included.

DATES	OFFICERS
1824–1835:	Barnet Lyon Joseph.
1844–?:	A. Alexander.
1851–1853:	Levy Levy, president;
	J. Rousseau, gabbai;
	A. Mosely, hon. secretary.
1853:	Joseph Abraham.
1854–1855:	J. Rousseau, gabbai.
1854–1856:	Joseph Michael, parnass.
1856–1859:	Levy Levy, seventh time parnass;
	John Braham, several times gabbai.
1859–1860:	Levy Levy and John Abraham, wardens.
1860–1862:	Moses Blanckensee, parnass;
	John Solomon, gabbai.
1862–1863:	Joseph Michael, president;
	Joseph Platnauer, warden;
	P.D. Alexander, hon. secretary.
1863–1864:	John Solomon, parnass;
	Joseph Platnauer, gabbai.
1864–?:	Levy Levy and Henry Simmons, wardens.
1870–1871:	M.J. Platnauer, president.
1878–1879:	Henry Simmons and S. Platnauer, wardens.
1879–?:	M.Blanckensee, president;
	A. Jessel, vice-president;
	P.D. Alexander, treasurer;
	G. Mosely, hon. secretary.
1884:	J. Rousseau, president.
1884–1890:	Henry Simmons, president;
	S. Platnauer, vice-president;
	Jack S. Platnauer, hon. secretary.

199

1890–1891:	John Jessel, president; Maurice Nathan, vice-president; Jack S. Platnauer, hon. secretary.
1891–1895:	Henry Simmons, president; Samuel Platnauer, vice-president; Jack S. Platnauer, hon. secretary.
1895–1897:	I.M. Jacobs, president; A. Lazarus, vice-president; Frank Goldman, hon. secretary.
1897–1898:	I.M. Jacobs, president; S. Lazarus, vice-president; Frank Goldman, hon. secretary.
1898–1903:	S. Lazarus, president.
Feb. 1903:	I.M. Jacobs, president; M. Epstein, vice-president and hon. secretary.
Jan. 1904:	S. Barder joined as hon. secretary.
Dec. 1904:	M. Fine, president; L. Goldberg, hon. secretary.
Jan. 1906:	L. Fine joined as vice-president.
Dec. 1906:	M. Nathan, president; S. Lazarus, vice-president; F. Goldman, hon. secretary.
Dec. 1907:	M. Bertish, vice-president; A. Goldsmid, hon. secretary.
Dec. 1908:	H. Barder, hon. secretary.
Dec. 1909:	Samuel Epstein, hon. secretary.
July 1911:	M. Bertish, president; S. Lazarus, vice-president.
Jan. 1913:	M. Nathan, president; S. Lazarus, vice-president; S.H. Jacobs, hon. secretary.
Nov. 1913:	S. Fine, president.
Dec. 1913:	S. Lazarus, president; S. Fine, vice-president; S.H. Jacobs, hon. secretary.
Nov. 1915:	D. Levy, vice-president; A.J. Goldsmid, hon. secretary.
Jan. 1917:	H.R. Levy, hon. secretary.
Jan. 1919:	D. Levy, president; P. Cirelstein, gabbai; H.R. Levy, hon. secretary; A. Harrisberg, parnass.
Feb. 1919:	Dr. S. Brodetsky, president; A. Harrisberg, vice-president; A.J. Jacobs, treasurer; H. Barder, hon. secretary.

Dec. 1919:	Rev. J. Polack, chairman of meeting to 1935; S. Rowland, president; A. Harrisberg, vice-president; H. Salanson, hon. secretary.
Nov. 1920:	S. Rowland, president; W.S. Morris, treasurer; H. Salanson, hon. secretary
Dec. 1921:	Frank Goldman, president; Morris and Salanson re-elected.
Dec. 1922:	A. Harrisberg, vice-president, others re-elected.
Feb. 1924:	L. Ryness, president; A. Harrisberg, vice-president; F. Marcus, hon. secretary; W.S. Morris, treasurer.
Dec. 1924:	B. Spielman, treasurer.
Dec. 1925:	C.J. Tanchan, president; B. Spielman, vice-president and treasurer; F. Marcus, hon. secretary.
Oct. 1926:	N. Sacof, hon. secretary.
Oct. 1927:	W. Fox, president; B. Spielman, vice-president and treasurer; N. Sacof, hon. secretary.
Nov. 1928:	Officers all re-elected.
Nov. 1929:	B. Spielman, president; L.A. Melcher, treasurer; Maxwell Levy, hon. secretary.
Dec. 1930:	H. Fox, president, with L.A. Melcher and Maxwell Levy.
Jan. 1932:	A. Mass, president, with L.A. Melcher and Maxwell Levy.
Mar. 1934:	S. Fox, president; W. Dembo, treasurer; M. Miel, hon. secretary.
Jan. 1935:	A. Mass, president; H. Amsel, hon. secretary.
Feb. 1936:	A. Mass, president; Maxwell Levy, treasurer; I. Freeland, hon. secretary.
Jan. 1937:	Officers all re-elected.
Feb. 1938:	C.J. Tanchan, president; B. Spielman, vice-president.
Feb. 1939:	B. Spielman, president with Maxwell Levy and I. Freeland.

Thereafter officers re-elected until:

Aug. 1942:	B. Spielman, president; S. Jacobs, treasurer; I. Freeland, hon. secretary.

Jan. 1945:   B.W. Dembo, president;
                  joined S. Jacobs and I. Freeland
May 1946:   A.E. Morris, treasurer, replaced S. Jacobs.
Apr. 1948:   S. Jacobs, president;
                  C.J. Tanchan, vice-president and treasurer;
                  A.E. Morris, hon. secretary.
May 1949:   Officers re-elected.
July 1951:   A. Mass, treasurer;
                  A. Steinberg, hon. secretary joined S. Jacobs.
Oct. 1954:   C.J. Tanchan, vice-president;
                  A.E. Morris, treasurer;
                  M.N. Mass, hon. secretary joined S. Jacobs.
Thereafter officers re-elected until:
Apr. 1958:   Alan Cohen, vice-president.
Mar. 1960:   Prof. J. Yoffey, president;
                  Alan Cohen, vice-president;
                  A.E. Morris, treasurer;
                  L. Gould, hon. secretary.
Mar. 1961:   S. Bloom, hon. secretary.
Mar. 1962:   Officers all re-elected.
Mar. 1963:   Alan Cohen, president;
                  Dr. S. Curwen, vice-president;
                  A.E. Morris, treasurer;
                  J. Burke, hon. secretary.
Thereafter officers re-elected until:
Nov. 1966:   J. Burke, president;
                  M.C. Berkovitch, vice-president;
                  A.E. Morris, treasurer;
                  Dr. S. Curwen, hon. secretary.
Dec. 1967:   L.G. Gould, president;
                  M.C. Berkovitch, vice-president.
Dec. 1968:   L.G. Gould, president;
                  S. Bloom, vice-president;
                  M.C. Berkovitch, treasurer;
                  Dr. S. Curwen, hon. secretary.
Nov. 1969:   Dr. S. Curwen, president;
                  S. Bloom, vice-president;
                  M.C. Berkovitch, treasurer;
                  I. Kushner, hon. secretary.
Feb. 1971:   M.C. Berkovitch, treasurer;
                  S. Bloom, vice-president;
                  I. Kushner, hon. secretary.

Jewish Burial Ground, Barton Road, Bristol

(Original research by David and Simon Jacobs and Lynne Edwards on 19th February 1984. Update by Judith Samuel [1989 or 1990], additions by Dr. B. Susser on 30th July 1992.)

Starting from the left-hand side by the warehouse wall. See plan on page 215.

All are standing stones except where mentioned otherwise.

Row I

1 Dinah, daughter of Barnett and Maria Lazarus who departed this life March 6th, 1944-Adar 11th, 5704. Sadly missed by all. May her dear soul rest in peace. HEB. Betulah Dina daughter of Dov.

2 In loving memory of Julia Champeny, wife of Herbert and mother of Lewis Champeny; born 1867; died November 17th, 1920-Kislev 6th, 5681. May her dear soul rest in peace.

3 In loving memory of Hannah Levy, widow of Solomon Levy, who departed this life April 2nd, 1912, in her 79th year. Her children rise up and call her blessed – Proverbs, 31:28. HEB. Hannah wife of Solomon.

4 In affectionate remembrance of Nelson Platnauer who died on September 30th, 1903–5664, aged 80. May his soul rest in peace. HEB. Nathan son of Joseph.

5 In memory of Annie Lyon, of North Street, Stokes Croft, daughter of the late Solomon and Rosetta Lyon died 20th June, 1903, aged 54 years. Peace to her soul. HEB. Daughter of Solomon.

Row II

6 HEB. Joseph son of Jacob the Priest.

7 Sacred to the memory of Isaac Monat Jacobs who entered into rest July 29th, 1914/Ab 6th, 5674. HEB. Isaac son of Abraham Ephraim.

8 To the memory of Hinda Sarah Campbell, beloved wife of Aaron Campbell who departed this life August 14th, 1914/Ab 22nd, 5674. This stone is affectionately dedicated by her sorrowing husband, sons, daughters and grandchildren. May her soul rest in peace. 'Her children rise up and call her blessed, her husband also, and praise her.' HEB. Hinda Sarah daughter of Abraham Ephraim, wife of Aaron son of Isaac.

9   In loving memory of Aaron Campbell who departed this life July 12th, 1926, aged 69 years. This stone is erected by his beloved sons, daughters, sons-in-law, and grandchildren. May his soul rest in peace. A founder of Achai Brit. HEB. Aaron son of Isaac.

10 [Square plinth with writing on all four sides] In loving memory of Samuel Lazarus, son of Barnett and Maria Lazarus who died March 6th, 1921, aged 63 years. May his soul rest in peace. 'The Lord gave and the Lord hath taken away, blessed be the name of the Lord.' HEB. Samuel son of Dov.

11 In loving memory of Henry Simmons who died January 16th, 1904, aged 77 years, HEB. Tsvi son of Joseph: and his beloved wife Selina who died May 15th, 1920, in her 73rd year, HEB. Shoshana daughter of Jacob. Works not words be proof of love.

Row III

12 Sacred to the memory of Jacob Schwartz died March 24th, 1895, aged 66. May his dear soul rest in peace. HEB. Jacob son of Moses.

13 Sacred to the memory of Maurice Michael who departed this life May 2nd, 1893–5653, aged 83 years. May his soul rest in peace. HEB. Meir son of Joseph.

14 Sacred to the memory of Michael Joseph Platnauer who died February 26th, 1893-Adar 10th, 5653, aged 75. A devoted husband, a self-sacrificing father and trustworthy friend., HEB. Michael Joseph son of Joseph.
    Also of his wife Sophie who died February 7th, 1896, aged 64. Her works praise her in the gates, HEB. Blumah daughter of Aaron Jacob.

15 [Square pillar] Sacred to the memory of Samuel Platnauer, a beloved husband and father, who departed this life June 17th, 1900-Sivan 20th, 5660, in his 80th year. 'He did justly, loved mercy and walked humbly with his God'. HEB. Samuel son of Joseph.
    And of his dearly beloved wife, Fanny, who passed from this life Kislev 28th, 5666-December 26th, 1905, aged 74. 'To live in the hearts of those we leave behind is not to die.' **Side panel**: 'Lord I have hoped for thy salvation and done thy commandments; yea, though I walk through the valley of the shadow of death I will fear no evil, for thou art with me.'

A & B: [Fallen stones]

16 In loving memory of George Harris who died March 1st, 1891, aged 53 years. May his soul rest in peace. HEB. Elchanan son of Michael Tsvi.

17 Elizabeth Churchill died 26th November, 1891, aged 72 years.

204

C [In pieces]

18 Sacred to the memory of Rose, relict of the late Frederick Levy of Birmingham, who departed this life April 29th, 1890–5650, aged 64. HEB. Rose daughter of Solomon.

19 Sacred to the memory of Abraham Solomon, died 28th April, 1890–5650, aged 35. 'Help me, O Lord my God, O save me according to thy mercy.' HEB. Abraham son of Joel.

20 In beloved memory of Maurice Moore who departed this life 30th March, 1899, aged 77 years. A man of truth, sincere and pure, he walked with God, upright and sure, in age full green and ripe he died, we mourned his loss, we grieved, we sighed. May his soul rest in peace.

21 In loving memory of Rosetta Sarah, wife of Maurice Moore, died 19th January, 1887–5647.

D [Completely eroded]

Between Row III and IV

22 [facing warehouse] In memory of Moses Aaron Finklestein (Jacob Saunders) died June 23rd, 1880-Tammuz 14th, 5640, aged 46 years. HEB. Moses Aaron son of Abraham. [Eroding]

Row IV

23 In memory of Hannah Zachari who departed this life December 2nd, 1881–5642, aged 75 years. HEB. Hannah daughter of Samuel, wife of Mordecai.

24 [A tall stone] In memory of Adam Louis Sametband, who died January 16th, 1883–5643, aged 45 years. HEB. Abraham Yerachmiel son of Ze'ev Isaac from Warsaw.

25 In loving memory of Isaac (John) Phillips who departed this life June 11th, 1883-Sivan 6th, 5643, aged 25 years. HEB. Isaac son of Mordecai the Priest.

26 In memory of Fanny Berce who departed this life December 13th, 1883–5644, aged 64 years. HEB. Halshah Feiga daughter of Meir.

E [Totally illegible]

27 In memory of Fradella Schwartz died 22nd January, 1886. HEB. Freda daughter of Jacob. [Deteriorating]

28 [Huge stone, falling] In memory of Miriam, wife of Maurice Michael, died 3rd April, 1886–5646, aged 67 years. May her dear soul rest in peace . . . [rest illegible] HEB. Miriam daughter of Solomon, wife of Meir.

29 In loving memory of Rebecca, dearly beloved wife of Joseph Hellering, who died July 20th, 1897, aged 62 years. HEB. Rebecca daughter of Moses Aryeh.

Also in everlasting and devoted memory of Joseph Hellering who entered into rest May 28th, 1910/5670, aged 80 years. HEB. Joseph son of Ze'ev.

30 [generally illegible] . . . Michael A. Jessel . . . February . . . in his 88th year. HEB. Michael son of Nathaniel, died 23th Shevat (5656). (*Jewish Chronicle* obit: 7th February, 1896)

F [illegible]

31 Sacred to the memory of Henrietta Sternberg who departed this life Tebeth 18th, 5672-January 8th, 1912, aged 90. 'I will say of the Lord, he is my refuge and my fortress, my God, in His will I trust.' HEB. Marat Hannah daughter of Simon.

32 Sacred to the memory of David Sternberg who departed this life September 5th, 1889-Ellul 9th, 5649, aged 72. 'Into thy hand I commit my spirit, thou hast redeemed me, O Eternal God of Truth.' 'The memory of the just is blessed.' HEB. David son of Solomon.

Row V

33 In loving memory of Amelia Solomon who departed this life July 3rd, 1893–5653, aged 60 years. 'I will lay me down in peace and take my rest for it is thou, Lord, only, that makes me dwell in safety.' Verily there is a reward for the righteous. HEB. Malkah daughter of Jacob.

34 In loving memory of Joel, beloved husband of Henrietta Solomon, who died Sivan 27th, 5651-July 3rd, 1891, aged 69 years. 'The Lord is good, a stronghold in the day of trouble'. Nahum, 1:7. HEB. Joel son of Simon.

35 In loving memory of Henrietta Solomon, wife of Joel Solomon, died December 3rd, 5649–1888, aged 56 years. Lord, I have hoped for thy salvation and done they commandments. HEB. Yuta daughter of Solomon the Levite.

36 In affectionate remembrance of Bertha Jessel who departed this life November 17th, 1888-Kislev 14th, 5649, aged 38 years. [Deteriorating]

G [Illegible, broken]

37 Maria Sternberg, born Nissan 13th, 5589-April 16th, 1829; died March 2nd, 1906, aged 77 years. 'He only is my rock and my salvation', Psalm LXII: 6. HEB. Miriam daughter of Simon.

38 Sacred to the memory of Deborah Jessel who died November 3rd, 1883–5644. HEB. Betulah Deborah daughter of Michael.

39 Sacred to the memory of Moses Blanckensee who died November 3rd, 1883-Cheshvan 3rd, 5644, aged 72 years. HEB. Moses son of Judah the Levite.

206

40 In loving memory of Mary Anne Blanckensee who departed this life December 8th, 1891–5652, aged 72 years. HEB. Miriam daughter of ??? [Deteriorating]

41 In memory of Matilda Lazarus died March 24th, 1883–5643, aged 67 years. HEB. ? daugher of Eliezer.

42 Sacred to the memory of Joseph Rothschild died January 4th, 1881–5641, aged 75 years. HEB. Joseph son of Samuel.

43 In memory of Rosetta, widow of the late Solomon Lyon who departed this life April 2nd, 1880-Nisan 21st, 5640, aged 66 years.

44 Sacred to the memory of Joseph Benjamin who departed this life 29th Shevat, 5640-11th February, 1880. For nearly 40 years 2nd Reader and Faithful Servant of the Bristol Congregation, he earned the love and commanded the respect of all who knew him. May his dear soul rest in peace. HEB. Joseph son of Benjamin.

45 Fanny, beloved wife of Barnet Harris, died Nissan 5th, 563(5)9.

46 Elizabeth Rousseau, A.E. 63 obit December 2nd, 1889.

H [Completely eroded]

Between Row V and VI

47 [Lying against warehouse wall] In loving memory of Minna Rebecca, daughter of Joseph and Sophia Polack, died February 7th, 1891–5651, aged 2 years. 'The Lord called the child,' 1 Samuel.

48 [Facing warehouse] HEB. Marat Bila daughter of Matathias.

Row VI

49 Sacred to the memory of Samuel John Morse, who departed this life September 4th, 1878-Elul 6th, 5638, aged 15 years. HEB. Samuel Jacob son of Abraham.

50 In memory of Joseph Michael, died January 1st, 1878-Teveth 26th, 5638, aged 75 years. HEB. Joseph son of Meir.

51 Sacred to the memory of Matilda, for upwards of fifty years the devoted wife of Joseph Rothschild, died July 22nd, 1878–5638, aged 71, by whom and her bereaved children this stone has been erected in loving remembrance. HEB. Martel daughter of Abraham.

52 [Eroded] . . . memory of . . . Michael, . . . life . . . 88. HEB. Mordecai son of Michael, died Tuesday, 21 . . . 1831.

53 Sacred to the memory of Levy Levy who departed this life April 5th, 1876, aged 86 years. HEB. Levi son of Moses.

And Elizabeth Levy, widow of the above, who departed this life November 4th, 5637–1876, aged 79 years. HEB. Marat Bila daughter of Abraham the Priest.

54 [Eroded] In loving memory of Solomon . . . 1876 or 1878.

I [Illegible]

55 In loving memory of Rose Goldman who died September 3rd, 1894, aged 52 years. Peace to her soul. HEB. Marat Blumah wife of Naphtali Ze'ev.

56 In loving memory of William Goldman who died March 17th, 1906, aged 64 years. HEB. Naphtali Ze'ev son of Tsvi, the Levite.

57 Sacred to the remembrance of John Solomon who departed this life June 10th, 1886. We will not forget, we loved thee living, . . . Death took thee suddenly, we'll not (forget). Our earthly loss is thy eternal gain. May his soul rest in peace. HEB. Jacob son of Simon. [Eroding]

58 In affectionate remembrance of our dear aunt Jane Moore, who was gathered to her people Sivan 4, 5699, aged 90, May 22, 1939. HEB. Marat Sheina daughter of Menahem.

59 In loving memory of Abraham Morse who departed this life July 18th, 1888, aged 53 years. May his blessed soul rest in peace. HEB. Abraham son of Samuel.

60 In loving memory of Clara, widow of Abraham Morse, who departed this life August 21st, 1891–5651 aged 59 years. May her blessed soul rest in peace. HEB. ? daughter of Jacob.

Row VII

61 In affectionate remembrance of Edward Abraham Alexander, second son of William Wolfe Alexander and Angelina Israel Alexander, who died on the 9th of July, 5637/1877 aged, 39. [From Collyer Ferguson papers, tombstone no longer legible] HEB. Abraham son of Jacob Ze'ev, died 9th Av, (5)637 [19 July, 1877].

62 Sacred to the memory of Joseph Michael who departed this life January 6th, 1888–5648, aged 75 years. Deeply lamented by his many children and numerous friends. May his soul rest in peace. HEB. Joseph son of Joseph.

63 [Square plinth with broken pillar] Sacred to the memory of Sara, deeply beloved daughter of Samuel and Fanny Platnauer, who departed this life September 22nd, 1887-Tishree 4th, 5648. **Side panel**: This lovely bud, so young and fair, . . . lived but to show how sweet a flower in paradise would bloom.

J [Totally eroded]

64 [The next two stones are surrounded by an iron railing] In loving memory of Barnett Lazarus who died July 10th, 1894-Tamuz 6th, 5654,

aged 70 years. May his dear soul rest in peace. the Lord gave and the
Lord hath taken away, blessed be the name of the Lord. HEB. Dov son
of Abraham.

65 In loving memory of Maria, widow of Barnett Lazarus, who departed
this life April 13th, 1902-Nisan 6th, 5662, aged 75 years. May her dear
soul rest in peace. Into thy hand, I commend my spirit, the Lord is with
me, I will not fear. HEB. Eshet Miriam daughter of Abraham.

66 [Small stone] In memory of Jacob Moses Alman who departed this life
January 2nd, 1876, aged 88 years. HEB. Abraham Jacob son of Moses
Joseph.

67 In memory of Solomon Levy, died July 30th, 1875, aged 50 years. HEB.
Solomon son of Abraham the Levite.

68 HEB. Tsvi son of Jacob, died aged 68 on 16th Nisan, 5635 (21st April,
1875).

69 HEB. Solomon Zalman son of ?Abraham, died aged 19, on Wednesday
24th Adar, 5635? (probably 5638 = 27th February, 1878.)

K [Illegible]

70 In memory of Michael Alman departed this life August 6th, 1874, aged
52 years. HEB. Meir son of Abraham Jacob.

L & M: [Illegible]

Row VIII

71 Sacred to the memory of Charlotte Alexander died June 7th, 1912-Sivan
22nd, 5672. For thou art my help, O Lord God, thou art my trust from
my youth; Psalm LXXI:5. HEB. Betulah Hayah daughter of Jacob Ze'ev
the Levite.

72 Sacred to the memory of Rosetta Emma Alexander born May 14th,
1831, died September 22nd, 1910-Ellul 18th, 5670. Blessed is everyone
that feareth the Lord, that walketh in his ways; Psalm 120:1. HEB.
Betulah Reizel Emma daughter of Jacob Ze'ev the Levite.

73 Sacred to the memory of Annette Lydia Alexander, born May 14th,
1831, died September 22nd, 1880-Tishri 17th, 5641. May her soul rest
in peace. I will both lay me down in peace and sleep for the Lord only
makes me dwell in safety; Psalm 4:89. HEB. Hannah Leah daughter of
Jacob Ze'ev the Levite.

74 Sacred to the memory of Angelina, relict of William Wolfe Alexander,
born 15th April, 1808-18th Nissan, 5568; died 18th December, 1882-
8th Tebeth, 5643. Her children rise up and call her blessed; Proverb
XXI:28. HEB. Halshah Angelina daughter of Joseph Israel.

75 In memory of William Wolfe Alexander who departed this life on
Saturday, August 1st, 5634–1874, aged 76. HEB. Jacob Ze'ev son of
Asher the Levite.

76 Sacred to the memory of Isaac Frankel Alexander, son of Abraham and Matilda Alexander, who died at Clifton on 18th June, 1876, aged 40 years. HEB. Isaac son of Abraham the Levite.

Row IX

N & O [Totally eroded]

77 [Flat stone] Sacred to the memory of Rebecca Michael who departed this life August 11th, 5633–1873, aged 51 years.

78 In memory of Julia, youngest daughter of Maurice and Miriam Michael, died February 10th, 5627–1867, aged 12 years.

79 [Flat stone] To the beloved memory of John Solomon who departed this life November 6th, 5629–1868, aged 79 years. 'Return unto thy rest, O my soul, the . . . shalt bountifully . . .' [Eroding]

80 In memory of Joseph Hart who departed this life December 16th, 5629–1868, aged 72 years. [eroding]

81 [Pillar memorial, most plaques have fallen off] Joseph Platnauer, who departed this life 13th August, 1871, aged 97 years.

82 In memory of Solomon Lyon departed this life February 1st, 5631–1871, aged 65 years.

P [Illegible]

Row X

83 Julia Hart

Q R S T & U [All flat stones, illegible]

84 In memory of Isaac Solomon who departed this life October 15th, 1872–5633, aged 53 years.

85 In affectionate remembrance of Louis Lionel, fourth son of Joseph and Matilda Rothschild, who departed this life 6th July, 1865, aged 23.

86 . . . aged 20 . . . [otherwise illegible]

87 [Flat stone – eroding] In memory of Henrietta Braham departed September 9th, 5603–1842, aged 63.

V [Illegible]

88 Phoeby Lewvy, relict of M. Lewvy, who departed this life Dec. . ., 5607–1846.

89 In memory of John Braham departed this life August 14th, 5624–1864, aged 64.

Row XI

90 In memory of an affectionate mother, obit 21st December, 5603–1842, as a tribute of love by her sons, John, James and George Braham. HEB. Rosa daughter of Isaac.

W [Illegible]
91 In memory of Henry Essinger departed this life October 19th, 1854, aged 30 years. [Eroding]
92 Samuel Rotchchield who departed this life July the 24th, 5615–1855, aged 72 years. HEB. Samuel son of Isaac.
93 Joseph Alexander Millerman departed this life April 3rd, 5613–1853, aged 36 years. HEB. Alexander son of Abraham, died 25 Adar Sheni, 5613.
94 HEB. Matathias son of Moses, died 28 Sivan, 5612 (= Tuesday, 15 June, 1852).
95 In memory of Fanny Platnauer who departed this life March 18th, 5612–1852. HEB. Betulah Frieda daughter of Joseph.
96 Sacred to the memory of Simon Solomon who departed this life September 21st, 1856, aged . . . HEB. Simon son of Solomon. [Eroding]
X [Flat stone, totally eroded]
97 In memory of Ellen, beloved wife of Isaac Solomon, departed this life June 9th, 5623–1863. HEB. Eshet Rebecca Telza daughter of Joel, wife of Isaac son of Samuel.
Y [Flat stone, eroded]
98 HEB. Mrs. Gutla, daughter of Asher the Levite, wife of Joel son of Isaac.

Row XII

99 Morris ?? , 1861. HEB. of Faringdon, Meir son of Eliezer, died 20 Iyyar, 5621 (= Tuesday, 30th April, 1861).
100 In memory of Caroline Jacobs departed this life February 10th, 5624–1864. HEB. Kreinala daugher of Isaac.
101 Rosetta ? Marks. HEB. Reichka daughter of Moses, wife of ? George Marks.
102 In memory of Matilda, beloved wife of Abraham Alexander . . . 15th March, 1859. HEB. Telza daughter of Isaac.
103 In memory of Abraham Alexander, who departed this life at Clifton on the 22nd of July, 1870–5630, in his 81st year. He represented Russia as Consul in the city of Bristol for forty-two years. HEB. Abraham son of Asher the Levite.
104 [Flat stone] Sacred to the memory of Charlotte, wife of Jacob Moses Alman, who departed this life on the 13th day of Shebat, 5619–18th January, 1859, aged 75, in whom were united the virtues of a daughter, wife, mother, sister and friend, with a pious and fervent trust in the Great God of Israel.

211

Z [Flat stone, illegible]

105 [Flat stone] . . . Solomon Joel . . . HEB. Joel son of Isaac, buried 27th Kislev, 5610. [erosion nearly complete]

106 [Flat stone] To the memory of Sarah, the beloved wife of John Solomon, departed this life October 3rd, 5611, aged 43 years.

107 Joseph Solomon obit December 25th, 5610–1849, HEB. Died Asarah B'Tevet, 5610 = Tuesday, 25 December, 1849)

AA [Standing stone, now on the ground, illegible]

108 In memory of Martha Chapman, who departed this life July 17th, 5615–1855, aged 37 years. HEB. Betulah ? Motak daughter of Moses.

109 In memory of Jane Chapman, who died 2nd November, 1850, aged 74 years, wife of the late Joseph Chapman. HEB. Beracha or Bluma daughter of Moses son of Solomon.

BB [Illegible – could be Joseph Chapman?]

110 To the memory of Sarah, the beloved wife of John Solomon, departed this (life) October 3rd, 5611, aged 43 years. HEB. Sarah daughter of Abraham, wife of Jacob son of Meir.

Row XIII

111 [Eroded except:] . . . to the memory of Lionel Emdin . . .

112 Abraham Levy who departed this life September 2nd, 5607–1847. HEB. Abraham son of Moses.

CC [Flat stone, illegible]

113 Lydia Mosely departed this life Saturday, December 27th, 5605–1844, aged 60; HEB. A woman of valour, Leah daughter of Isaac.
And in memory of Bessie, daughter of A. and E. Mosely, died December 17th, 5615–1854, aged 2 years. HEB. Bila daughter of Abraham.

114 Sacred to the memory of Rosetta, wife of Simon Solomon, who departed this life May 20th, 5607–1847, aged 56 years. HEB. Reiza daughter of Abraham, wife of Simon (?).

115 [First of three pillar memorials] In memory of Joseph Frankel Alexander, Royal Hanoverian Consul for the City of Bristol for 31 years, who departed this life on the 27th day of Cheshvan, 5609–23rd November, 1848 aged 61 years. HEB. Joseph Frankel son of Asher the Levite.

DD [Illegible]

116 To the memory of Joseph Alexander who departed this life on the 3rd day of Sivan, A.D. 5571–26th May, 1811, aged 99 years. HEB. Anshel son of Joseph Moses Frankel the Levite.

117 Gertrude Nathan, ?1850. HEB. relict of Solomon Nathan died ? October, 5610 aged 38, Gella daughter of Moses.
EE FF & GG: [Illegible]

Remaining tombstones along right hand wall, *only stones with legible inscriptions have been noted*

118 To the memory of Lissman Lazaruss who departed this life July 13th, 5609–1849. HEB. Lipman son of Eliazar drowned in the waters.
119 HEB. Abraham son of Simon, the righteous Priest, died 17 Sivan, ...
120 HEB. Nehunia son of Avraham died on 18th Kislev, 5553 (Monday 3rd December, 1793), aged 96 years.
121 HEB. Mrs. ? daughter of Jacob, wife of Lekkish, died 2nd day New Moon, Heshvan, 5523 (18th October, 1762).
122 HEB. Woolf Benjamin, born Falmouth, Cornwall, died 9th October, 1851 (or 1831?).
123 . . . e Ballin, died the 9th of Shebat, 5563-1st February, 1803, aged 57 years.
124 Henry Emanuel Ansell, son of Wolfe & Phoebe Ansell, of Pontypool, who departed this life March 5th, 5601/1841, aged 11 years.
125 HEB. ? daughter of Isaac, wife of Judah Leib, died the intermediate Sabbath of Passover, 5533 (10th April, 1773).

Remaining tombstones along the back wall

126 [Right hand corner] M.S. Lazarus departed this life on Sunday, September 5th, 5622–1851, erected by his children 5652–1891. HEB. Moshe Eliezer son of Samuel.
127 To Miriam Jackson. HEB. died 22 Sivan, 5582 (11th June, 1812). Also Jacob Jackson. HEB. died 5 Adar, 5598 (2nd March, 1838).
128 In memory of Betsy Solomon, relict of Solomon Solomon, native of Falmouth, aged 68 years. HEB. Beilah, daughter of Isaachar Jakob, wife of Isaac son of Israel the Levite.
Also in memory of Solomon Solomon who died and is interred at Lisbon the 25th day of Shebat, 5579-20th February, 1819, aged 55.
129 Philip Morris, died at Abergavenny the 24th June, 1841, aged 59 years. HEB. Pheivish son of Moses.
130 In memory of Joseph Barnett, departed this life February 17th, 5600–1840, aged 38 years. HEB. Joseph son of Isaachar.
131 To the memory of Catherine, Relic of the late Moses Dight, who departed this life January 22nd, 5603–1843, aged 73. HEB. Gitel, daughter of Asher the Priest, wife of Abraham Moses son of Meir Dight.

213

Remaining tombstones along the left hand wall

132 Sacred to the memory of Mr. Abraham Symons, who departed this life June 10th, 5589–1829, A.M., aged 78 years. HEB. Avraham son of Simon.

133 [Left hand corner] In memory of Joseph Emdin who departed this life July 12th, 1851, aged 57.

JEWISH BURIAL GROUND, BARTON ROAD, BRISTOL

Row numbers

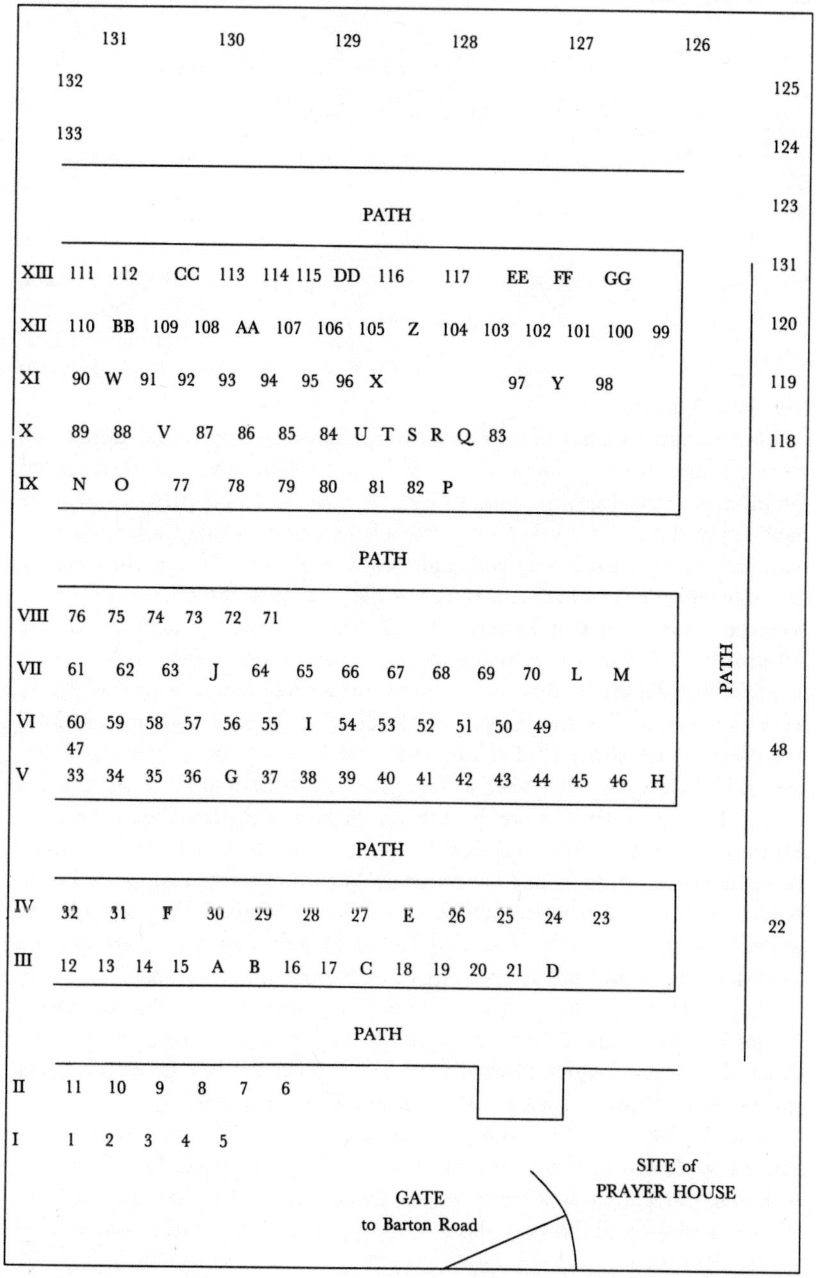

```
        131        130        129        128        127      126
    132                                                               125

    133                                                               124
    _____

                            PATH                                    123

XIII  111  112     CC   113  114 115 DD  116      117    EE  FF  GG   131

XII   110  BB  109 108  AA  107 106 105  Z   104 103 102 101 100  99  120

XI     90  W  91  92   93   94   95  96  X              97   Y   98   119

X      89  88  V  87   86   85   84  U  T  S  R  Q  83                118

IX     N   O      77   78   79   80     81  82  P

                            PATH

VIII   76  75  74  73  72  71

VII    61  62  63   J    64   65   66   67  68  69   70   L   M

VI     60  59  58  57  56  55  I  54  53  52  51  50  49
       47                                                            48
V      33  34  35  36   G   37   38   39  40  41  42  43  44  45  46  H

                            PATH

IV     32   31   F   30   29   28   27   E   26   25   24   23        22

III    12  13  14  15   A   B  16  17   C  18  19  20  21   D

                            PATH

II     11  10  9   8   7   6

I      1   2   3   4   5
                                                        SITE of
                                                     PRAYER HOUSE
                            GATE
                         to Barton Road
```

PATH (vertical, right side)

215

Letters from Mrs. Rachael Brandon to Mrs. Angelina Alexander

Mackay's Hotel,
19 Princes St.,
Edinborough[1]
July 7th, 1833

My dear Angelina,

I wrote you this day week from Liverpool which I make no doubt you received and trust it found you, William, Robert and my dear grand Children in perfect health. Thank God, we have all [kept] perfectly well, we have enjoyed our Tour very much. We left Liverpool Sunday last, I must say with some regret for it was with difficulty I could get excused from dining that day with Lewin Mozley, it is impossible to express the attention we have received from all of that Family. Mr. Charles Mozley, the night before we left sent your Father a very polite letter, saying should it be his fate to meet us again how happy he shall be to renew our acquaintance, begged when we write we would give his respects to William and thank him for his kind introduction; he also included two letters of Introduction to friends of his, one in Edinborough, the other in Glasgow, which he hoped we should find useful. They all regretted our having [to go and] said they should be most happy to see more of us and from us I must own to you I like the family exceedingly well from what I have seen and heard of them. I compare Lewis' Wife to you in her manners and Elias's Wife to Matilda, they are all very genteel, live in good stile. The Old Father and Mother I lunched with on Saturday, they could not see me before as the old gentleman had been very ill, they seem plain, chatty and good kind of people. One of the sons being Parnas he asked your Father if he would go to Synagogue, he did so, an offer which they seemed much pleased with. We supped at Elias' on Friday night and we parted quite pleased with each others acquaintance.

Now for Mr. Franklin who I could get no rest from, and was at last obliged to dine with them on Saturday last, the young man himself is very well, but the Father is a most vulgar looking man. We had an excellent Dinner, and they all did everything in their power to make us comfortable. I

---

[1] Mrs. Brandon's spelling has been retained throughout.

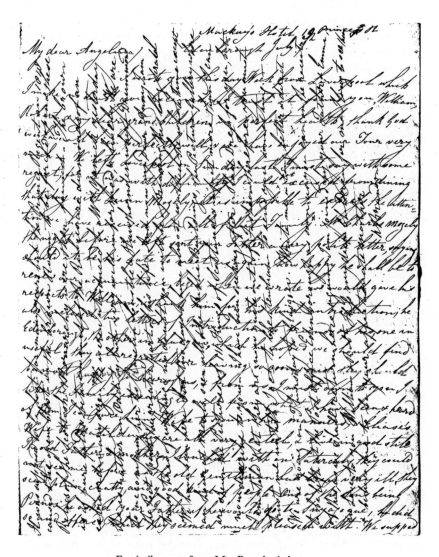

Facsimile page from Mrs Brandon's letter.

really think the young man is jealous of Mozley, for he paid Emma every attention, danced with her, wished her to join his Sister and himself, and go to the Theatre, and to the Races, they both entreated me to let her return in September as they are then very gay in Liverpool. All I refused, I do not like quite so much attention. Mozely is attentive and gentlemanly, the other intruding, and there is a very great difference in their Families throughout. Old Vanovan and his Daughter dined at Franklins, a lady from Holland who sang and played beautifully and 2 French Gentlemen were of the party. We did not leave there until one o'clock.

Now for our journey from Liverpool. We arrived at Bowness in Lancaster, stayed there two days, we went in a Boat on the Lake of Windermere. The scenery is Lovely and the water calm. We landed at two of the inhabited Islands and were rowed about for three hours. The sun shone on the mountains and we were delighted with our luck. The next day we went on the Keswick Lake, one of the Mountains here is supposed to be 3,000 feet above the level of the sea. We landed to see the fall of Lador, our boat Man, a fine handsome fellow, played on the Key Bugle to shew the effect of the echo on some part of the Lake; after which we fished on the Lake. Emma caught several, so did your Father, but I was left minus. We next proceeded to Penrith, Carlisle and Longholm, this last place is the first town in Scotland. Here they speak broad scotch and all the middling people go barefooted, they tuck up their gowns and you see nothing but their flannel pettycoats and their bare feet, they wear no shoes, nor stockings, but their Gowns and Hats, which are made of Plaid are good. They cut an odd appearance and you can scarcely understand what they say. We arrived at Edinborough on Sunday evening. It is truly a splendid City, and the largest I ever saw next to London. The Houses are curiously built, some six and seven stories high, with different families living in them. There are no street doors to them, but you at once ascend a narrow stone staircase, after getting up half way in some of them you would be surprised to see what large rooms they contain. We saw Holyrood House or Palace; it was the burial place of the Kings of Scotland. They shewed us the apartments where Queen Mary was sitting with Rizzio at supper when her Husband Darnly and his accomplices rushed in and murdered the former, Darnly being jealous of him. We also visited the Castle; there is but little shewn here except the Room where Mary, Queen of Scots, was delivered of her only son, James the First of England and Sixth of Scotland. From there we were conducted [to] the Crown Room, here are deposited the Scottish Regalia. These consisted of a sword, Sceptre, and Crown. It was supposed to be lost for many years but the Prince Regent in 1818 caused the Open Chest in the Crown Room to be forced open and these Relics of the Scottish Monarchy were then found. The Crown is of pure Gold, between each of the Rubies are diamonds of an extraordinary size.

218

We were introduced to Mr. Yanick yesterday. He is rather an Oddity but very well informed and lively. We are to accompany him to Rozelin Castle and Hawthornden, where Drummond the Poet spent the greater part of his life. And now, my dear Anny, I am truly tired of writing and no doubt you will be of reading this long screed. We have been here but two days and have almost walked the whole time except an hour at meals, seen all the Public Buildings, the Picture Gallery where are shown the Pictures of three Kings of Scotland and in fact more than I can now describe to you. I have been seeking after a Plaid Dress for you, but I am told that they are now quite out of fashion, therefore you must trust to me until I get to Cheltenham to send you something. We are going on Thursday to Glasgow. Write me a long letter and direct to be left at the Post Office in Edinborough as soon as you can on receipt of this, as we shall return here again.

I am joined by your Father and Emma in love to you, William and Robert. Kiss my dear Children for me, I long to see them, believe me to be your affectionate mother,

R. BRANDON.

I forgot to tell you they feast us too well, your Father is grown stouter from eating so much Scotch Marmalade and Currant Jelly; which we have every day for Breakfast and Tea with Plum, Fowls, Eggs, Broiled Fish, &c., &c.

Your Father says I have not described properly all I have seen but really I should take a Week to describe all. I must therefore tell you no more when, please God, we meet.

Our love to Joe, Caroline, Abraham and Matilda. Write me how Robert gets on.

Donners Hotel,
Scarborough,
July 29th, 1833

My dear Angelina,

Your letter, as well as Williams, came duly to hand, and afforded your Father and self much pleasure to find it left you both and my dearest Grand Children in perfect health. I hope your next will be a little longer one, and pray tell me if my darling Emily has forgotten her Grand Mama and Grand Papa, or if she often names us in any way? I am happy to hear the twins, and Baby, have so much improved. Your remaining at Clevedon will no doubt strengthen them very much and improve Annette's walking. Your Father and myself are glad to hear that Robert is well and continues to like his Profession and that he behaves himself as you could wish, no doubt with you he will continue so make our kind love to him and say we shall write him soon.

My last to you was from Edinburgh, which place we left for Glasgow. This is a large town but I do not admire it after seeing Edinburgh. The Exchange

219

is certainly the finest in size and Workmanship I ever saw and it contains several other fine Buildings, it is more a place of business than the former and not so Clean. At five in the morning after I got there we had to take a coach and drive down to the River side where we took places in the Steam Packet and sailed for Loch Lomond. The Scenery here, while navigating these extensive Lakes, was the greatest break we have had, and *will* repay you for going so far. You see Mountain after Mountain rising in succession on every side, whose stupendous height inspires the mind with sentiments of awe and admiration and as you proceed on the Scenery is diversified all equally grand and sublime. We stopped to Breakfast at Dumbarton and had to take another coach to get to the water side and after re-embarking we continued our delightful sail to the end of the Lake, when we were let down in a Boat and crossed over the Tarbat about two miles from this Lake. We then had to go in a Cart to Arochan when we embarked in another steamer for Loch Long. This Lake is exceedingly beautiful also, but the Scenery is quite of a different kind to Loch Lomond and we were out on this last Loch until half past ten at night, and could get nothing on board to eat, which was rather too long a journey. We had at six in the Evening to leave the Steamer, we were to get on board another, which has five hundred passengers. This rather alarmed your Father as it was generally supposed that there was danger from having so many on board. I assure you, your mother was very active in getting from one ship to another, and going into the Cart Chase with a lot of straw in the bottom, all these adventures make it the pleasanter. As to Emma she had a companion, a very gentlemanly young man who was of our party, and who paid her every attention, and she thought of no dinner nor danger.

We staid four days at Glasgow and returned for one day to Edinborough. But before we reached Edinborough we went to Callender and the Trossaks through a beautiful Park, and sailed in a boat on Loch Earn Head, landed to see the House that the Lady of the Lake used to sit in which is so beautifully described by Sir Walter Scot. I assure you I had some difficulty to get up this hill and I was much laughed at to see the Boat Man so gracefully handing me down the Hill. We proceeded to Dunkel to view the Rambling Bridge and Immense Waterfalls, you here sit in a beautiful summer house to see the falls through various mirrors to great advantage. We then crossed the Queen's Ferry in a steamer to South Queen's Ferry and got to Edinborough. The road from this last place to Scarborough is much worse than in Scotland and to get here we were obliged to have four Horses all the way. We arrived here only yesterday. It seems to be a very fashionable Sea Port. I think I shall like it. The Band plays three times a Week on the Pier and it appears to be visited by very genteel people. The sands are very fine to walk on and the cliffs around are beautiful. We shall remain here a few days before we proceed to York and Harrogate. I think it will be the beginning of August before we shall reach Cheltenham as we shall not hurry back, the weather has truly favoured us since us two have been out.

James has very carelessly left a Tippit of Emma's at the Inn at Bonas, I wrote for it, described it to be forwarded to you in George Street, should it come I shall thank you to pay the Carriage and keep it for me until, please God, we meet at Cheltenham. If you write me again direct to the Post Office, Harrogate. We shall stay there a few days and write me all the news. I am happy to hear your Sister was well when you last heard from her. I wrote her from Glasgow. I expect a letter from her at Harrogate. I beg you will render our best and kindest regards to Abraham, Matilda, Joe and Caroline, kiss my dear Babies for me, give Emily an extra one after, and often your Father and myself have said how we wished for you and our dear William to have been with us and as often hear and talked of Emily and he of the Twins and of her. Tell William I shall be obliged to him if he will write me the exact address of David as I wish to write him soon.

We called as we passed threw Muckleberry upon Mr. Porchas, Johnson's Brother married his Daughter. He received us very kindly, and shew[ed] us his Cottage which he has lately let, and also his manufactory, asked us to lunch but we had not time to stay. Remember us to all Friends, your Quarter of the Globe and with the most Parental affection of which your Father and self have for William and yourself, I shall subscribe myself

Your affectionate Mother.

Your Father's kindest love to R. Brandon, and
you both. He says you must excuse his writing,
he never has his journal to talk over at Cheltenham.

Rachael Brandon's will records that her sister was Mary Ann, wife of Abraham Mocatta; her children were Lydia, wife of Henry Hyman Cohen, Angelina (named Angel) wife of William Wolfe Alexander, Emma (named Eve) wife of Charles Mozeley, and David Israel Brandon, Gabriel Israel Brandon, John Israel Brandon and Robert Israel Brandon named Abraham.

GLOSSARY

Adar: a month in the Jewish calendar, generally corresponding to February or March, including the festival of Purim.

Adar Sheni: a month in the Jewish calendar, which appears only in leap years, generally corresponding to March.

The **Ark**: contains the Sefer Torah (the five books of Moses – Genesis to Deuteronomy – written on a parchment scroll). It is a reminder of the Ark of the Covenant in which the two stone tablets of the law were placed. It is the most holy part of a synagogue, as it was in the Tabernacle, and later in King Solomon's Temple. As a reminder of these places of worship, where a curtain was hung before the Holy of Holies, a velvet curtain is hung in front of the Ark. For the High Holydays, the curtain is white to symbolize forgiveness and atonement. In large synagogues the Ark will contain several scrolls donated by members of the congregation.

Ashkenazim: Jews of Germany, who lived there from Roman times, later in northern France and thereafter Eastern Europe generally. c.f. Sephardim.

Av: a month in the Jewish calendar, generally corresponding to August.

Bar Mitzvah: when a boy reaches thirteen years and one day and becomes responsible for keeping all the commandments of the Torah, and is thereby entitled to read the Torah in Synagogue.

The **Bimah**: the central platform in the synagogue, from which the Torah is read aloud to the congregation.

Beth Din (Jewish Court): governs matters of law between Jews. Once Jews were not living in the ancient state of Israel, the Rabbis said that a Beth Din could only deal with matters not covered by civil law.

Beth Olem (House of Eternity): the Jewish cemetery.

Ba'al Koreh: reader of the Scrolls of the Law.

The **Board of Deputies of British Jews**: founded in 1760. After the Sephardi and Ashkenazi congregations had together congratulated King George III on his accession, they realized that thereafter they would work better together, and have been doing so ever since. Nowadays, the Board's members come from all congregations, be they Orthodox, Reform or Liberal, in Great Britain and the colonies. It is to all intents and purposes the Jewish Parliament.

A **Burgess**: a person holding privileges conferred by municipal corporations or representing the same in Parliament, a citizen.

A **Cantor**: the man who leads the service in Synagogue, chanting the prayers.

Chanukah: a festival which starts on the 25th Kislev. The lighting of the candles on the eight days of the Festival, one on the first day and one more on each succeeding day, commemorates the miracle of the cruse of oil. When Judas Maccabeus and his seven brothers prevailed against the heathen foes, they found in the Temple only one undefiled cruse of oil intact with the seal of the high priest. This contained sufficient oil to light the Menorah for one day but miraculously it lasted for eight days. The following year they designated these eight days to give thanks to God for the rededication of the Temple after it had been defiled by pagan worship of Greek Gods.

Chazan: the Hebrew name for a Cantor.

Cheder (a room): a school for teaching children the elements of the Jewish religion approximating to 'Sunday School'. See **Sabbath School** below.

Chirogaphers: the people, one Jew and one Christian, in charge of the Chirograph chests. They each held a key and both had to be present at the opening of the *archa*. Chirograph chest: refers to the chest or *archa* in which medieval deeds recording financial transactions were kept. (Chirograph = manuscript)

Chumash: the version of Torah with the Haftorah as used in Synagogue during the annual cycle, which starts with Genesis in the autumn (usually October) and ends with Deuteronomy 51 weeks later.

Common era: the period that in other circumstances is named Anno Domini.

Domus Conversorum: the Latin term for the House of Converts established to house people after their conversion. The house in London was founded by Henry III in 1232 to provide board and lodging for Jews who had converted to Christianity.

Eliezer bar Jakov: the Hebrew name of Lazarus Jacobs, meaning Eliezer son of Jacob. It has always been traditional for Jews to be named after their fathers in this way.

Ellul: a month in the Jewish calendar, generally corresponding to August or September.

Gabbai or Treasurer of the Congregation: one of the Wardens of the Synagogue. The Wardens are the laymen who organize the services in the Synagogue beside running the everyday affairs of the community.

The **Gemara:** comprises the second part of the Talmud after the Mishnah (see below). The Gemara is the interpretation of the Mishnah by later writers who were active in Babylonia and Palestine from the third century until the two works were put together in the Talmud.

The **Hebrews:** the word used in the local press to describe the Jews who lived in Bristol in the seventeenth, eighteenth and nineteenth centuries.

Iyyar: a month in the Jewish calendar, generally corresponding to May.

Kislev: a month in the Jewish calendar, generally corresponding to December including the festival of Chanukah.

223

Kosher: fit to eat according to the dietary laws.

Ma'oz Tsur: a special Chanukah hymn sung after the kindling of the lights, probably written in the thirteenth century. It refers to the deliverance of the Jews from Egypt, Babylonia, Persia and Syria.

The **Maranos:** those Jews who publicly converted to Christianity rather than leaving Spain in the expulsion of 1492. Many continued to practise Judaism in secret. Jews were expelled from Spain in 1492 and from Portugal in 1497.

Marcheshvan (or Heshvan): a month in the Jewish calendar, generally corresponding to November, which contains no festivals.

The **Menorah:** the seven-branched candlestick set up in the Tabernacle, later in the Temple. It is commemorated in the Ner Tamid in modern Synagogues.

Mikveh: a ritual bath constructed in accordance with Jewish law, in which women must immerse themselves every month before resuming marital relations. Some men go to a Mikveh, particularly on the eves of Sabbaths and Festivals. Converts must do so once before becoming a Jew.

Minchah: the afternoon service.

Minyan: a quorum for prayers of ten males over the age of 13.

The **Mishnah:** compiled at the beginning of the third century; includes commentaries of Jewish law and ethics collected over four centuries. It and the **Gemara** form the basis of the Talmud.

Mitzvot (singular Mitzvah): 'divine commandments' and signifies special commands in Torah. Colloquially the word has come to express any act of human kindness, corresponding to a good deed.

Mohel: performs circumcision on boys on the eighth day of their lives unless medical reasons advise postponement.

Ne'ilah: the concluding service of the Day of Atonement.

Ner Tamid or perpetual light: burned in the Tabernacle, later the Temple and is a feature of modern Synagogues. It recalls the commandment to the Israelites to keep a lamp burning in the Tabernacle (Exodus 27:20 and Leviticus 24:2).

Nisan: the first month in the Jewish calendar, generally corresponding to April including the festival of Pesach.

Parnas (President): with the Gabbai, one of the wardens of the community.

Pentecost: see Shavuot below.

Pesach (Passover): commences on 15th Nisan with the Seder service, which commemorates the exodus from Egypt and the birth of the Jewish nation. The festival lasts for eight days.

Porger: the man who removes forbidden fat and sinews from meat.

Purim: celebrates the story of Esther. Because of a grudge against Mordecai, the Jew, Haman presented the Jewish people as a whole to King Ahasuerus as a danger. Haman asked that the Jews be massacred. But Mordecai asked his cousin, Queen Esther to intervene and the Jews were saved. The Festival is an opportunity for rejoicing, feasting and masquerading.

Rabbi (plural Rabbonim): came into use in the first century. They are teachers of Torah who receive ordination (Semichah). Their function is to teach the community, for which they were not originally paid, while holding down a regular trade or profession during the day. From the fifteenth century Rabbonim were paid.

Rosh Hashanah: marks the Creation of the World, the Jewish New Year and occurs on the first day of Tishri, the seventh month, the holiest month of the year. The period from Rosh Hashanah to Yom Kippur is the time when mankind stands before the divine throne for judgement.

Sabbath School: (cf. **Cheder** above) When education was not compulsory, Hebrew Schools attached to Synagogues were general.

The **Seder:** a family ceremony at which the Haggadah containing the story of the Exodus is read and unleavened bread is eaten.

Sephardim: the Jews of Spain and Portugal who were expelled in the fifteenth century. They resettled in North Africa, Turkey and Italy. Some later went to Amsterdam and London. They regarded themselves as the aristocracy of the Jewish people. Their successors in modern Israel came from North Africa and other countries of the Middle East and are gaining in numbers.

Shabbat (Sabbath): starts on Friday evening at sundown and lasts until nightfall on Saturday. It is a time when a Jew may not work, a time of rest and an opportunity for families to eat and pray together as, so often, they cannot do during the week.

Shabbat HaGadol: the Great Sabbath before the festival of Pesach.

Shammas or Beadle: the caretaker of the synagogue.

Shavuot (Pentecost): commemorates the giving of the Torah to Moses on Mount Sinai and occurs in May. It is often referred to as Pentecost in the Jewish press in the nineteenth century.

Shechita: slaughter of animals for food by the method prescribed in the Torah.

Shevat: a month in the Jewish calendar, generally corresponding to January or February. (**Shevat 5615** lasted from 20th January to 18th February 1855. The years are numbered from Creation.)

Shiur: a gathering where study takes place, sometimes accompanied by refreshments.

The **Shochet:** the person authorised to kill animals for food according to Jewish law. The method is basically very quick and therefore as pain-free as humanly possible.

Shul: Yiddish for Synagogue.

Sivan: a month in the Jewish calendar, generally corresponding to June, including the festival of Shavuot.

Shomer: the person who is qualified to check the Kosher quality of food sold

225

in shops or used in communal functions, especially weddings and Bar Mitzvot.

Starr (or Shtarr): a Jewish legal deed. The mortgage documents entered into by medieval Jews in England were collected together and stored in the building that existed on the site now occupied by the Public Record Office in Chancery Lane, London. The room was later named the Star Chamber and became notorious in the days of Queen Elizabeth I.

A **Sukkah:** the booth in which Jews spend their time during the Festival of Sukkoth. This commemorates the protection the Israelites received from the weather throughout their wanderings in the desert. The festival lasts for seven days and is held five days after Yom Kippur.

The **Synagogue:** a place of worship, an innovation of the Exile in Babylon in the sixth century before the common era. After the destruction of the Second Temple in 70 C.E., synagogues came into their own as the centre for Jewish worship. In Hebrew, they are known as a House of Study. The term 'Synagogue' is Greek.

The **Talmud:** a compendium of Jewish learning, both law and lore; comprising the Mishnah and Gemara.

Tammuz: a month in the Jewish calendar, generally corresponding to July.

Tanakh: the Hebrew Bible, an abbreviation of the initial letters of 'Torah', the five books of Moses, 'Nevi'im', the books of the prophets and 'Kethuvim', the writings (e.g. Psalms, Proverbs, Chronicles etc.). The order of the last two are different in Tanakh to that in the English bible.

Teveth: a month in the Jewish calendar, generally corresponding to January.

Tishri: a month in the Jewish calendar, generally corresponding to September or October including the festivals of Rosh Hashanah, Yom Kippur and Sukkoth.

Torah: the first five books of the Hebrew Bible. Also more generally all facets of Jewish learning. Learning Torah is a religious duty required of every Jew according to his or her ability.

Treasurer: see Gabbai.

The **Wardens:** the President and Treasurer of the community. (See Parnas and Gabbai above)

Yizkor: the memorial service for close deceased relatives recited as part of various festivals.

Yom Kippur (10th Tishri): the climax of the ten-day period that starts with Rosh Hashanah. One is constantly reminded that this day brings pardon for sins between man and God. It cannot bring forgiveness as long as no attempt has been made to repair any injury inflicted upon one's fellows. This is a day of self-denial, a twenty-six hour fast, but at the end one is full of well-being from the exertions of the day.

Zionism: a political movement for the re-establishment of a Jewish community in the land of Israel. It was started by Theodore Herzl, an Austrian journalist, after he attended the trial of Dreyfus. Small groups of Jews went to settle in Israel from the 1890s.

BIBLIOGRAPHY

ABELSON, Rev. J., 'Some Reminiscences of Bristol Jewry', *Jewish Chronicle*, 5th April 1907.

ABRAHAMS, Israel, 'Israel Joachim Gaunse - A Mining Incident in the Reign of Queen Elizabeth', JHSE *Transactions* IV, 1899–1901.

ABRAHAMS, Israel, and STOKES, H.P., *Starrs and Jewish Charters*, for the JHSE at the University Press, Cambridge, 1930.

ABRAHAMS, Lionel, 'The Economic and Financial Position of Jews in Mediæval England', JHSE *Transactions* VIII, 1915–1917.

ADLER, M.A., 'The Jews of Bristol in Pre-Expulsion Days', JHSE *Transactions* XII, 1928–1931.

ADLER, M.A., *The Jews of Mediæval England*, Jewish Historical Society of England, 1939.

ALDERMAN, Geoffrey, *Modern British Jewry*, Clarendon Press, Oxford, 1992.

BARNETT, Arthur, *The Western Synagogue through Two Centuries*, Vallentine Mitchell, 1961.

BARRETT, W., *History of the Antiquities of Bristol*.

BELL, Adrian, *Yesterday in Bath*, Pitman Press, Bath, 1972.

BRAYBROOKE, Marcus, *Children of One God*, SCM Press, London, 1991.

BROWN, Malcolm, 'The Jews of Norfolk and Suffolk before 1840', JHSE, *Transactions* XXXII, 1990–1992.

BROWN, Malcolm and SAMUEL, Judith, 'Jews in Bath', JHSE, *Jewish Historical Studies*, XXIX, 1982–1986.

BUSH, Graham, 'Bristol and its Municipal Government: 1820–1851', *Bristol Record Society's Publications*, Vol. XXIX.

DOBSON, R.B., *Jews of Medieval York and the Massacre of March 1190*, Borthwick Papers, No. 45, 1974.

DUNSCOMBE, Max, 'Established 1797', *The Bristol Templar*, Bristol, Spring 1989, (magazine of the Temple Local History Group).

EMANUEL, R.R., *The History of Bristol Jewry*, Newsletter, No. 4/88, (Temple Local History Group, Bristol).

EVANS, John, *A Chronological Outline of the History of Bristol*, published by the author, 1824.

FELDMAN, David, *Englishmen and Jews*, Yale University Press, New Haven and London, 1994.

GOMME, JENNER and LITTLE, *Bristol: an Architectural History*, Lund Humphries, London, 1979, in association with Bristol & West Building Society.

GROSS, C., *Exchequer of the Jews of England in the Middle Ages*.

GWYER, John, 'The Case of Dr. Lopez', JHSE, *Transactions* XVI, 1945–1951.

HUME, Martin, M.A., *The So-called Conspiracy of Dr. Ruy Lopez*, JHSE, *Transactions* VI, 1908–1910.

HUNT, William, *Historic Towns, Bristol*, Longman Green, 1902 & 1909.

HYAMSON, A.M., *A History of the Jews of Oxford*, 2nd. ed., 1928.

JACOB, Alex M., 'Aaron Levy Green, 1821–1883', JHSE, *Transactions* XXV, 1977.

JACOBS, Dr. Joseph, *The Jews of Angevin England*, David Nutt, London, 1893.

JESSOP and JAMES, *The Life and Miracles of St. William of Norwich.*

JEWISH YEAR BOOK, 1900/5660

JEWISH YEAR BOOK, 1902/5662 (Harris)

JOSEPHS, Zoë, 'Jewish Glassmakers', JHSE, *Transactions* XXV, 1977.

LATIMER, John, *Annals of Bristol*, Kingsmead Reprints, 1970.

LELAND's *Itinerary.*

LIPMAN, V.D., *Medieval Norwich*, W.E. Heffer & Sons for the JHSE, Cambridge, 1967.

McGRATH, Patrick, *The Merchant Venturers of Bristol*, The Society of Merchant Venturers, Bristol, 1975.

MADOX, T., *Exchequer of the Jews.*

MARGOLIOUTH, Moses, *The Jews of Great Britain*, James Nesbit & Co., London, 1846. Also a version in three volumes published in 1851.

NEALE, W.G., *At The Port of Bristol*, vol. 1, *Members and Problems, 1849–1899*, Port of Bristol Authority, 1968.

NICHOLLS, J.F., & TAYLOR, John, *Bristol, Past and Present*, vol.I, J.W. Arrowsmith, 1881.

PARSONS, Ian, ed., *The Collected Works of Isaac Rosenberg*, Chatto & Windus, London, 1979, reprinted 1984.

PRYCE, George, *A Popular History of Bristol*, W. Mack, Bristol, 1861.

PRYNNE, W., *A Short Demurrer*, 1655.

RICHARDSON, H.G., *The English Jewry under the Angevin Kings*, Methuen, London, 1960.

RIGG, J.M., *Calendar of the Plea Rolls of the Exchequer of the Jews.*

RIGG, J.M., *The Rolls of the Exchequer of the Jews.*

ROTH, Cecil, M.A., *Short History of the Jewish People*, East and West Library, 1953.

ROTH, Cecil, M.A., 'The Middle Period in Anglo-Jewish History', JHSE *Transactions* XIX, 1960.

ROTH, Cecil, M.A., *A History of the Jews in England*, John Trotter Publishers, 1989.

SCHLESINGER, Alex, 'A Tribute to Rev. Max Modell', *Recorder*, April 1992, (magazine of Bristol Hebrew Congregation).

SEYER, Samuel, *Memoirs, Historical and Topographical, of Bristol*, vol.i, John Mathew Gutch, 1821.

STOKES, H.P., *Studies in Anglo-Jewish History*, for the Jewish Historical Society of England by Ballantyne, Hanson & Co., Edingurgh, 1913.

TOMLINSON, C., *Isaac Rosenberg of Bristol*, Bristol Historical Association.

TOVEY, *Anglia Judaica*, Weidenfeld & Nicholson, in association with Martin Green, London, 1990. Originally published in London in 1738.

WOLF, Lucien, 'The Case of Thomas Fernandez before the Lisbon Inquisition', found among his unpublished papers, printed in JHSE, *Miscellanies* II, 1935.

WOODWARD, Sir Llewelyn, *Age of Reform, 1815–1870*, (2nd ed.), The Oxford History of England, Vol.13, at the Clarendon Press, Oxford, 1962.

INDEX

[See also appendices]

230

233

France 17
Frankfort-am-Main 101
Frankfurt 140
Freeland, Anne 179, 180
Freeland, I. 179
Free Port 152
Friends' Meeting House, Hampton
Road, Redland 191, 193
Fripp, S.C. 72
Frome 143

Gabbai 105
Gaunze, Joachim 42, 43
Germany 17, 22
Giffard, William 34
Glass 101 et seq
Glassmaker(s) 101 et seq
Glassware 101
Gloucester 16, 25, 26, 33
Gloucester Gaol 186
Gloucestershire 184
Gloucester Museum 103
Goldberg, H. 158, 159
Goldberg, Rev. H. 124
Goldberg, L. 149, 164, 165
Goldberg, Louis 164
Golders Green, London 184
Goldman, Frank 146, 148, 149, 174
Goldman, Messrs. F. & S. 146
Goldman, M. 164
Goldsmid, Alfred J. 162
Goldsmid, Miss E. 149, 162
Goldsmid, Michael J. 162
Goldstein, Rabbi Dr David 192, 194
Gollancz, Rabbi Herman 94
Goodman, F. 149
Goodman, Mrs H. 148
Goodman, Rev. Hyman 97, 98, 148,
195
Goodman, Tobias 83
Gordon, Miss Sara 94
Grand Hotel, Bristol 169
Gravesend 178
Great Exhibition, 1851 106
Great Gardens 74, 102, 103
Great Gardens burial ground (in Rose
Street) 103
Great George Street 62, 140
Great Portland Street 85
Great Synagogue 85, 94
Great Western Railway 78, 135

Greater London 184
Greaves, Rev. Talbot A.L. 122–124
Greece 140
Green, Rev. A.A. 85
Green, Aaron Levy 78, 83–87, 92, 112,
132, 195
Greenwich 128
Green, William (Friese-Green) 60
Griqualand West Congregation 89
Guild of Kalendars 21
Guttenberg, Marcus 59, 60
Gyna, widow of Abraham Russell of
Huntingdon 36

Haberfield Crescent 62
Hagin son of Isaac 30
Hak (Isaac) son of Meyrot (Meir) 35
Hak le Prestre 31
Hamburg 154
Hamburg House, Clifton College 153,
154
Hamilton Rooms 164
Hammersmith Synagogue, London
98
Hands, Miss L. 175
Hanover 140
Hanover Street 62
Harris, Anita 165
Harris, Emanuel 165
Harris, Henry 193
Harris, Messrs. W.J. (later Wise &
Harris) 167
Harrisberg, Aaron 96, 164, 165, 171,
172
Harrisberg, David 171
Harrisberg, Michael 171
Harrisberg, Mrs. Rachel 195
Harrisberg, Rose 171
Harrisberg, Sarah 171
Harrison, Colonel 61
Harrow School 154
Hart, Len 190–192
Hebrew passim
Hebrew Boarding Schools 78, 80
Hebrew Ladies' Benevolent Society 81,
114, 168, 176
Hebrew lessons 78
Hebrew and Religion Classes 81, 93,
185
Hebrew School(s) 80, 114, 164, 172
Hebrew School, Congregational 148

235